"[Ann Hood's] entertaining, thoughtful, and heartfelt storytelling is what keeps her loyal readers always wanting more." —Robin Kall, *Providence Journal*

"Hood's early ambitions to be a writer . . . clearly helped her to manage the job's exhausting schedule and no less exhausting sexism, with an Ephronian approach of turning it all into copy. . . . [Her] love for air travel . . . is infectious and undying." —Joanna Scutts, *Air Mail*

"[Hood's] detailed recollections of her year[s] in the skies are delightful, and she is keenly insightful about how her training and experience as a flight attendant were essential to her personal growth." —*National Book Review*

"Dynamic. . . . Hood's recollections are charged with airline history, as well as personal reminiscences. . . . Hood still 'flies' in her vivid memories and invites readers to become airborne, if only in imagination." —Barbara Bamberger Scott, *Bookreporter*

"Lively. . . . Colorful anecdotes make for an entertaining memoir of travel and self-discovery." —*Kirkus Reviews*

"Sparkling. . . . Hood's companionable storytelling paired with her bold skewering of an oft-glamorized world . . . make for an enthralling account. . . . From takeoff to landing, this entertains and inspires." —*Publishers Weekly*

"Hood's delightful memoir of her stint as a TWA flight attendant in the late 1970s is full of amusing trivia, hilarious stories, and all the warmth of her novels. . . . An engaging memoir perfect for fans of Hood's and readers interested in aviation history or who love a good coming-of-age memoir." —*Library Journal*

"*Fly Girl* soars: Ann Hood's memoir of her experiences as a flight attendant is a love letter to the years when flying was a dream—and the 747s ruled the skies. I was catapulted back in time and savored every second and every story from 35,000 feet in the air." —Chris Bohjalian, #1 *New York Times* best-selling author of *The Flight Attendant* and *The Lioness*

"Winning and compulsively readable, *Fly Girl* is like a first-class ticket to the sadly bygone days when air travel was stylish, sexy, and deliciously rarified. What a pleasure to see another side of this best-selling author—the small-town girl with a passion for adventure who earns her flight-attendant's wings while decidedly discovering her own."      —Paula McLain, *New York Times* best-selling author of *The Paris Wife* and *When the Stars Go Dark*

"In this warm and engaging memoir, Ann Hood captures the heady thrills as well as the grueling realities of life as a flight attendant during the golden age of air travel. Over eight years, Hood walked a million miles, explored far-flung cities, and learned invaluable lessons that shaped her as a writer and a person. A brisk history lesson, an affectionate homage, and a thoughtful critique of the airline industry, *Fly Girl* soars."
                      —Christina Baker Kline, *New York Times* best-selling author of *The Exiles* and *Orphan Train*

"*Fly Girl* is a sheer pleasure. A hilarious and often moving look back at a bygone era and a young woman's coming of age."
                      —Dennis Lehane, *New York Times* best-selling author of *Since We Fell*

"At first blush, *Fly Girl* is a charming, layered memoir about Ann Hood's life as a flight attendant who knew the industry in its glory days—and its-not-so-glorious days post-deregulation. But it's also something much more, nothing less than a manifesto calling us to embrace joy and adventure, however we define them. I have always loved Ann's stories and now I know why she has so many: She has *lived*, in the best, fullest sense of that word. She can't make the sun stand still, but, boy does she make it run."
                      —Laura Lippman, *New York Times* best-selling author of *Dream Girl* and *Lady in the Lake*

"As a young woman in the late 1970s, Ann Hood's determination to seek an adventurous life propelled her into this contradictory profession. Now she flies readers through that era—of flight, American history, and her own life—and into the present with warmth, humor, and insight in a memoir that sparkles."                      —Julia Cooke, author of *Come Fly the World: The Jet Age Story of the Women of Pan Am*

# FLY GIRL

*A Memoir*

Ann Hood

**W. W. NORTON & COMPANY**
*Celebrating a Century of Independent Publishing*

Copyright © 2022 by Ann Hood

For information about permission to reproduce selections from this book, write to Permissions, W. W. Norton & Company, Inc., 500 Fifth Avenue, New York, NY 10110

For information about special discounts for bulk purchases, please contact W. W. Norton Special Sales at specialsales@wwnorton.com or 800-233-4830

Manufacturing by Lakeside Book Company
Production manager: Devon Zahn

Library of Congress Cataloging-in-Publication Data

Names: Hood, Ann, 1956– author.
Title: Fly girl : a memoir / Ann Hood.
Description: First edition. | New York, NY : W. W. Norton & Company, [2022]
Identifiers: LCCN 2021062280 | ISBN 9781324006237 (hardcover) |
ISBN 9781324006244 (epub)
Subjects: LCSH: Hood, Ann, 1956– | Flight attendants—Biography.
Classification: LCC HD6073.A43 H66 2002 |
DDC 387.7/42092 [B]—dc23/eng/20220201
LC record available at https://lccn.loc.gov/2021062280

ISBN 978-1-324-05041-4 pbk.

W. W. Norton & Company, Inc.
500 Fifth Avenue, New York, N.Y. 10110
www.wwnorton.com

W. W. Norton & Company Ltd.
15 Carlisle Street, London W1D 3BS

1 2 3 4 5 6 7 8 9 0

*For Kate Heckman*
*and*
*Matt Davies*

# CONTENTS

# PROLOGUE

A FRIEND OF MINE recently said to me, "I love when you start a story with 'When I was a flight attendant . . .' because I know it's going to be a good story." At dinner or cocktail parties, when someone asks what I do, they often look at me blankly when I say that I'm a writer. "Have I read anything by you?" they ask, often accompanied with a narrowing of the eyes. Or: "Have you published anything?" Sometimes even people I know ask me if I'm still writing, as if it's a hobby and not a career. But once I say those magic words, "When I was a flight attendant . . ." everyone is interested.

What did I actually do on those planes? What was the scariest thing that ever happened? The weirdest? Was the job fun or boring? Did I actually get to see any of the places where I flew? Was there really a mile-high club? Did I date pilots? Passengers? Famous people? Flight attendants still hold the mystique they had back in the golden age of flying, even though, as one flight attendant described it, "I started to fly when every passenger was treated like they were in first class, and stopped flying when most passengers felt like they were riding a Greyhound bus, not a jumbo jet." I have the unique experience of starting as a flight attendant at the end of those glamour days, and stopping just as service, legroom, and meals began to disappear. I flew through the start of deregulation, an oil crisis, massive furloughs, start-up airlines, corporate takeovers, and a labor strike. I didn't see it all, but I saw a lot.

Why did I, a smart, twenty-one-year-old woman in 1978 choose to become a flight attendant rather than a banker or pharmaceutical salesperson or teacher or social worker as my college friends had? Flight attendants were still stereotyped as not-very-smart sex kittens in airline advertising and in many people's minds back then. Yet the only job I applied for during my senior year of college was flight attendant.

The love of flying, the romantic connotations of flight, the dreams of adventure were planted in me when I was very young. I literally and metaphorically had my eyes on the sky. At night, in 1958 or '59, in Arlington, Virginia, at the Shirley Park Apartments, we kids sat on the grassy hill between the apartment buildings and stared up at the sky to watch spotlights sweep across it. A new airport, so modern that moving pods would take passengers to their airplanes, was being built. I don't know why those lights swept the sky sometimes, but when they did it was always an event. Our parents hustled us outside and everyone lay down on blankets and watched.

A year or two earlier, the Russians had launched Sputnik into space, where it had orbited for a couple months, looking down at us. Although I was too young to remember that, ever since it happened, all everyone talked about was space—going into it, imagining what was there, landing on the moon like President Kennedy promised we'd do. It was no wonder that I became fascinated, obsessed even, by the idea that something was *up there*, circling, watching, seeing. Seeing what? Stars, certainly. Planets—the rings of Saturn, angry red Mars, comets with their flaming tails. The moon that was possibly made of blue cheese, or maybe was an actual face staring down on us. "See the Man in the Moon?" my mother would ask, her finger pointing out the wavy eyes and grin. But what else? Martians? Angels? Saints? I thought about the sky. What was it made of? Could I stand on its clouds? I took to gazing upward.

The year after I was born, the Russians launched a dog named Laika into space in Sputnik 2 to see if it was possible to survive being launched into space in a rocket. Laika died six days later because she ran out of oxygen. (Or so we thought; half a century later we learned she'd actually died within hours.) We didn't hear much about Laika's fate, just that the Russians were ahead of us in the Space Race. Laika was a folk hero of sorts, like Lassie and Rin Tin Tin, and kids whispered about her with a combination of awe and sadness for years after she went to space. The Russians had launched a satellite, too, Sputnik I, and the adults worried over the implications of the Russians beating us into space. But I thought of Laika as I watched the sky on those autumn nights. I thought of space and rockets and moving pods. The year I was three, and again the next year, I dressed as a space girl for Halloween. My mother used aluminum foil to make the costume, adding pipe cleaner antennae to the top of my head because no one really knew what a space girl might look like.

Sometimes on Sunday afternoons we drove out to Chantilly, Virginia, twenty miles from the Shirley Park Apartments, to watch them work on the new airport. We parked our enormous green Chevy station wagon in an empty field and stared out at the cranes and construction equipment, oddly excited. My father knew everything about the airport. The architect, he told us, was Eero Saarinen, and he was from Finland. The airport was being built to accommodate new airplanes called jets. They had big engines—two on each wing—instead of propellers and, my father told us, they were going to change the world. "A person could get on a jet at this airport," he said, sweeping his arms toward the piles of concrete and equipment, "and be in Paris France in seven hours." That was less time than it took us to drive to visit my grandmother in Rhode Island.

And then, the most exciting thing of all happened. On October 17, 1958, President Eisenhower christened the first Boeing 707 at the other airport in Washington, DC—National Airport. That was followed by the first flight of a 707 jet, a VIP-only trip from Baltimore's Friendship International Airport to Le Bourget in Paris, with a stop to refuel in Gander, Newfoundland. It is no exaggeration to say that this was all people talked about. Jets. Progress. Tomorrowland come to life.

Once again, all of the children in the Shirley Park Apartments were hustled outside. Down the stairs from our second-floor apartment, out the door, onto the grass. "Watch the sky!" our parents instructed, their necks craned, their eyes gazing upward. I, too, dropped my head back and set my sight on the blue, blue sky. It seemed that for a very long time there was just that blue sky and puffy white clouds. Until in the distance came a rumbling and all of the parents pointed to the sky and the jet cut across it, leaving a long white tail behind. Even after the 707 disappeared, that tail of white remained. I remember staring at it until it disappeared, a habit I still have today.

Although it can be argued that the Jet Age began a week later, when a Pan Am 707 took off from Idlewild Airport—

now JFK—in New York, headed to Paris on its first daily scheduled flight, for me the Jet Age began the day I watched that Boeing 707 cut across a Virginia sky.

Five months later, TWA followed Pan Am with its first regularly scheduled jet flight from San Francisco to New York. That flight took five and a half hours, half the time it had taken on the Constellation prop planes. Soon, Boeing 707s dominated air travel, and led to changes in everything about it, from airport runways and catering to baggage handling and air traffic control systems. By 1970, Boeing had to create a new, bigger jet—the 747—to accommodate the growth of air travel that the 707 had begun.

When Dulles Airport opened in November of 1962, we had moved from Virginia back to Rhode Island, missing what we had so carefully watched grow. Eero Saarinen didn't get to see it open either; he died of a brain tumor at the age of fifty-one, a year earlier. He hadn't lived to see the TWA International Terminal at Idlewild Airport in New York open earlier that year, in March of 1962. That terminal, designed to capture the spirit of flight, resembled an enormous bird with wings spread, preparing for landing. It was one of the first airport terminals that had enclosed jetways, a PA system, baggage carousels, and those mechanical split-flap Arrivals and Departures boards whose clicking sound quickly became synonymous with air travel.

With the lens of six decades, I marvel at how all of these seemingly disconnected things—trying to glimpse Sputnik, seeing the first 707 leave a jet stream in the sky, watching Dulles Airport being built—shaped that little girl who tossed her head back and stared up at the sky as the Jet Age began. I grew up wanting nothing more than to fly. As I got older, flying offered a way out of my small hometown and into the big world beyond.

I couldn't know that I would come of age at a remarkable time for aviation. Flying was still glamorous, and flight attendants were considered to be beautiful and sexy ornaments even as they fought relentlessly for women's rights against age and gender discrimination and for career professionalism. I was hired as a flight attendant the same year deregulation began and changed how we flew forever. Over the next eight years, I would experience the end of the golden age of flying, watch major airlines go bankrupt, endure layoffs and a labor strike, and walk over a million miles in high heels on flights, smiling as I served thousands of passengers. I worked in one of the most demanding, sexist, exciting, glorious jobs a person can have. I was a flight attendant.

FLY GIRL

# TAKING FLIGHT

M Y FAMILY, like most Americans in 1972, was a car-trip kind of family. In 1965, only 20 percent of Americans had flown in an airplane. The reason was simple: flying in those pre-deregulation days was too expensive. The government, through the Civil Aeronautics Board, or CAB, set and regulated fares. In 1974, it was actually illegal for an airline to charge less than the CAB-dictated $1,442 in inflation-adjusted dollars for a flight between New York and L.A. That was one reason why every summer, my parents, my brother, and I piled into our green Chevy station wagon and left Rhode Island, where we'd moved when I was in first grade, for places like Amish Country or Hershey in Pennsylvania, or Niagara Falls. Most of these trips were actually just stopovers on the way to visit my father's relatives in Greensburg, Indiana, a small town in the southeastern corner of the state, filled with corn, fried chicken, and cousins.

In 1967, we booked a week's stay at Expo 67 in Montreal, a kind of world's fair built on an island in the St. Lawrence River. To me, this was even more exciting than the free Kisses in Hershey or the shoofly pie in Lancaster, Pennsylvania. For one thing, Canada was another country. I would actually be somewhere outside the United States, albeit much closer to

Rhode Island than Disneyland. For another, I was still upset that my parents had refused to take us to the 1964 World's Fair in New York. "Too crowded," my mother said every time I begged them to take us. "The traffic!" my father said. But I had seen pictures of it in the magazines and newspapers that came to our house—picture phones, a robot Abraham Lincoln reciting the Gettysburg Address, and a ride in a boat through canals lined with animatronic dolls dressed in traditional outfits from around the world, dancing and spinning as they sang "It's a Small World"—and I had wanted to see it all for myself. But there was no convincing my parents.

Three years later, we were headed to Canada and Expo 67. Expo 67 had more than ninety pavilions, a geodesic dome, a biosphere, and a sleek glass-and-metal exhibit built by the USSR, which featured a bust of Lenin and a replica of the satellite that had carried Yuri Gagarin, the first person who went to space. Not as exciting as watching a life-size, robotic Lincoln give a speech, but still exciting to me.

Other than how expensive flying was, another reason that we always took car trips was that my mother—who had flown exactly twice, both times in a navy cargo plane to and from Naples, Italy, where my father was stationed in the early '50s—hated flying. She was terrified of being thousands of feet in the air and reportedly kept her eyes closed for most of the time. My mother was afraid of many things, probably because of her older sister's sudden death from an allergic reaction to anesthesia a decade earlier, when Mom was twenty-one and Ann, my namesake, was twenty-three. There were no grief support groups or grief counseling then, so my mother had to navigate her grief and her fear of catastrophes alone. Only two years a bride when her sister died, and with a baby son, she had to meet my father in Italy, flying for the first time alone with a toddler, leaving her bereaved family behind and establishing a lifelong dislike of airplanes and a nagging fear that at any moment something could go terribly wrong.

That summer of 1967, as we arrived in Montreal, Expo 67 rose dramatically from its island, a testament to modernity with its spires and spheres and elevated mini rail glistening in the sunlight. I had been waiting all summer for this, and suddenly here it was before me.

"We're not going," my mother announced.

"You've got to be kidding me," my brother Skip said with all the sarcasm a teenager could muster, which is to say a lot. He had just gotten his learner's driving permit and had spent most of the trip so far begging to practice. My mother refused to let him drive at all, and he had been sulking for hours.

I stared at the Expo, seemingly within arm's reach, so close I could almost taste the exotic food the brochure promised: "Breakfast in Tokyo, lunch in India, tea in Ceylon, and dinner in France or Mexico or Switzerland or Czechoslovakia . . ."

"Babe," my father said patiently, "we came all this way. The kids are so excited."

My father indulged my mother all her superstitions—*No shoes on the bed! You have to leave from the same door you entered!*—and ghosts (she believed her dead relatives visited her regularly) and fears of heights and water and looming catastrophes.

"Jeane Dixon predicted the thing is going to sink and thousands of people are going to die, and I just cannot go there," my mother explained, her voice growing more panicked with every word.

Jeane Dixon was a famous psychic and astrologer whose columns in the newspaper my mother read religiously. She had predicted President Kennedy's assassination, and she was a devout Catholic, which was all my mother needed to believe her.

"I cannot go there and have all of us die when it sinks," Mom cried.

By now she was hyperventilating, so my father exited and turned away from Expo 67 and into the city.

"We're not going?" Skip said. "I don't believe this." He put on his new black Wayfarer sunglasses, blocking us all out.

"Sorry, kids," Dad said—and I knew he was sorry because he was looking forward to it as much as I was. "We'll just find a nice hotel and go for a fancy dinner right here in Montreal." He patted my mother's arm. "Sound good, babe?"

She lit a cigarette and took a long draw, then exhaled slowly. The smell of my childhood was cigarette smoke, and soon the car was filled with it as Mom smoked one cigarette and then another to calm down from the tragedy we'd just escaped.

I watched Expo 67 disappear out the back window. Like Jeane Dixon's other false predictions—the Soviets would land the first man on the moon, World War III would begin in 1958, and, years later, that George Bush would defeat Bill Clinton, Expo 67 never did sink, and the geodesic dome and several of the pavilions still stand. I glimpsed them once many years later driving over that same bridge. But that day in 1967, I had the feeling that if I waited for my parents to do anything exciting, I'd be too old to enjoy it. I was only ten, but I was ready to go, to soar, to see things. That night, in my twin bed in the Montreal hotel, I began to plot my own adventures. No car trips in a Pall-Mall-smoke-filled station wagon. Unlike my mother with her fears of bridge collapses and islands sinking and airplanes, I would fly. And I would love it. I would fly everywhere, to every state I'd written down in my careful log of license plates we passed—Land of Enchantment and Sunshine State and Beehive State—to every country on the pull-down map in my fifth-grade teacher Mrs. Kennedy's classroom.

In his twin bed across from me, my brother worked math problems on his slide rule and hummed a Beach Boys song. I closed my eyes and pictured that big blue sky I loved to stare at. A jet appeared with its white jet stream behind it. On that plane, a combination of what I'd seen in the movie *Boeing Boeing* (Tony Curtis, airline stewardesses in hats and gloves) and advertisements in magazines (smiling men in suits and ties drinking martinis, smiling stewardesses lighting men's cigarettes), there I sat, going somewhere.

Six years and many more miles logged in family car trips later, in June of 1973, I took my first flight on Delta Airlines to Bermuda. I was sixteen years old and traveling with my friend Nancy. My father drove us the hour to Logan Airport in Boston, giving us travel advice as we navigated I-95 traffic and the Callahan Tunnel: *Always ask for directions. Don't panic if you forgot something, just buy it there. Stick together. Don't get in cars with strangers. Be careful. Have fun.* Some of this advice seemed to contradict itself. But I latched on to *have fun* and prepared for my first great adventure.

As the airport came into view, the sweeping Boston skyscrapers rose beyond Logan Airport, and Boston Harbor glittered beside it. Iberia and Pan Am and TWA and Alitalia 747s waited at gates; cars and taxis lined the curbside; passengers in business suits and summer dresses filed into terminals; and above it all the traffic control center loomed, a giant rectangle of windows and concrete.

This was long before roller bags (only flight attendants had them as part of their crew luggage back then) and TSA checkpoints. I lugged my Harvest Gold American Tourister suitcase—my Christmas present that year—to the check-in line, showed my tickets and my proof of United States citizenship card, and was handed a boarding pass. My father walked us to the gate and waited until we boarded before he headed home. When I looked out the airplane window, there he still stood, waving goodbye. I couldn't know then that this was a ritual that would be repeated for decades to come, my father seeing me off or waiting for me to arrive at airports as I wandered around the world. There he would be, his blue eyes sparkling, a big grin on his face. Even now, when I get on or off a plane, a small part of me expects to see him there, waiting for me or sending me off.

For the previous two years, I'd worked as a model for the Jordan Marsh department store in the local Warwick Mall and in its flagship store in downtown Boston. Other than movies, records, and ice cream, there was not a lot for a teenager to spend money on in my small town, so most of the money I made from modeling and the hours I worked at the store itself went straight into my savings account. Every Friday night I took my passbook to the bank with my father and deposited my paychecks, getting a stamp in it with the date and total amount. Models, even teen models at a local department store, made very good money, and I felt a thrill watching my savings account grow and grow.

I had ended my junior year by breaking up with my steady boyfriend and vowing to start having a big, exciting life. Although I wasn't sure what exactly that meant, it was clear to me that I would have to leave West Warwick, Rhode Island, in order to do it. Somehow I convinced my friend Nancy to join me on a trip somewhere, anywhere. Nancy had a savings account, too, built by scooping ice cream after school and on weekends at the Newport Creamery in the mall, which was also bursting with money. She went to her mother with our scheme, and I went to my father— the two people most likely to say yes. We both obtained permission with one caveat: we could go anywhere except New York City, which my father believed to be the most dangerous place for two sixteen-year-old girls—or anyone—to go.

As luck would have it, our ninth-grade French teacher, Mr. Lautieri, now worked as a travel agent at Midland Travel in the mall. Nancy and I went to him, and without hesitation he booked us on a flight to Bermuda—$99 roundtrip on Delta from Boston to Hamilton—and a hotel room in the Hamilton Princess, a pink Grande Dame overlooking the Hamilton Harbour. He sent us off with plane tickets and brochures of beaches with pink sand, happy people having high tea and shopping in St. George, and tropical fish swimming beneath a glass-bottomed boat.

To me, even though it sat only 751 miles away, off the coast of North Carolina, Bermuda seemed as exotic as Katmandu or Mozambique. I shopped for weeks for the perfect outfit to wear on the plane. In 1973, people dressed up when they flew.

Men wore jackets and ties; women accessorized their outfits with matching shoes and handbags. I had to find something that made me look stylish, older, worldly. After many hours at the mall, I finally bought a one-piece shiny polyester jumpsuit, white with a fake inset blue-and-white polka dot blouse. White platform sandals. White hoop earrings. White clutch. How sophisticated I felt in that outfit! Like a person ready to see the world.

ON BOARD MY Delta flight to Bermuda, I studied the stewardesses in their navy-and-red uniforms with white ribbed mock turtlenecks and wings pinned to their jackets as they moved about the cabin. I had wanted to be an airline stewardess since I was eleven years old and read a 1964 book called *How to Become an Airline Stewardess*, by Kathryn Cason. "The airline stewardess leads a life completely different from the routine of any other working girl," Cason wrote. "Breakfast in New York on a winter morning and lunch in Miami under palm trees is all in a day's work . . . Dinner could be in London, Amsterdam, Stockholm or Rome. Could be? It is, every day." For a girl growing up in a small, depressed mill town with outsized dreams, this sounded enchanting. Deep down, I wanted to be a writer, and writers, I believed, needed adventures. They needed to run with the bulls in Spain and jump into fountains in Paris. What better way to have adventures than being a stewardess and getting paid to have them?

Of course, on page 1, Cason also warns that in the airline industry, men write the rules and set the standards, do all the interviewing and hiring, and fill all the top jobs. "So face it from the start—you'll never make a Vice-Presidency. But who cares? . . . [they] are running the biggest non-profit marriage market in America . . . the average stewardess keeps her job for 27 months. Within that time, 85% resign to marry!" Cason goes on to list the assets of girls lucky enough to become stewardesses—liking people, a friendly outlook on life, tact, and patience. "Now, when that kind of girl learns to cook too, what kind of man in his right mind wouldn't rather see her standing in *his* doorway than an airplane?"

When I read these words as a seventh grader, they probably held little impact. Everyone I knew wanted to get married, sooner rather than later. Even girls my age practiced writing their names as "Mrs." before the name of whichever boy they had a crush on. I'd watched my older girl cousins finish high school and maybe a two-year program in nursing or at Katharine Gibbs for secretarial training, then appear at our door to show off their diamond engagement rings and nervous fiancés. In no time, they walked down the aisle in complicated, beaded white gowns, we younger cousins in our own pink or maroon gowns and odd headpieces—giant bows or straw hats—trailing behind them. If this was our fate, why not marry one of those businessmen in the airline ads instead of the guy who sold us deli meat or fixed our cars?

I focused instead on all the cities Cason promised I'd visit, all the friendships I'd form, all the things I would learn about the big world out there beyond the factory roofs outside my window. But as the sixteen-year-old who boarded that Delta plane that summer morning, what did I think about the stereotypes of stewardesses? Of women in general? In the few years since I'd first read *How to Become an Airline Stewardess*, my attitude had started to shift. Did marriage have to be my fate? What would life be like if I *didn't* get married and lived a single life in a fancy penthouse apartment in a big city somewhere? One of the reasons I broke up with my high-school boyfriend was a fear of stepping onto that marriage track before I had a chance to live my own life. In just five years, I would be the one in the uniform at the boarding door greeting passengers, hired at a time when perceptions of the job and women's roles began to shift, as well as the start of airline deregulation, arguably the most crucial turning point for the airline industry.

But all of that lay ahead of me in the sunny, blurry future I imagined for myself. "Outdoors the sun is shining, the sky is clear and blue, the crew car is waiting, filled with girls, all young, all excited, chattering like magpies, with the whole world ahead of them . . . In you get and off you go," Cason tells us at the end of the book. That first flight felt a little like that already. *In you get and off you go.*


ALTHOUGH I WAS an avid and indiscriminate reader, I somehow missed the Vicki Barr Flight Stewardess books of the late '40s and early '50s, which follow Vicki and her glamorous friends on adventures and dates. I also never read the 1951 *Skygirl: A Career Handbook for the Airline Stewardess*, written by Mary F. Murray with an introduction by the very first flight attendant, Ellen Church. Murray, the director of stewardess training at the Aviation Training School in Boston, wrote the book "for the girls who want to be airline hostesses and wonder whether they qualify." She gives matter-of-fact information about everything from training, uniforms, domiciles, and even the drawbacks of the job, including smiling and poise that are "her most valuable asset."

I did, however, read the 1967 bestseller *Coffee, Tea or Me?: The Uninhibited Memoirs of Two Airline Stewardesses* by the time I was sixteen. "Stewardessing is the ideal job for girls looking to travel and see other places, make many new and varied friends, feel at home in hundreds of strange cities, and get paid for these things to boot," the narrator Trudy Baker tells us on the first page. Trudy Baker and Rachel Jones were actually pseudonyms for the ghostwriter, Donald Bain, an American Airlines PR executive. The book is peppered with illustrations by Ben Wenzel of stewardesses in miniskirts and high heels being leered at by male passengers as they stuff men's briefcases into the overhead bin, leaning over a grinning pilot with a large breast squashed against his cheek, or hanging out in cocktail lounges or fancy restaurants with cleavage spilling out of a tight-fitting dress. "A stewardess," Trudy—Donald Bain—writes, "is a girl. She wears a uniform and works at thirty-five thousand feet. But above all she is a girl, female and subject to all the whims and desires of all females." To Donald Bain, Ben Wenzel, and the book's publishers, that meant stewardesses—and all "girls"— wanted to be ogled and objectified. When Trudy attempts to put a soldier's bag in the overhead, her "pull proof" blouse pulls and reveals her bare belly. The soldier puts his nose in her belly button, and all Trudy thinks is, "It tickled."

The stewardesses on my flight to Bermuda had big smiles and short, styled hair. To my relief, they didn't match up with the buxom sexpots in *Coffee, Tea or Me?* In fact, they looked pretty wholesome, like me. One of the qualifications for being a teen model at Jordan Marsh, called a Marsha Jordan Girl, was a wholesome look. I wore my dirty-blond hair long and straight and, other than lip gloss for special occasions and Jordan Marsh fashion shows, didn't use any makeup. Watching the stewardesses, I could easily see myself as one of them, and the thought thrilled me.

My excitement at actually flying was so great that I didn't listen to a word they said over the intercom (until I actually went to flight attendant training myself, I thought there were parachutes under the seats). To my delight and surprise, after takeoff the stewardesses donned paisley aprons and appeared with full breakfasts for us—coffee, orange juice, scrambled eggs, sausages, and fruit. It was, I thought, the most delicious breakfast I'd ever eaten.

THE LIST OF everything I didn't know on that first flight was long: I didn't know there were two cabins, separated by a blue curtain, one rarefied and elegant and the other for everyone else; I didn't know that while I ate my eggs and sausage there were people just a few years older than me behind that blue curtain, sipping champagne; I didn't know what the life of a stewardess was really like—"Food under your fingernails, sore feet, complaints and insults," as well as that "it was like going to graduate school for the world"; or which airlines flew where; or that this was not only the golden age of flying but also the golden age of airplane hijackings, with sometimes as many as two a day. All I knew was that so far traveling was everything I'd hoped it would be, and more. And there wasn't just the excitement of the flight itself, of looking *down* at clouds, but also the marvelous things at the airports—watching luggage drop onto the baggage carousel and slowly spin toward me, the people rushing past who seemed to being going *somewhere*, the line of taxis in front of the terminal waiting for passengers. Behind me were the days of overly chlorinated motel swimming pools; of hours in a smoke-filled car and soggy sandwiches from the cooler in the way-back. Getting on an airplane meant perfect trays of food and gentle Muzak in the background, playing cards with the airline's logo on them, reclining seats and little jets of air tickling your face.

Just a few years earlier, all of us seventh graders at John F. Deering Junior High School were required to visit our guidance counselor, Mr. Stone, and tell him what we wanted to do after high school. It seems like a strange thing to do, but our answer shaped our future through high school. Combined with our IQ scores, whatever we announced that day—nurse, teacher, secretary, mechanic—tracked us toward either college prep courses or commercial courses that focused on typing, shorthand, bookkeeping, wood shop, and auto repairs. Seventh grade was also the year our school allowed girls to wear pants to school. Our hemlines were getting shorter, and the administration instituted a policy for teachers to measure the distance between our hem and our knees. If our skirts looked short, we were ordered to climb onto a desk so the teacher could measure. More than three inches and we were sent home. It seemed that the world was changing, what with girls in pants and miniskirts, notebooks with peace signs on the covers, lava lamps and Make Love, Not War posters bought from Spencer Gifts at the newly opened mall.

Mr. Stone was young, maybe fresh out of college, with the mutton-chop sideburns and droopy walrus mustache that were so popular in 1968. All male teachers were required to wear suits and ties every day, and Mr. Stone always wore a brown corduroy suit, even in warm weather. When it was my turn to visit his office, he asked me what I hoped to do when I grew up. I was a straight-A student, the kid who always raised her hand in class, who joined clubs and started new ones, a go-getter.

I had a grand plan. I would be a stewardess, travel the world, have adventures, and then write novels about my travels and adventures.

"I want to be a writer," I told Mr. Stone.

He looked baffled. "Ann," he said, "people don't do that."

"Don't do what?"

"Become writers," he said. Although I didn't understand it then, Mr. Stone was saying what anybody in my small mill town might say about becoming a writer: it was impossible. Writers came from different kinds of places, lived different kinds of lives.

I looked around his office. "Then how do we get all these books?"

Mr. Stone followed my gaze across the bookshelves. "All of those writers are dead," he said.

Melville. Hemingway. Fitzgerald. He was right. After I died, someone would find my unwritten novels and I would be published posthumously, I thought, putting plan B in place.

"Then I want to be an airline stewardess," I announced.

Mr. Stone peered out at me from behind his aviator glasses and said, "Ann, smart girls do not become airline stewardesses."

But Mr. Stone was dead wrong. Some smart girls do become airline stewardesses. And writers. And after my first flight, I knew I would be one of them.

# FLY GIRLS

IN MANY WAYS, I was the most stereotypical type of girl who became an airline stewardess. Small town. Love of travel. Big dreams. Craving excitement. In 1937, TWA's chief hostess, Ruth Rhodes, believed that flying was the most romantic thing a woman could do. According to Barry in *Femininity in Flight*, she said: "Women don't have enough adventures in their lives." Just seven years earlier, a twenty-six-year-old registered nurse named Ellen Church had walked into United Air Lines' district manager Steve Stimpson's office in San Francisco looking for a job as a pilot. She was refused the job because she was a woman, even though she had her CAA pilot's license. Determined to work in aviation, she pitched Stimpson the idea of having registered nurses, like her, to serve passengers. After all, nurses were trained to keep people calm and to handle emergencies. Plus, seeing women on board would send the message that air travel was safe, something many people did not yet believe.

Passenger air travel was still new in 1930. Those early airline passengers endured a lot: deafening noise, extreme temperatures, and turbulent flights due to flying at low altitudes. When you consider that in 1910, fewer than a thousand Americans had even seen an airplane, these first passengers were considered foolhardy by many. "Don't you think it would be good psychology to have women up in the air?" Church said. "How is a man going to say he is afraid to fly when a woman is working on the plane?"

Although the first scheduled passenger service between Tampa and St. Petersburg, Florida—just eighteen miles apart—started in 1914, for most of the 1920s airlines were used to carry mail. That first passenger service didn't catch on, lasting only three months. But just a month later, Western Air Express, which started carrying mail in April 1926, allowed passengers to fly on its mail route between Salt Lake City and Los Angeles via Las Vegas, if there was room on the plane. The flight took eight hours, cost $180 and the passengers sat on the mailbags. Two years later, Maude Campbell of Salt Lake City became the first female passenger. It was such big news that she was met with flowers when the plane landed in Los Angeles and newspapers across the country covered it.

The following year, Jane Eads, a twenty-one-year-old reporter for the *Chicago Herald and Examiner*, flew from Chicago to San Francisco. The flight took twenty-four hours and included two plane changes and stops in Iowa City, Omaha, North Platte, Cheyenne, Rock Springs, Salt Lake City, Elko, and Reno. The cabin of the Boeing Model 40 was cramped, and in order to board she had to climb a stepladder onto the wing and then climb through an opening into the plane—wearing a skirt, of course. Eads wrote: "Before landing I was too frightened to write. The plane tipped and tilted and dropped. It was the most exhilarating feeling I've ever experienced in my whole life."

Despite these discomforts and hardships, throughout the 1920s and '30s airlines began carrying passengers. Pan Am and KLM, the Royal Dutch Airline, were among the first; KLM even had Lady Heath, the first woman to pilot a passenger plane. By 1934, there were 450,000 airline passengers, up from just 6,000 in 1930. Qantas Airlines operated the world's first international passenger service in 1935 between Brisbane and Singapore.

The first flight attendant was actually a man named Heinrich Kubis, who began working as a steward eighteen years before Ellen Church. The professional waiter served passengers on zeppelin flights between Germany and the United States beginning in 1912. (Kubis was serving passengers on the *Hindenburg* when it burst into flames in New Jersey in 1937 and managed to help some passengers and crew members to escape out a window.) The British airline, Imperial Airlines, hired stewards, called cabin boys, for passenger service, and airlines in the United States soon followed their lead. These stewards dressed in uniforms that brought to mind naval officers or ship captains. Airlines also borrowed a lot of terminology from ships, words that are still used today—pilots are called captains, the cockpit is the flight deck, and the kitchen is called the galley. Even the word "steward" was borrowed from ship terminology.

Transcontinental Air Transport, which merged with Western Air Express and eventually became TWA, hired the young sons of investors who financed the airline to work as air couriers. Their duties included picking up passengers and bringing them to the airport with a stop along the way to get the catered meals, weighing and loading baggage, and boarding the fourteen passengers. In flight, the couriers pointed out the location of the lavatory, handed out gum to prevent passengers' ears from popping and cotton balls to block out the noise, and distributed magazines and maps. They relayed messages to people on the ground, written by passengers on airline stationery and passed from the courier to the pilot.

Couriers, dressed in wool double-breasted jackets with brass buttons and blue-and-gold braided epaulets inspired by the uniforms worn on ships, also provided meal services. TAT used custom-made gold-plated dinnerware and flatware, designed to complement lavender tablecloths and napkins. The Fred Harvey Company, a chain of hotels and restaurants developed in the western United States to cater to train passengers, provided the food, which consisted of cold sliced meats, sandwiches, salads, olives, fruit, and warm chicken that had been precooked and put in thermoses.

With men doing the job, it was no surprise that at first management rejected Church's idea. Women? On airplanes? But Stimpson, who knew Boeing needed to attract more customers and show people that flying was safe, persevered, and finally the airline agreed to a three-month trial of female attendants on flights between Oakland and Chicago. Not only would passengers find comfort in the fact that the crew was medically trained, but Stimpson and his colleagues also believed that women were better at serving food and taking care of passengers. Church was hired at a salary of $125 a month.

On May 15, 1930, Ellen Church became the first stewardess. She had recruited seven other nurses from hospitals in Chicago and San Francisco and designed their dark-colored suits and green capes and hats. Church also invented the jump seat, where even today flight attendants sit for takeoff and landing. She quickly realized that the knobs on the cabin doors and the bathroom doors were the same, which could lead to a confused passenger opening the wrong door in flight and dropping outside 11,000 feet. Putting fold-down jump seats by the cabin doors kept passengers away.

On board, the eight stewardesses—known as the Great Eight—removed their suit uniforms and changed into their white nurses' uniforms to perform the tasks the male couriers had done. Except for those hired as head flight attendants, called pursers, to run the service on international flights, men would not become flight attendants again until 1971, when the Supreme Court ruled against Pan Am and declared that airlines could not prevent men from becoming flight attendants.

We're so used to seeing male flight attendants now that it's hard to believe how new and unusual it was in the '70s. My friend David had always loved airplanes, so when he graduated from college in 1975, he wrote to TWA about possible jobs. He was surprised when they suggested he apply as a flight attendant. Just a few years later, when my friend Matt boarded a Delta flight from Boston to Fort Lauderdale for spring break, he didn't even know there were male flight attendants until he saw one on that flight. By the time I started flying the following year, about 14 percent of flight attendants were men. My training class of twenty had three. Today, more than 25 percent of flight attendants are men, and it's common to see male flight attendants, or even all male crews.

But long before men became "stewards" again, the first stewardesses could not weigh more than 115 pounds or be taller than 5'4", restrictions based not on standards of beauty but on the small size of the cabin. Like the stewards before them, their job included not only greeting the passengers at the door and serving them in-flight but also tightening the screws that held the wicker passenger seats in place, refueling airplanes, weighing passengers and baggage, loading and unloading baggage and mail, and pushing the airplane into the hangar at night. Due to the low altitude where early planes flew—under 10,000 feet at about 100 miles per hour—airsickness was a common occurrence, and handing out airsickness bags was a big part of the job. On layovers, stewardesses were often required to sleep on the plane, even though the pilots got hotel rooms.

FIVE YEARS AFTER United Airlines hired Ellen Church and American Airlines also hired stewardesses, TWA followed suit. Jack Frye, the airline's president, believed passengers were choosing American and United over TWA because they employed pretty girls. "There will be women in the air," Frye wrote to management, "and they will be called hostesses." The word "hostess," he believed, conveyed the charm and domestic skills needed to welcome passengers on board as if they were her guests.

Two thousand women applied for the first sixty TWA hostess jobs. If hired, they would be sent to a three-week training at hostess school in Kansas City. An ex-army pilot and TWA copilot, LeRoy Rainey, was their instructor in hostess school, where they studied the theory of flight, meteorology, in-flight hostess duties, and how to work the DC-2's heating system. Rainey informed them that they would not be able to fly after they turned twenty-eight. "If you haven't found a man to keep you by the time you're twenty-eight, TWA won't want you either," he explained.

Upon passing the course, hostesses were given gray flannel uniforms with red silk blouses, gray topcoats fitted with red lining, and a hat with the TWA logo printed inside wings. Their manual stated that they could not wear perfume or nail polish, makeup had to be conservative, and they could not accept tips. Passengers had to be addressed by name and doted on. In a hostess-instruction letter from 1937, they were ordered to obtain one Packard electric razor to keep in their hostess kits at all times. Directions for how to sterilize it were included, so that the razor could be loaned to more than one passenger on a flight for shaving. The list of what else was in that hostess kit included everything from six TWA pencils to a sewing kit with several colors of thread, scissors, straight pins, safety pins, and a variety of buttons.

By 1936, uniforms became less severe. Skirts had kick pleats, the TWA logo was stitched in red on the hat and jacket pocket, and white silk scarves were added. A year later, TWA added sleeping accommodations to their planes—wide, twin-sized berths with separate dressing rooms for men and women. That meant more duties for the hostesses: cleaning lavatories, emptying ashtrays, serving hot meals, and even putting their passengers to bed. United's instructions for making up a berth had thirty-eight steps that had to be repeated twelve to fourteen times per flight. Flying over the Rockies required dispensing oxygen and checking passengers for signs of hypoxia.

Despite the reality of the hostesses' work, the media glamorized the job. "The flying hostess may well expect a career of romance and adventure," a front-page story in the *New York Times* said. The *San Francisco Call-Bulletin* described "sky school" as the most exciting school any student ever attended. TWA, and every other airline, required stewardesses to be unmarried.

"TWA announced that it will have vacancies for some twenty hostesses," the article continued. "The prime reason is that Dan Cupid had turned his darts into 'anti-aircraft' arrows and virtually decimated TWA's sky girls." When World War II began and nurses were needed for the war effort, the nursing requirement was removed, and stewardesses became the airlines' best marketing tool.

IN MANY WAYS my friend Kate Ferguson Heckman epitomized this second wave of stewardesses. I met Kate many years after I'd stopped flying at an outdoor concert on a summer night in Providence, Rhode Island. Everyone sat on blankets on the lawn of the historic John Brown House and ate picnic food as a band played big-band music. During the concert I noticed an attractive older woman glancing over at me from time to time. By then, I was a pretty well-known writer and it wasn't unusual for someone to recognize me in the grocery store or coffee shop. When the concert ended and people began folding up their blankets and heading off, the woman came up to me. Kate was in her eighties then, still pretty, with twinkling blue eyes and a big smile.

"Are you Ann Hood?" she asked me.

I told her I was, then waited to hear which book of mine she'd read or where she'd heard me give a talk.

Instead, she said, "Well, you and I have something in common. We were both TWA stewardesses."

Kate had read an op-ed I had in the *New York Times* about flying and recognized me from my book jacket photo. Imme-

diately we began sharing stories of our days flying for TWA—
Kate back in the '40s and me in the '70s and '80s.

When Kate was six years old, her older sister came home from
her job as a department store buyer in Chicago and gave Kate
the Christmas present that would change her life—a twenty-
eight-minute train ride to Sioux Falls, where they ate Chinese
food (Kate for the first time). That brief trip planted the desire
to travel and see the world. When I heard Kate's story, I immediately thought of my old TWA roommate, Diane. Her elementary school in the small town of Fremont, Ohio, sat near a
railroad track. "I used to hear the train go by and wonder where
it was going, and I'd think, I'm going to see the world someday."

As a junior living with her sister in Chicago and studying
child psychology at DePaul, Kate saw an ad in the paper for
TWA hostess interviews in the Loop. She went for the interview and was brought into a room where two men asked her to
walk back and forth. "I knew they were checking out my legs.
But so what? I wanted to fly." The next day she was called in
for a physical and an IQ test, and just that like she was on a
train from Chicago to Kansas City for hostess training.

Her class in 1946 had sixteen women from eight states, and
after six weeks of training Kate was working her first flight—a
Kansas City–Chicago turnaround on a DC-3, the only hostess for twenty-one male passengers. One of her classmates was
quickly fired for deplaning dressed in street clothes instead
of her uniform—a medium blue skirt and jacket with the red
TWA logo, hat, and gloves. She'd changed so she would make a
date and found the check hostess at the bottom of the airplane
stairs waiting.

Kate and most of her class volunteered to train on the new Lockheed Constellation. The Connie, as it was called, had the first pressurized cabin, which gave the plane the ability to fly at high altitudes, thus reducing airsickness and forever changing the flight time of long-haul journeys. Howard Hughes, the owner of TWA, was looking for a way to beat United and American, and the Connie was his answer. He bought thirty-five planes in a secret deal with Lockheed that prevented them from selling to the other airlines. Kate was in the third class of hostesses trained to work on the Constellation, which flew eight hours from New York to Gander, Newfoundland, where crews changed, and then continued on another eight hours to Shannon Airport in Ireland. Very soon afterward, flights continued on to Paris, Geneva, and Rome, with new cities added all the time.

In Cairo, Kate had dinner with King Farouk. Buddy Rogers, a wrestler and the husband of Mary Pickford, read her palm on a flight. Howard Hughes himself was a frequent passenger. Back in New York, on their days off, Kate and her roommates traveled from their apartment in Jackson Heights to Manhattan to go to the Copacabana and the El Dorado. For a young woman from a small town in South Dakota, being a TWA hostess in 1948 offered a life other girls only saw in the movies. But she and her coworkers also knew, "We were the biggest sales force the airline had."

IN 1958, *LIFE* magazine called an airline stewardess one of the most coveted careers open to young women in America. "The chance to fly, to see the world, and meet all sorts of interesting people—mostly the kind of men who can afford to travel by plane—gives the job real glamor." The qualifications were listed as between twenty-one and twenty-six years old, unmarried, reasonably pretty, especially around the hips, which is eye level for the passengers . . ."

Thanks to movies like *Boeing Boeing* in 1965—a favorite on my television's *Sunday Afternoon at the Movies* for most of my childhood—and books like *Coffee, Tea or Me?* in 1967, the sexpot image continued to grow. In *Boeing Boeing*, suave Tony Curtis is simultaneously engaged to three stewardesses—"delectable creatures," we are told in a voice-over. The opening credits show the actors in stewardess uniforms with their real names below them, and below that, their measurements: 42-32-36. Curtis makes sure that their layovers never overlap, affording him the pleasures of three beautiful fiancées. Until the start of jet travel throws a kink in his plans—suddenly their flight times are reduced and they can all be home more. All three stewardesses arrive at his apartment in Paris at the same time, along with his buddy, played by Jerry Lewis, and pandemonium ensues.

This was the climate of my childhood—the stewardesses in books and movies and advertisements were sexy and glamorous. Russell Baker wrote in the *New York Times* in 1965, "In the present enlightenment, few people will be shocked to hear that the airlines have been subtly trading in sex. Where the modern spirit of tolerance rebels, however, is the point at which the flying industry starts trying to dictate their clients' taste in women." But they did, and the taste they dictated was for sexy women, like the gold-uniformed Continental stewardesses who promised: "We really move our tails for you."

In 1967, the same year that I read *How to Become an Airline Stew-*

*ardess,* United Airlines ran a recruitment ad that read: "Marriage is fine. But shouldn't you see the world first?" And National Airlines ran the now-infamous commercial of a pretty woman in a stewardess uniform saying, "I'm Cheryl. Fly me." A magazine ad for Eastern Airlines that same year featured a picture of a group of beautiful, dejected, sad women with Twiggy haircuts or teased shoulder-length hair, all of them dressed in miniskirts and high heels beneath the headline: PRESENTING THE LOSERS. The ad copy reads: "Pretty good aren't they? We admit it. And they're probably good enough to get a job practically anywhere they want. But not as an Eastern Airlines stewardess." Why did these "girls" not get picked? Eastern explained that sure, they want her to be pretty . . . "Don't you? That's why we look at her face, her makeup . . . her figure, her weight . . . her legs . . ." but also "her voice, her speech . . . her personality, her intelligence, her intentions . . ."

Braniff Airlines' ad asked: "Does your wife know you're flying with us?" and Pan Am's asked: "How do you like your stewardesses?" Famous designers like Oleg Cassini and Emilio Pucci added that panache that was attributed to stewardesses, though uniforms actually became part of the sexualized marketing. This was the '60s, and hot pants and miniskirts were the style, of course. National Airlines' stewardesses wore fake tiger-fur hats and jackets—"Uniforms that purr." TWA had their stewardesses wear paper stewardess dresses that reflected the flight's destination: French cocktail, British wench, Roman toga, and Manhattan penthouse pajamas. Unfortunately—or maybe fortunately?—the uniforms were so impractical, ripping and shredding, that the gimmick lasted only seven months. Perhaps most outrageous of all, Braniff introduced "the Air Strip," with stewardesses beginning the trip in a space-age bubble hat and cape on the runway, then removing it in full view of passengers to reveal a Pucci suit, and then removing that to reveal underneath a yellow serving dress, and finishing the "Air Strip" in casual wear of culottes and a sporty top because on those long flights she should be "slipping into something more comfortable."

As a kid who logged in many hours in front of my family's Zenith television, I saw those ads on TV, and I saw the print ads in the magazines my parents subscribed to, like *LIFE* and *Time*. Sitting here five decades later, a sixty-four-year-old woman who has traveled extensively, lived in big cities, done the kinds of things my younger self dreamed about, I can see the blatant sexism used in these marketing campaigns. I can feel insulted and outraged at the projection of every stewardess as being buxom and naughty. But to that twelve-year-old small-town girl, those attributes—*Fly me!*—were as exciting as the promise to have "Breakfast in New York on a winter morning and lunch in Miami under palm trees [be] all in a day's work . . . Dinner could be in London, Amsterdam, Stockholm or Rome." In many ways, my dreams were vague. I just knew they happened far from West Warwick, Rhode Island.

# HOW TO BECOME AN
# AIRLINE STEWARDESS

THE HISTORY and the culture of being an airline stewardess that I stepped into was a combination of women fighting for equal pay, fair work rules, and respect for their jobs as flight attendants while those same women were being portrayed as sex symbols, used to dress sexy, act demure, and lure businessmen onto airlines. It seemed, in 1977, to pretty much capture the role of women in general.

During winter break from college during my senior year in 1977, my parents sat me down at the kitchen table and asked me what exactly English majors did once they graduated. My parents were mostly hands-off. Or maybe the ambition and work ethic I had shown since I was a kid convinced them I would do just fine. Not only was I the one with my hand always in the air to be called on with the right answer; the one who wrote plays and forced classmates to perform in them; who edited the yearbook and school newspaper, starred in drama club plays, and got straight A's, I worked as a Marsha Jordan Girl; was the Rhode Island teen rep to *Seventeen*, sending monthly dispatches on fashion and trends in my school—"Everyone is wearing Dr. Scholl's sandals now that the weather is warm. Red is the most

popular color!" "Astrology is really a hot topic at West Warwick High School!"—and a Bonne Bell Girl, sitting in the mall
demonstrating how Ten-O-Six Lotion helped your complex-
ion or making lipstick from scratch by melting special wax and
adding dyes to it. I fought for more relevant English classes. I
fought for recycling. I fought for the end of the Vietnam War.
My parents sat back and watched, dazed and proud, at fashion
shows and school plays and awards ceremonies.

When I left for college in 1974, I wanted to major in English
so I could learn how to write novels. After my meeting with
Mr. Stone back when I was twelve, I had eventually returned
to my original plan to become a stewardess and then a writer.
Run with the bulls! Jump naked into fountains! Shop on Carn-
aby Street! Becoming a flight attendant—by then they were no
longer called stewardesses because of the increase of men in the
job—would offer me adventure, the chance to travel for free,
glamour and excitement, all while I hatched plots and charac-
ters for my novels. But my father tried to convince me to major
in business, a new frontier for women. "If you're a business
major, you'll be able to write your own ticket," Dad said. What
I didn't tell him was that I was interested in a different kind
of ticket, one that gave me unlimited flights on 747s heading
everywhere in the world.

That December day that my parents asked me what I
intended to do with my BA in English, my mother expected
me to announce that I would become an English teacher. To
her, that was a very good job—summers off, benefits, home by
three or four in the afternoon. Besides, why else would someone major in English? My father probably still held out hope
that I would enter the business world. I knew plenty of young

women who majored in the mysterious new field of marketing. They had taken special classes on how to write a résumé and they'd bought suits—knee-length skirts and matching jackets with floppy bow ties—for interviews with banks and insurance companies and IBM, the dream place to land a job back then. Dad frequently dropped tidbits about businesses that were hiring managers. "And they want women!" he always added. Even English majors.

"I want to be a flight attendant," I told my parents.

They looked at each other. They looked at me.

Then my father asked, "If you're a flight attendant, do we get free tickets?"

"I think so," I said.

"Sounds like a good plan," Dad said. Like me, he had wanderlust.

He told me to get in the car. We were going to Logan Airport to pick up applications.

DAD AND I drove the hour to Boston and I went from terminal to terminal at Logan requesting flight-attendant applications at the ticket counters, where there seemed to be an endless supply, and he idled in the car curbside. By the time we were back home, I had a big stack of applications. Alleghany, American, United, Eastern, National, Northwest, Delta, Republic, Air New England, and many more that I no longer remember. Only two really mattered to me. I didn't want to fly around the Ohio Valley or between Washington, DC, and Boston. I wanted to see the world, and in 1977 only two airlines flew internationally: Pan Am and TWA. True, Delta had taken me to Bermuda, and Eastern had flown me to the Bahamas the following year. But I wanted pyramids and the Wailing Wall, the Eiffel Tower and the Coliseum. I wanted to gobble up every city on every continent.

Back at home, my father and I sat at the kitchen table while I read through the applications. Some were just one page, others were several pages long.

"Now, fill them all out," my father said in his slightly Southern drawl.

I looked at all of those beautiful logos of clouds and globes and wings and said, "I think I'll just apply to these." I plucked TWA and Pan Am from the stack, then added Eastern for good measure because they flew to the Caribbean and Latin America.

"Apply to all of them," Dad said. "You never know. For example, I just read in the paper that United is trying to get routes to China."

With all my twenty-one-year-old bravado I wanted to tell him that I did indeed know. Instead, I picked up a pen and began to fill out every application, Dad instructing me along the way. The applications were mostly the same: name and birthdate, level of education, height and weight, vision, and the perplexing question "Can you swim?" (Later I would learn that this was a requirement for most airlines in the unlikely situation of an ocean ditching.) They also asked if you were willing to relocate (definitely!), if you spoke any languages (French, *un peu*), and for a list of jobs you'd had (salesgirl, waitress, model).

That same year, Anna Quindlen wrote in the *New York Times*, "They are attractive and good-tempered . . . they are flight attendants, and the occasional air traveler who still thinks of them as the coffee-tea-or-me type is in for a jolt. Beneath the faultlessly groomed exteriors—'It is still our contention that cosmetics are necessary for all women,' said one training specialist—there is a different kind of person." That person, Quindlen went on to describe, was "older, better educated." Combine that with travel benefits, a salary competitive with other entry-level jobs, and the chance to work with many kinds of people, and the job of flight attendant was perhaps even more appealing than in the early days.

Height: 5'7"
Weight: 120 pounds
Hair: Blond
Eyes: Green
Vision: Corrected to 20/20 with contact lenses
Education: BA English, University of Rhode Island, 1978
Work Experience:
    Marsha Jordan Girl, teen model for Jordan Marsh department stores, Warwick, RI, and Boston, MA, 1971–1976
    Salesgirl, Jordan Marsh, 1971–1974
    Waitress, Dunes Club, summer 1976, 1977
    Student Body Treasurer, paid position on student government, University of Rhode Island, 1976–1978
    Freshman Orientation Leader for incoming freshmen at the University of Rhode Island, summer 1977

Languages: English, French
Are You Willing to Relocate: YES
Can You Swim? YES

The first response I received was from American Airlines. They were having preliminary interviews at TF Green Airport in Warwick, ten minutes from my parents' house. (The airport uses Providence as its name—or PVD in airport code—but it actually sits about seven miles away in Warwick.) The same week that I filled out applications, my mother and I went to Casual Corner at the mall to buy an interview suit. No shoulder pads or floppy ties like the business majors I knew had bought. We left the mall with a black suit—polyester, pencil skirt, fitted jacket, white blouse, and a black, white, and pink patterned scarf to tie jauntily around my neck, just like a flight attendant.

Like almost every girl I knew, my hair was cut short in a Dorothy Hamill wedge, named after the 1976 Olympic figure-skating champion who sported that haircut. Standing in front of the full-length mirror on the back of the door of my childhood bedroom in my black suit and that scarf and black high heels, my short hair highlighted to look sun-kissed, I saw a flight attendant looking back at me.

My father had told me a story that a friend of his from work had shared with him about his daughter's flight-attendant interview. She'd been led into a room and invited to sit across from the interviewer. For the next excruciating five minutes the two of them sat in silence. Then the interviewer stood and thanked her for coming. She never heard from the airline again.

"They're looking for friendly people," my father told me. "Walk in there. Shake hands. Say your name and ask them how they are. Don't just sit there waiting for them to do something."

The story of that interview gone wrong scared the hell out of me. I would do as my father instructed, but what if the interviewers surprised me with something else?

"Just have your answers ready," Dad said.

Sure. But answers to what?

"Well, why do you want this job?" he asked.

"I want to travel," I said.

He laughed. "So does everybody. They aren't hiring you to give you free vacations."

"I like people?" I tried.

Dad grinned. "There you go. You love people and you love to travel."

At the airport, I was led into a small waiting room with half a dozen other applicants, and one by one we were called in for a preliminary interview. *I love people and I love to travel*, I kept repeating until my name was called.

My interviewer was a woman with big hair that looked as if it were hair-sprayed into a helmet. She had on more makeup than I'd had to wear during fashion shows at Jordan Marsh, and she did not look like she loved people. She looked angry.

I put on my best smile—her lips were covered in very red lipstick, mine in pale-pink lip gloss—and shook her hand. "Hi! I'm Ann. How are you?" I said.

She frowned and looked over my application. Then she asked me to walk back and forth across the room, the same request given to Kate Ferguson back in 1946. I walked back and forth, stopping when I was in front of her again, still smiling.

"Thank you," she said in a way that let me know we were done.

"That's it?" I said, surprised. I hadn't even been asked to sit down.

"Yup," she said, and opened the door for me. "Thank you for coming."

Needless to say, I never heard from them again. I went over and over what I had done wrong but couldn't come up with anything. My father said that I simply didn't have the look they wanted. I thought of how certain I'd been when I'd stared in my mirror that I looked exactly like a flight attendant. "Every airline has a look they're after. This one wasn't for you."

Neither was Alleghany, but I decided that on my own when I got the letter to come for a preliminary interview at TF Green. They'd included a brochure that explained I would train and be based in Pittsburgh. The route map on the back was a series of lines radiating from Pittsburgh all through Pennsylvania and the Ohio Valley, up to Detroit and cities like Binghamton, Albany, and Buffalo in upstate New York. I studied that map and knew that this wasn't what I wanted. Jumping into a fountain in Binghamton didn't have quite the same pizzazz as jumping into a fountain in Paris.

I soon realized that for various reasons other airlines weren't the right fit for me either. Midwest Airlines would have me based in Milwaukee and flying around the Midwest; Air Florida had routes mostly around Florida; Southwest flew predominantly in Texas; and yet another, PSA, flew up and down California. Many of those smaller airlines eventually grew or merged with other airlines and today are still flying.

But in 1978, I had my sights set on Pan Am and TWA. I wanted to see the world, and they were the airlines that could show it to me.


MY FATHER CONVINCED ME to interview with United too, because they were a solid company with plans for expansion internationally. Besides, he said, I needed a safe bet just in case TWA, Pan Am, or Eastern didn't hire me. Didn't hire me? Despite my disastrous American Airlines interview, it hadn't occurred to me that I might not actually get my dream job. My father must have seen the look of terror on my face because he quickly added, "It's always good to have a choice." I decided he was right. I liked the idea of living in a big city like Miami, Eastern's home base, or United's home base of Chicago. Their routes, though not as far-reaching as Pan Am's or TWA's, were extensive nonetheless. I'd flown to Hawaii with my girlfriends on United the past summer, and the flight attendants, dressed in sarongs and wearing leis, served us Mai Tais and coconut chicken. Honolulu? Buenos Aires? Caracas? I accepted interviews with all four airlines—Pan Am, TWA, Eastern, and United.

Although none of the preliminary interviews for these airlines asked me to walk across the room, they were pretty well all standard: one or two interviewers, often in their flight attendant uniforms, looked over my application and asked very few questions. In ten minutes or less, I was walking back out in my black polyester suit, scarf tied around my neck, and the next applicant was on his or her way in. Unlike the disastrous American Airlines interview, all four of these led to the next phase of hiring.

Eastern Airlines sent me a letter congratulating me on being invited to a final interview in Miami. Tucked inside was a round-trip ticket. If I had any doubts about pursuing a job as a flight attendant, that ticket sealed the deal. Free tickets were apparently going to fall in my lap once I worked for an airline! I went back to Casual Corner and bought the exact same suit in white with a scarf in tropical colors. I was going to Miami, after all, and I wanted to look the part.

Eastern flight attendants wore bright blue or yellow polyester dresses decorated with a pattern of the airline logo. To me, they all seemed tanned, with peachy or pink lipstick, like girls who spent a lot of time at the beach. Lolling on a tropical beach on my days off sounded fine to me. With that ticket in hand, I knew I could be one of those girls, sipping cocktails under palm trees, driving a convertible, jetting off to South America. When I arrived in humid Miami, I went straight to the hotel— also paid for!—and met up with other applicants in the lobby. A bus with EASTERN AIRLINES written across it in huge letters whisked us off to corporate headquarters for physicals, height and weight measurements, and tons of forms to fill out.

Although this was my first experience at a final interview, it was consistent with all of my interviews to come—everyone traded stories and tips about who was hiring and how many flight attendants they needed, what different airlines were looking for, like "All American" or "Sexy" or "Sophisticated," and the different interview practices each had. There was an immediate camaraderie with the other applicants. After all, not just one of us would get the job. Airlines were hiring hundreds or even thousands of new flight attendants. Plus, we had gotten this far because, in part, we were friendly. After just a couple interviews, I began to see the same faces, like seeing old friends.

The tone of the letter and the official business of the afternoon made me feel like the job was already mine. The next morning, we took the bus back to Eastern headquarters and one by one were invited into an impressively large office to have our final interview. "I love people and I love to travel!" I said. I smiled big. I talked about how much I liked Eastern Airlines. Yes, I answered, I was happy to relocate to Miami or their new base in San Juan.

Then the interviewer leveled a serious gaze at me and said, "Ann, what will you do if you don't get this job?"

Don't get the job? But they had flown me to Miami! They asked me for my uniform size!

I stuttered and said *um* too many times. I didn't think telling him that I wanted to write novels would go over very well, so I said, "Um, I don't know? Maybe go to grad school? In English?" That surprised even me, as I had no desire at all to go to graduate school. I was going to be a flight attendant and have adventures and write novels.

"That sounds like a good plan for you," he said, and I felt like I might throw up right there in that sunny office. Wasn't my plan to be a flight attendant for Eastern Airlines? On the flight home, I realized I should have said that if I didn't get the job, I'd reapply. All I wanted to do was work for them!

Still, I held on to the hope that what had happened wasn't what I thought had happened. I couldn't have flubbed the interview, could I? A month later my mother called me at college to tell me I had a letter from Eastern Airlines. Did I want her to open it? Not really, but of course she had to. No airline ticket this time, just a form rejection letter. I remember sitting in the phone booth of the student union and crying.

"Sweetie," my father told me, "you're just not the type they're looking for. I just know United and the others will love you."

By then I'd had other preliminary interviews and I was

already getting second interviews for Pan Am and United and TWA. One of them had to take me, didn't they?

PAN AM WAS the only airline at that time that required a second language. I heard about a German major at my college who had gotten hired by them, but surely I didn't need that level of proficiency. I spoke terrible French, despite studying it from seventh through twelfth grade and always getting an A. I'd been taught by wonderful, smart teachers who suffered the curse of a strong Rhode Island accent, which led to strange French pronunciations. Still, I could manage OK—or so I thought. After all, I had read entire novels and written papers in French.

At the second Pan Am interview, we were required to take a written language test, which I passed. We were also given a math test and some kind of personality test and then participated in a group interview. A few days later I got a letter congratulating me on making it to the final interview, which was in New York City in the Pan Am Building, a fifty-nine-story skyscraper at Forty-Fifth Street and Park Avenue in Manhattan. No ticket this time. I had to get myself to New York City. Somehow I convinced my very reluctant mother to drive there with me, both of us terrified of driving in the city and of the city itself. This was the place my father had deemed too dangerous for Nancy and me to visit alone. I'd been there exactly twice—once on a family day trip when I was eight and we went to Macy's, the Empire State Building, and an automat; and one night in college when a group of us decided to drive the three and half hours there, only to arrive in Times Square around midnight, glimpse the sex shops and creepy people, and get too scared to get out of the car. We turned around and drove all the way back to Rhode Island. Although I loved the Manhattan of Doris Day/Rock Hudson movies, and books like *Marjorie Morningstar*, the real city terrified me.

Somehow, before Google maps and GPS, Mom and I managed to drive to Manhattan, find the Pan Am Building, and park the car. I don't remember where she went while I took the elevator up that gleaming skyscraper, but I do remember feeling like I had landed right in one of those Doris Day/Rock Hudson movies I loved. Here I was in a suit and high heels, moving through a fancy building in Manhattan, suddenly feeling literally on top of the world. Maybe I did belong here, I thought, gaining confidence with every step. By the time I walked into the office, I decided that Pan Am was the airline for me. After the interview, Mom and I would go for lunch, to celebrate. Surely fancy restaurants were on every corner.

The final interview that day was a huge success. Without actually saying *You're hired*, the two interviewers let me know that I was just what they were looking for. They shuffled some papers and told me when training—in *Honolulu!*—would be starting, and that I would be based there or at JFK. I imagined myself in that Evan Picone pale-blue uniform, moving through the aisles of a 747 on my way to Paris. I imagined living in one of these skyscrapers, or in a high-rise on Waikiki Beach.

"The final thing," one of the interviewers said, "is the language test."

"Oh, I took it in Boston," I said.

"Right. And passed with 100 percent. But now you need to take the oral test."

Panic did not set in right away. I knew my accent was bad, the accent of someone who had learned French with a blue-collar New England twist. But I had a good vocabulary and mostly still remembered verb conjugations. Plus, I had passed the written test. They could see that I knew French. Kind of.

Down the shiny, polished hallway, I went to another office, where a man in a suit greeted me effusively.

"This'll be a breeze," he said after we sat down. "Pretend I'm a passenger and tell me to please put my suitcase in the overhead compartment."

I stared at him. I knew how to say *monsieur* and *s'il vous plaît*. Maybe "suitcase" was *valise*? But overhead compartment? Of course, as soon as I walked out of that office and down that hallway to the elevators, I realized I could have just said a simple sentence like, "Mets ta valise la-haut"—*Put your bag up there*. But I panicked and couldn't think of anything at all.

"How about, 'Fasten your seatbelt, please'?"

"Seatbelt?" I repeated.

At which point we both looked at each other and silently acknowledged that I could not, indeed, speak French.

"I'm so sorry," he said as we shook hands, that pale blue uniform and six weeks in Honolulu already fading.

UNITED AND TWA both proved to be my most successful interviews and the most intense ones. After the personal interview with United, I was called to Boston for a group interview that took an entire afternoon. Most of it remains a blur, except the psychological test. We all sat in a circle and were given face-down pictures of babies that we couldn't look at until it was our turn. At that point, we were to pick up the photograph, study it, and then pretend to be the baby in the picture.

"Forget you're at an interview with an airline," we were told. "Don't pretend the baby is on a plane. Just interpret that baby as you see it."

I still think this was one of the strangest things I had to do in an interview. The connection between babies and my psychology baffled me. In fact, I never learned why this test was administered to potential flight attendants. Perhaps it was a version of the Thematic Apperception test, which uses pictures of people in ordinary situations to measure and assess someone's personality and maturity. Of course, the TAT and versions of it are administered by trained psychologists, not flight attendants conducting interviews. Still, we had to do it.

A David Cassidy look-alike who had been at my Pan Am interview (he also failed the language test in New York) and at my preliminary TWA interview sat next to me. It was comforting to see a familiar face in such a stressful time, and we shared stories and gossip about who was hiring and how different interviews were conducted. I was certain that with his boyish, pop-star good looks combined with a perfect smile and an easygoing personality he'd be hired by someone.

When it was his turn, he looked at the picture of a baby with his face twisted into a full-on tantrum, and said, "I'm so unhappy! Flight attendant, come and help me!"

"No, no," the interviewer said gently. "Forget about the airline. Just be the baby."

He nodded, twisted his own face, and pretend-cried, "Flight attendant! My ears hurt!"

The interviewer gave him several more tries—"What if the

baby wasn't on a plane? What would he feel?"—until finally
she said in her bright flight-attendant voice, "Thanks! Let's
move on now." Needless to say, that was the last I saw of him.

I made it to the final interview, which was held at JFK. Even
though I was told I would most likely be based in Cleveland—
not Honolulu or San Francisco, as I'd hoped—and that I knew
United flew to many small cities around the United States, I
liked the interviewers and the whole feeling of the company.
Plus, there was that rumor of them flying to China soon. One
United ad during the '70s opened with waves washing up on
a beach lined with palm trees, then cut to a flight attendant
dressed in a Hawaiian sarong with a big flower behind her
ear, standing seductively at a United airplane boarding door.
After gorgeous shots of waterfalls, flowers, leis, and a beautiful
Hawaiian woman, the familiar jingle plays as a jet takes off at
sunset. *Fly the friendly skies of United!* I could definitely see myself
"flying the friendly skies."

A week before the final interview, the flight attendant who
had interviewed me called. She told me that I was what United
was looking for in their flight attendants and that this final
interview was really a formality to get weighed and measured,
fill out employment forms, meet some key management people.
I was as good as hired, she said. Except one thing.

"Your hair," she told me. "The highlights look too brassy.
United likes a more natural look. The girl next door. Which
you have, except those highlights . . ."

I carefully painted on those highlights every six weeks from
a kit called Sun In, which was supposed to give my hair a sun-
kissed look.

I don't remember what I said, but I do remember what she

said next. "Would you be willing to get rid of the highlights and restore your hair to its own honey color?"

"Of course," I said, because I wanted that job and if all it took was changing my hair color, why not?

Years later I would wonder if my hair with its golden highlights had really been an issue, or if the request itself was part of the selection process. A TWA flight-attendant personnel video from the same year lists the qualities they are looking for in a flight attendant as both "a unique personality" and someone who is "willing to conform." If that was the real purpose of the call, to make sure I would conform, I passed easily. A day later I was sitting in a hair salon having my hair stripped and then colored a shade called honey blond.

UNITED FLEW FROM Providence to New York, and so another round-trip plane ticket arrived for me. The ticket was open, which meant I just had to go to the ticket counter at the airport and tell them when and where I wanted to fly. I took an early flight so that I had plenty of time before my interview. How sophisticated I felt walking across the terminal at JFK as directed in the letter that accompanied my ticket, looking for a room that was tucked behind a particular counter. But in no time my confidence began to disappear. I couldn't find the counter or the room, and I was too nervous to ask for help. The rumor mill at all of the second and third interviews said that there were airline spies—possibly even one of us pretending to be an applicant!—watching you when you didn't know it in order to see the real you. Don't trust anyone was the advice.

As paranoid as this sounds, my friend and fellow TWA

flight attendant, Diane, sat next to a man in first class on her flight to Miami for her final interview with Eastern Airlines. Frazzled because she'd almost missed the flight, she hurriedly painted her fingernails right there in the first-class cabin. That man was an Eastern executive who sent word not to hire her because she was too disorganized and also so rude that she'd put on nail polish on the plane. She didn't get the job.

That day at JFK I passed ticket agents and gate agents and pilots and flight attendants, so many people dressed in United's polyester camel-and-rust western-style uniforms, their blouses decorated with random blue, orange, and red overlapping *U*'s. But any one of them could keep me from getting this job just because I couldn't find the location of where I was required to be. If I couldn't do this simple thing, how was I going to serve four hundred 747 passengers Mai Tais and coconut chicken, or evacuate a plane in an emergency?

Finally, I saw a ticket counter for a different airline. Surely that guy wasn't going to tell someone at United that I was lost. I asked him for directions and he looked puzzled.

"I don't know where that is," he said, shaking his head.

When I showed him the letter, his face lit up.

"Oh, you need to be at JFK," he said.

Now I looked puzzled.

"You're at LaGuardia," he said, and when he saw that didn't make any sense to me, he added, "the other New York airport."

"The other New York airport?" I repeated. All I had told the ticket agent back in Providence was that I was going to New York, and he didn't ask me *which* airport. Now here I was at the wrong one, with minutes ticking down until my interview.

The ticket agent must have seen the absolute terror I felt

because he told me to calm down and directed me to the Carey bus that went between LaGuardia and JFK. I thanked him and then I ran in my high heels and black polyester suit. I was no longer early; I was almost late. That traffic-clogged ride between airports that day was surely the longest hour of my life thus far. As soon as the doors opened at the United Terminal at JFK, I flew off the bus. With barely time to catch my breath, I found my way to that room behind the counter where my interviewer from Boston—the one who had called about my hair—sat waiting with two others. As soon as she saw me, she smiled. And minutes later, I was hired.

AT THE SAME TIME that I was interviewing with United, I was also having my first two interviews with TWA. Like most of the other airlines, the preliminary interview, held in a hotel in downtown Boston, was brief. But I left it feeling even more certain that TWA would be the perfect fit for me. The interviewer, in her sharp Ralph Lauren uniform, looked professional but friendly. We chatted for a few minutes, and then she stood, indicating the interview was over. But when we shook hands, she said, "I'll see you again very soon." A thrill shot through me, and lasted the whole hour back to Rhode Island. True to her word, I got a letter inviting me to a second interview the very next week.

That interview, also in the Boston hotel, was a group interview that lasted about an hour. We had to answer questions like "Would you rather *give* a party or *go to* a party?" I answered honestly, "Although I like going to parties, I'd rather give a party," and then had to tell the two interviewers—one male

and one female flight attendant—why. "I like to entertain people," I said, "and make them feel comfortable and have fun."
They both smiled and I knew I had given the right answer. We
also had to role-play with one another, take a simple math test
(back then flight attendants had to sell liquor and headsets for
movies and hand in accounting forms at the end of each flight),
and do a final one-on-one interview with both interviewers.
Again, as I stood to leave, I was told that I would be hearing
from TWA very soon for a final interview. Most airlines only
had two interviews, but TWA was unique in that they had a
three-interview hiring process.

I wanted more than ever to fly for TWA, but first I had to
get through their infamous final interview—two days at Breech
Academy, their training center in Kansas City—reputed to be
the hardest in the industry. Opened in 1969, Breech was named
for a TWA executive, Ernest Breech, who was responsible for
securing TWA's financing for its first jets. Breech Academy
immediately became the gold standard for training stewardesses. Its campus, which their website describes in detail, sat
on "thirty-four manicured acres in Overland Park, Kansas,"
about twelve miles from Kansas City. The campus consisted of
"living pods" for the trainees, which featured double en-suite
rooms circling a sunken living room, thirty-two classrooms,
mock-ups of all the planes TWA flew, grooming rooms, galley
trainers, a beauty salon, a dining room, offices, and a three-
hundred-seat auditorium. The classrooms were octagons with
one long horseshoe-shaped desk that allowed every student to
sit in the front row. Test questions were projected on a screen
at the front and students pressed one of the answer buttons in
front of them.

Three years after Breech opened, TWA hired two men—
their first—and hostesses, as TWA called us, or stewardesses,
were renamed flight attendants. For a young woman in 1978,
that change meant something. Stewardesses were sexy and flir-
tatious; flight attendants were professionals on the plane first
and foremost for the passengers' safety. The name was in fact
changed to reflect an Equal Employment Opportunity ruling
that removed work and pay inequalities. But when a former
stewardess recently posted on the Facebook page Stewardesses
of the 1960's and 70's asking if anyone besides her preferred
the word "stewardess," she got over 350 comments, overwhelm-
ingly in favor of being called stewardesses. Being a stewardess
reflected something special, women mostly hired before 1978
wrote. It was a status symbol. It meant class and graciousness.
More than one former TWA stewardess commented that TWA
called them hostesses because they were taught to treat the passengers like they were guests in their homes.

When I arrived for that final interview process, I was
escorted to a pod in one of the dormitories. Each pod had a
common room with ten double rooms circled around it, two of
us in each room. It looked like something out of *The Jetsons* with
its mod colors and futuristic design. To me, it was the perfect
place to step out of a college classroom and onto a jet.

FOR OUR THREE DAYS at Breech Academy, we were tested—psy-
chologically, mathematically, physically—weighed and measured, given drug tests, and split into different groups for
interviews, role-playing exercises, and team building. We all

marveled at how intense this final step was. What were they looking for anyway?

In the 1979 video for In-flight Services Personnel Selection (obviously not available to us at the time), Daphne Halderman, a Kansas City–based flight attendant dressed in a brand-new Ralph Lauren uniform, hair permed and makeup flawless, asks the very same question we did: "What in the world are we looking for?" Her answer: someone who is attractive and well groomed, has a pleasing personality as well as good judgment and common sense, flexibility, excellent communication skills, a unique personality while willing to conform, sensitive to the needs of others and service oriented. That year, TWA hired 560 new flight attendants.

There were also of course the other qualifications of height and weight, age and education, and willingness to relocate. About one-third of the twenty-five applicants who attend the preliminary interview move on to the second interview, in which six to eight applicants are questioned by an interviewer who is looking to see if they possess those qualities they are seeking. Statistically, 50 percent of these applicants go to the final interview at Breech Academy and the majority of them do get hired. In 1978, over 14,000 people applied for 550 positions. Every one of us at Breech Training Academy for those two days wanted nothing more than to be in that 4 percent who heard the words "You're hired."

My roommate for those days at Breech was from San Francisco. Like all of the people at the final interview, she looked like she was ready to put on a uniform and greet people at the boarding door of a TWA jet. When we left for home on the final day, we hugged and promised to stay in touch. "See you in training!" I called to her as she went to her flight. When my acceptance letter arrived the next week, I immediately wrote her a gushing, excited letter, adding, "I hope we are in the same class." I was stunned when I received a letter from her telling me that she didn't get hired. "I'm glad you did though," she wrote. "You're perfect for the job. So perfect that we all thought you were a spy for TWA, watching us during our unguarded moments." I wasn't sure if I should be insulted or pleased. Me? A spy? But then again, spies were commonly believed to be flight attendants on a secret mission. If nothing else, her words illustrated how much I fit the ideal of a TWA flight attendant.

A FEW MONTHS EARLIER, I had worried that no airline would hire me. Now I had two job offers—TWA and United. United had the advantage of being a stable, growing company, but TWA offered me the glamorous life I so badly wanted. For most of its life, TWA was infamous for financial instability. As Jerry Cosley, who worked various management positions with TWA from 1960 to 1965, told *St. Louis Magazine*, "The news stories always started with 'Financially troubled airline TWA . . . '"

All around me, my friends were getting jobs in the usual way. One of my friends, a marketing major, had been taught in her "How to Interview" seminar to research the companies with whom you interviewed, not only to sound knowledgeable but also to ascertain their viability to survive. She researched both United and TWA for me and returned with advice.

"Work for United," she told me with no hesitation.

"But they fly to Boise and Milwaukee and Pittsburgh," I

reminded her. "I'll be based in Cleveland, the city that just went bankrupt? Where the river actually caught on fire?"

"TWA exists on the verge of bankruptcy," she said.

Although I hadn't done the due diligence of a marketing major, I did know that TWA, which had been owned by Howard Hughes, was known as the airline for celebrities. Black-and-white pictures of movie stars like Ava Gardner and Elizabeth Taylor drinking champagne on a TWA Connie with Hughes still appeared in magazines, and movies always featured TWA planes. Even with its permanently shaky financial situation, I figured, TWA could never really go under.

"I'm telling you," my friend said. "Go with United."

I, with the wisdom of a twenty-one-year-old with stars in her eyes, chose to ignore her.

MY ACCEPTANCE LETTER from TWA came with a ticket to Kansas City, a booklet to study for a test upon our arrival at training, and a phone number to call to accept the position. I didn't hesitate. I wrote a letter to United thanking them for the opportunity to interview with them but declining the job. Then I picked up the avocado-green rotary phone that sat beside the plaid La-Z-Boy reclining chair in my parents' living room, and just like that, I was on my way to becoming a TWA flight attendant.

The test on the first day of training would be on the three-letter codes every airport used. Most of us have seen those three letters on our checked baggage tags or airline tickets, but I had no idea what they meant when I looked at the fat packet of the airport codes for every city TWA flew. Even that was exciting, like learning a new, mysterious language. Some of them were easy—BOS for Boston, AMS for Amsterdam, CAI for Cairo. But many of them seemed to have no connection to the city in which they lay—ORD for Chicago, FCO for Rome, and MCI for Kansas City, my home for the next six weeks.

The packet also included a brief explanation of airplane terminology and an even briefer explanation of how airplanes actually flew. Airplanes had *engines*, not *motors*. The rotating red beacons on the wings meant those engines were on, and these were never to be called lights—they were rotating red beacons. I read about *lift*, which keeps the plane airborne, and *thrust*, which moves the plane forward. We would be tested on these things, too, on our first day.

Over margaritas with two old friends, I joked that the stuff I had to learn for this flight-attendant test was harder than some of my college exams.

They exchanged glances.

"What?" I said.

"Well," my friend Lynn said, "I mean, you're going to be an airline stewardess."

"A *flight attendant*," I reminded her. "For TWA," I added proudly.

"I guess if being a glorified waitress makes you happy," my friend Denise said.

Lynn shook her head in disdain or disgust, or both.

It hadn't occurred to me that some people would disparage my choice.

They were headed off to graduate school, one in philosophy and one in comparative literature, and were certainly more knowledgeable than I was on feminist theory. But I didn't view the job as one of glorified waitress. True, I wouldn't be analyzing literature or learning pedagogy, but I would be out in the world—often on my own—learning to navigate different cities and cultures. I'd also be in charge of hundreds of people on a flight, learning to navigate human nature. To me, the job fostered confidence and independence.

Before I could begin to explain that, Lynn asked me why it took *six weeks* to learn how to serve meals and put on makeup.

"And airport codes," Denise said, not even trying to hide her sarcasm.

"There's a lot more to learn that that," I said.

"Sure," Lynn said.

To them, I was stuck in time, entering a world that demeaned women and obstructed progress in women's liberation. Of course, this stung back then as I was embarking on a new, exciting career. I knew, too, that in some ways they were right. Despite a preference at TWA for new hires with college degrees, flight attendants were still chosen in no small part for good looks, and with height and weight requirements. But over the years, flight attendants had fought hijackers, formed strong unions, and even given their lives.

Those friends of mine were shortsighted. Flight attendants were trained in much more than beauty routines and airport codes. We were taught how to think on our feet, deal with difficult people and situations, find our way around airports and cities—sometimes all alone—and handle all kinds of emergencies, from hijackings to medical issues to plane crashes. Some of these things came easily to me. I found it easy to deflect annoyed or angry passengers and to even have them leave the flight satisfied. But I had to learn how and when to be authoritative, how to assess people and situations. These skills helped me in everything I've done in my life—being a flight attendant, of course, but also a teacher, a writer, traveling for book tours, and with a family of five or more, even being a parent. Plus I know how to make a terrific cocktail. Ultimately, though I could not yet say any of this to the friends who told me I would be nothing more than a glorified waitress, being a flight attendant would empower me and make me a strong woman. That was all still to come.

No matter what they thought, I was happy for them and my other friends as they began their first steps toward traditional lives in academia or with nine-to-five jobs, promotions and tenure, paid vacations. But I also knew somehow that unpredictability, flying to different cities and countries, even the crazy work schedule and a job where anything could (and did) happen suited me. Although I've separated the different airline interviews here for clarity, in reality they overlapped. Preliminary interviews, second and final interviews, all happening all the time. And this actual process—putting on that black suit and tying that scarf just right around my neck, going to Boston or checking in for flights to different cities, talking and smiling and being my most confident self—was a rehearsal of sorts for why I wanted to be a flight attendant in the first place. Getting hired by TWA was the culmination of all of that. Once TWA said *You're hired* and I accepted, my life did begin.

But first, I had to actually complete six weeks of training.

# BREECH TRAINING ACADEMY

As I STARED out the window on the flight from Boston to Kansas City, I felt something settle in me. I've had that same feeling only a few times—when I moved to Manhattan a few years later, the first time I saw my novel on a bookstore shelf, when I held each of my children for the first time, and when I married my husband, Michael, on an April afternoon in Abingdon Square Park in Greenwich Village. *Yes, this is right.*

Who was I as I sat on the plane heading toward six weeks of flight-attendant training at Breech Academy? I had graduated from the University of Rhode Island, twenty-one miles from my hometown, with a BA in English. I'd read my way through college, falling in love with Shakespeare, Willa Cather, F. Scott Fitzgerald, and E. E. Cummings. I'd also fallen in love with two boys, both a couple of years older than me. The one I loved most loved me least, the one I loved least loved me most. There had been boys in between these ricocheting relationships, wrong choices made out of boredom mostly. I was happy to be unattached as I started this new life. Ready for anything, for everything. I had wanted to leave my little hometown and my little state for so long, and finally I was. When we had to select our preferences for which city to be based in, I picked the ones that were the farthest away from Rhode Island—San Francisco, Chicago, L.A. Exciting things happened in those places—theater and art and readings by famous writers. I imagined attending openings and literary events, wearing a chic black dress and high heels, sipping martinis.

In college, I'd given up dorm life because I didn't like the inertia that came with the pot-smoking that was so prevalent there. For most of my life, I'd felt like an oddball—the only one who read so voraciously, who longed to live in a big city and to see the world. I always had good friends, but usually I wanted to do different things than they did. A secure job, marriage and kids all seemed like they belonged to someone else's life, not mine. As a junior, I pledged the sorority that some of my friends had joined two years earlier because they always seemed to be in motion, having fun and being busy with dances and social hours and community service projects.

Sorority life was not for me, but I didn't know myself well enough back then to realize that. I learned to ski so that I could join friends on snowy weekends in Vermont. I traded my faded blue jeans for khaki pants and sherbet-colored Izod shirts (worn over striped turtlenecks in winter), cut my hair in that Dorothy Hamill wedge after a sorority sister told me my hair was too long and looked unhealthy. I still have a picture of myself with three other Alpha Xi Deltas, and it takes me a moment to figure out which one I am, so alike did we all look. I'm still not sure why I didn't make friends with other English majors or join the staff of *A Good Five Cent Cigar*, the college newspaper.

Most of my friends didn't even know about my dreams to become a writer, or that I had composition notebooks filled with poems and stories I'd written. They didn't know that I minored in art history, or how much I loved sitting in the dark auditorium as the professor showed us slides of famous works of art. I almost passed on a class trip to the Metropolitan Museum of Art in New York City to view Monet's *Water Lilies* in an exhibition called *Monet's Years at Giverny* so that I didn't miss a social with Phi Sigma Kappa. In the end I did go on the trip, and I can still remember the astonishment I felt when I walked into that room and saw those paintings on every wall. Still, I continued to trade the things that pulled me in that direction for easier, more comfortable activities: happy hour at the campus pub on Fridays, jitterbugging in fraternity basements, drinking coffee in the Ram's Den at the student union with my friends. But now, finally, I was on my own, ready to discover the real me, the one I'd lost touch with in college.

ON A COLD JANUARY MORNING in 1979, I sat in an auditorium at TWA's Breech Training Academy in the Kansas City suburb of Overland Park with 120 new-hire flight attendants. Most of us were women with short or medium-length hair, makeup applied with varying skill, and wearing some form of business attire, a phrase that I, as a just-turned-twenty-two-year-old recent college graduate, had never heard before. The smattering of men were all freshly shaven with brand-new haircuts and suits and ties. Every one of us smiled nervously, and I'm sure, like me, had pounding hearts. It was our first day of TWA flight-attendant training.

"Look around you," the man on the stage told us. He was

the chairman of something—maybe personnel? I was too nervous to take it all in.

We all looked around the auditorium.

"Seventeen thousand people wanted to be where you're sitting today," he said. "By the end of the year, five hundred and sixty new hires will be in those seats." He paused. "Out of *seventeen thousand* applicants."

He paused again, letting it sink in. We were special. We were lucky. We had what it took to be a TWA flight attendant.

"It's easier to get into Harvard than to sit in your seat," the man said. He broke into a smile. "Congratulations. Give yourselves a round of applause."

All 120 of us clapped and smiled, bursting with pride. We'd made it. Or so we thought in that moment.

·   ·   ·

FLIGHT-ATTENDANT TRAINING has held a mystique and fascination for as long as there have been stewardesses. *Airline Glamour Girls*, a nine-minute 1940s stewardess-training film made by RKO, follows Mary from her job as a secretary—"Mary takes her last dictation!"—to stewardess training in Minneapolis, her spot won by sending a letter that included a recent photo. When she arrives, she gets nervous and asks herself:

"Are you pretty enough? Bright enough? Willing to work hard enough?" But Mary is determined and approaches her classes in theory of flight, aircraft, routes, and schedules with gusto. Two hours a day of comportment classes, meant to improve on their hire photos. The girls walk with books on their heads, move in a circle waving their arms gently, do knee bends, balance on teeter boards, joust, and even dance the conga, all "in the interest of grace, rhythm, and the body beautiful." These girls are five-two to five-seven, and "if they start with a few excess pounds, they graduate light enough to fly." The makeup courses are meant to enhance a girl's natural loveliness. "The airlines and the bachelors enjoy similar tastes—half the girls leave aviation for marriage each year."

Part of their training in hostess duties and procedures takes place on a mock-up plane. This course is to help the stewardess-to-be deal with passengers (like "Mr. Tipsy," who has smuggled a bottle of whiskey in his suit jacket pocket) and includes walking down the aisle with a big smile; how to give suggestions (not commands); serving (meal trays carried sideways, not front to back, to be more graceful); and how to use deep knee bends in the aisles. At night they have homework from seven to ten. Eight weeks later, Mary earns her wings, after lifting her skirt to show her legs and holding out her hands for inspection by airline management. On her first flight on a Constellation West, as the passengers approach, Mary gets a case of nerves. But she tells herself, "Better get that charm ready, baby," and she does. "What nice people!" Mary concludes.

Although the uniforms are mod and the planes are jets, not much else looked very different during American Airlines training at Stewardess College in 1968. "Our company is interested in all types of girls," the stewardess instructor in the film says, "as long as they live up to the high standards we have." Ten years earlier, American Airlines wanted stewardesses who looked like the All-American girl. That meant no makeup and no long hair. But by 1968, American Airlines stewardesses were more glamorous than they'd ever been. They not only took classes in psychology and service, but also in makeup—how to put on eyeliner and false eyelashes, for example. "Now," the voice-over says, "we are ahead of fashion." As the girls graduate and get their wings, one of them tells us, "Every man should marry an airline stewardess." In fact, when Carol Quinn, who was an American Airlines flight attendant from 1980 to 2001, and I talked about "the good old days" of flying, she still referred to her training—in 1980—as "The Charm Farm," a term leftover from the 1950s but still used thirty years later. In some ways, much of my flight-attendant training was the same as it had been for decades.

TWA retired its last Constellation and became the only all-jet airline in the United States in April of 1967. That year, they hired 1,600 air hostesses after screening 90,000 applicants—a lower acceptance rate than Harvard, as we were reminded on our first day of training. On TWA's all-jet fleet in 1967, for $1, passengers could choose from a menu that included gin, vodka, bourbon, Canadian, martini, Manhattan, vodka martini, daiquiri, or whiskey sour. Beer and sherry were fifty cents. TWA also instituted first-class meals, like chateaubriand carved in front of the passengers and served on Rosenthal china with the TWA logo, a service staple that was still in effect during my tenure.

At Pan Am stewardess training in 1969, they meant to turn a girl into a woman. To that end, the girls received beauty tips, classes on giving announcements, service training, safety training, and two hours of physical fitness a day. "Stewardesses, like airliners, must be slinky and sexy," they were told, "but pilots can be homely and bald."

A decade later, I arrived at Breech Training Academy for flight attendant training. How different would it be?

. . .

FROM 1935 TO 1985, 120 TWA new hires arrived for training every week. Like our predecessors, we also had to take classes in grooming, poise, food-and-beverage service, teamwork, and customer service. "Can a flight attendant have a bad day?" my friend Matt remembers his instructor asking, and then answering her own question with: "Of course. She just can't show it." I could picture those friends of mine, now sequestered in graduate school classes and university libraries, rolling their eyes as I sat with a professional makeup artist learning how to apply eye liner in a straight, even line, brush blush onto the apples of my cheeks, and swipe lipstick in the same maroon shade as the stripes on my uniform jacket correctly across my lips without a mirror. I could hear them groaning at the hours I spent practicing how to walk up and down the spiral staircase of a 747 carrying a tray of drinks.

For me up until then, makeup was something I'd mostly worn during my days as a teen model, applied with the help of my friend Beth; or the Bonne Bell Lip Smackers lip gloss I wore for fraternity dances. I never felt demeaned or objectified in training when I stood up from that makeup table wearing enough cosmetics to look professional yet still natural. But as my friend Diane told me all these years later, leaving grooming class was very strange. "Same blush. Same lipstick. Same uniform. It was almost frightening, like Stepford Flight Attendants."

The more important part of training, the part that took up most of our time and reminded us every day that we were not just there to sell airline seats, was safety. Our number-one role was to get all those passengers off a plane in case of an emergency, to administer first aid like CPR or the Heimlich maneuver, to literally extinguish fires. If we didn't pass the FAA's flight safety test, no amount of L'Oréal or Aqua Net was going to make us a flight attendant.

The year I was hired, TWA flew seven types of aircraft: the DC-9, the 727, the 727-200 (known as the Stretch), the 707, the 707-420 (also the Stretch), the Lockheed 1011, and the 747. The FAA test required that flight attendants know the safety practices for all the planes in the airline's fleet, how to locate and operate the emergency equipment, and how to evacuate each plane in case of an emergency.

TWA had so many different types of aircraft in order to accommodate their vast and varied route system. When I first saw a map with all the cities to which they flew, connected by spidery blue lines that radiated out of red circles, I was dazzled. Unlike Pan Am, TWA flew both short-haul flights, which are under six hours, and long-haul flights, which are over six hours. The DC-9 and both 727s flew passengers on short hauls—St. Louis to Pittsburgh or Kansas City to Detroit.

The 707, used for long-haul flights, was a relic from 1957. As Boeing's first jet, it started the Jet Age, and as the most popular plane in the 1960s it led to the development of many things we take for granted today, like baggage handling and airport terminal design. But by the time I was in flight-attendant training, the 707 was already becoming obsolete. They guzzled fuel so were hurt hard in the 1973 oil crisis, and they had noisy engines, which added to noise pollution. They were slowly being replaced by the larger, quieter, more fuel-efficient wide-bodied 747. Boeing stopped making 707s in 1978, though TWA continued to fly the planes until 1983. The 707 was the kind of plane I'd watched cut across the Virginia sky when I was a little girl. Now I'd be working on one.

The 707 seated 140 passengers; the stretch version held 189. I still remember the first time I stepped onto one—the seats seemed to go on forever, three seats on each side of a single aisle. Each wing had two of those noisy engines, and sitting at an over-wing seat was deafening. Once, I was working on a 707 that blew a tire on landing and sent us into a bit of a spin, leaving the plane leaning slightly when we finally stopped, one of the engines dangerously close to the ground. The flight attendant beside me on the jump seat let out a very long breath. "I was afraid that engine was going to hit the ground and explode," he said. In training, our instructors told us, "You're twenty times safer in a plane than a car," citing statistics of the number of car accidents versus plane crashes. That was good enough to allay any fear of flying for me. Still, every now and then—like this time—I was reminded of how close I actually was to something going wrong.

When 707s were new, and even when I first started as a flight attendant, flying was still glamorous and passengers dressed up for their flights. Unlike the shorts and flip-flops or sweatpants and sneakers people wear today, men wore suits and ties, women wore dresses or smart suits, and even kids dressed in their Sunday best. My husband remembers always putting on a blue blazer for flights when he was a kid. On one of my first flights, I still remember a family with three little boys, each dressed in khaki pants, penny loafers, and Izod shirts in different colors. In fact, so glamorous was flying on the 707 during its short life that under the title of the film *Boeing Boeing* read 707! 707!

Just as I learned that a DC-9 had two exits in the front and a rear tail-cone exit that dropped down to reveal a set of stairs for evacuating in case of an emergency, I learned that a 707 had six exits: two in the front, two in the rear, and two over-wing exits. I also learned where to position myself in the cabin during the pre-takeoff safety demonstrations, and how to point two fingers of each hand in the vague direction of those exits when the announcement was made.

Everybody who's ever flown can picture it, the flight attendant standing in the aisle pointing out the exits. Just like everything else, there was a class for learning how to do that. In it, we also practiced holding up a fake seat belt and buckling and unbuckling it, waved around the laminated safety instruction card from the seat pocket, showed where an oxygen mask would drop from and how to put it on and activate it. I always loved the line "Stay calm and place the mask over your nose and mouth while continuing to breathe normally." How were passengers supposed to stay calm and breathe normally when there was a decompression and a hundred or more masks dropped down in front of them? A friend of mine who was in a decompression said that he was in the galley when he heard a loud bang, loud enough for him to look around the curtain into the cabin, where he saw all those yellow masks dangling down and passengers screaming. "You know what they never told us in training?" he said. "During a decompression, the natural air in your stomach expands and people fart. A lot."

Flights that went over water—oceans, of course, but even ones that flew over just a little bit of water for takeoff and landing—required us to also demonstrate how to retrieve and don the life jacket that was tucked beneath the seats, tighten it, pull the tabs to inflate it, and blow into little tubes should it not inflate. A favorite trick played on new hires was to switch the demo life jacket, which didn't have the $CO_2$ cartridge in it to inflate it, with an actual life jacket so that when she pulled on those tabs, the thing actually did inflate, making a loud noise, puffing up all around her, and scaring the hell out of her. However, passengers always got a big laugh at seeing the startled flight attendant looking like the Michelin Man in the aisle.

My favorite part of the class on the airline safety demonstrations was how to use the intercom and to practice giving safety announcements. The high school actor in me loved having that microphone in my hand and telling everyone our altitude and flight time and where the emergency exits were. We were given laminated cards with the announcements printed on them for reference, but we were supposed to memorize them. Instead of a bedtime story, I used to say the TWA announcements to my niece Melissa to put her to sleep.

THE FIRST AIRPLANE to be called a jumbo jet was the 747, commissioned by Juan Trippe, Pan Am's president, who wanted a passenger aircraft twice the size of the 707. In just a little over two years, Boeing delivered its first 747s. On January 22, 1970, *Clipper Victor*, nicknamed "The Queen of the Skies," made the Pan Am 747's maiden flight from New York to London. Airlines used to follow the maritime tradition of naming their planes, just as ships were named. Some airlines still do that today, such as Jet Blue, which always uses the word "blue" in their plane's names—*Hopelessly Devoted to Blue, BluesMobile, Bluebird*.

Boeing's ads for *Clipper Victor* read "Welcome to the Spacious Age." With its twin aisles, 27 first-class seats, 292 economy seats, and humped upper deck, the 747 quickly became a status symbol. "Every airline wanted one," Bob van der Linden, a curator at the Smithsonian National Air and Space Museum, said. At first, the FAA didn't certify passengers to sit in the upper deck during takeoff or landing, so although not designed as one, airlines turned the upper deck into a first-class lounge—a "club in the sky"—serving caviar, foie gras, filet mignon, and, of course, fine champagne (usually Dom Perignon). Jeffrey Ruthizer, who flew to Paris on a 747 for his honeymoon in 1976 told the *New York Post*: "The stewardesses were beautiful and every single guy, and half the married guys, would be trying to grab one of them."

Those first-class lounges became legendary, with piano bars—Frank Sinatra Jr. played a show in an American Airlines lounge in 1971; Continental's Polynesian Pub offering a Cordon Bleu–trained chef; and Qantas's Captain Cook Lounge, a nautically themed "groovy" (as their ads boasted) lounge with purple, orange, and aqua seats, images of James Cook, replica tiki lanterns, and a ship's steering wheel where passengers sipped cocktails and champagne, smoked cigarettes, and ordered meals from a full restaurant. Flight attendants remember when Maxim's of Paris catered first-class meals on Pan Am, put orchids in the United Airlines cabin, and even created volcanoes with crème de menthe and dry ice. "It was all part of the pomp and circumstance that went along with flying the premier airplane of its day," former flight attendant Carole Tye told the *New York Post*.

At the height of a six-story building and with a wingspan equal to fifty parked cars, as Megan Specia once described the 747 in the *New York Times*, the plane was imposing and impressive. My friend Jackie once confessed to me that she loved 747s so much, found them so beautiful and even sexy, that she'd had a dream of walking in the TWA International Terminal at JFK and a 747 parked at a gate smiled at her. She moved nearer, and its wings beckoned to her, like arms. "That's how beautiful those planes are," Jackie said. "I even dream about them." Fifty years after they were introduced, British Airways retired its fleet of 747s, marking the end of an era. Once synonymous with luxury travel, even five decades after they started to fly, "the sight of 747s gliding into their docks, dwarfing other planes, could evoke a thrill in the most jaded passenger," the *New York Times* wrote.

When I began flying for TWA, we had seventeen 747s, all of them used on international flights. During training, we had to practice the proper way to walk in our high heels up and down the 747's iconic spiral staircase that led to the lounge, repeatedly bringing trays of cocktails and food upstairs on our mock-up plane with a particular—and difficult to master—ankle-crossing walk. Other than having to practice evacuating from the cockpit on a rope, which was about thirty feet high, I didn't set foot on a 747 for a long time. Since most new hires worked domestic routes, it would be years before I ever worked on one.

Since flying 747s was the province of senior flight attendants on international routes, the jumbo jet where I logged the most flight time was the Lockheed 1011. Eastern Airlines and TWA flew L-1011s; American opted instead for its competitor, the DC-10. Even in training, the L-1011 captured my heart and my imagination. Launched in 1972, it was a truly beautiful airplane. Its low-set wings and curved tail had many people compare it to a dolphin. With its twin aisles and Rolls-Royce engines (the flight attendant giving the boarding announcements always pointed these out: "We have a Rolls Royce engine on each wing . . .") the L-1011 had all the class and glamour of the much larger 747 but could be used for both medium- and long-haul flights. Instead of an upper deck, it had two elevators, or lifts, that took flight attendants below the main cabin to an area beside the cargo hold, where first-class supplies and meals were kept, along with extra items for coach. When I was alone, setting up the carts down there for first class, I'd hear dogs barking on the other side of the wall.

At first, flight attendants didn't like the L-1011 because it presented so many service challenges and gave them even more work to do. Timing the service with the use of the lower galley was difficult. The plane had thirty first-class seats with cocktail tables that could be converted into dining tables for as many as four passengers that proved to be tricky to open and close. First-class passengers were offered what was considered the largest menu in the industry at the time, with a choice of five entrees. There were 176 seats in the coach cabin, with only 2 per row. Unoccupied seats could be converted into consoles with more tricky maneuvering by flight attendants. Coach passengers had a lounge of their own and a choice of three entrees, making still more work. In the very back of the cabin, a press of a button—a button that frequently got stuck—made part of the rear bulkhead open and lift to reveal a closet for hanging garment bags.

Ultimately, TWA had six flight attendants write the service manual for the L-1011. But the manual didn't teach us how to fix that closet when it jammed while lifting garment bags or how to deal with any of the other new high-tech features that frequently went wrong. For some reason, for example, the lights and air vents were placed too high to be reached except with a special long rod. If a lightbulb burned out, only maintenance could change it, which sent passengers into an "I'll never fly TWA again" rant. Still, despite all of its quirks, it was always my favorite plane to work.

The Lockheed 1011 actually provided one of my more unusual experiences during training. We were told that there had been ghost sightings on board one of them, a plane that had repair parts from an Eastern Airlines 1011 that had crashed on December 29, 1972, on its approach into Miami Airport. *The Ghost of Flight 401* by John G. Fuller gives heartbreaking details about what happened after Flight 401's landing-gear indicator light did not illuminate when the landing gear was lowered. Even when the first officer attempted to lower it manually, the light did not come on. The pilots requested to be put into a holding pattern until they could fix the problem.

As they held over the Everglades, flight engineer Don Repo went below the flight deck to try to see if the landing gear was down while the two pilots in the cockpit put the plane on autopilot. Unbeknownst to any of them, the plane started to slowly lose altitude.

"We're still at two thousand feet, right?" the first officer asked Captain Loft.

"Hey!" Loft answered. "What's happening here?"

Ten seconds later, Flight 401 crashed.

Only 67 of the 167 passengers and 8 out of the 10 flight attendants survived. The captain and first officer both died, and Flight Engineer Repo, who had been below the flight deck when the plane crashed, died later of his injuries. During the session about Flight 401 and ghost sightings, our instructor, Paula, also pointed out the importance and bravery of the flight attendants. The plane had crashed into a swamp at night at a time when flashlights were not yet required emergency equipment. Flight attendants instructed the survivors not to light matches because of the jet-fuel spillage, then led them in loud rounds of Christmas carols to assist the rescuers in finding them.

The sightings of the ghosts of the captain and the flight engineer began just a few months later, and only on planes that used salvaged parts from Flight 401. Eastern Airlines issued a warning that any employee who talked about the ghost sightings would be fired. Reportedly, they also removed the parts from their other 1011s. Paula told us that if we saw something we should report it.

"I'm not saying if I believe it or not," she said. "I'm just here to tell you that some people have reported sightings on a TWA 1011."

I had been prepared for angry passengers and flight delays and missing commissary items. But ghosts? That was a surprise.

Our days at training were long, starting at nine a.m., and included classes on in-flight service, customer service, first aid, grooming and uniform standards, troubleshooting broken coffeemakers and film projectors, how to use the ovens and carts and lifts and doors, to name but a few. Then we would pause for dinner and often continue into the night. Part of each day was spent on learning the ins and outs of an aircraft, starting with our smallest, the DC-9, and ending with the 747. After we'd successfully completed all of the service and emergency procedures on an aircraft, we would take written multiple-choice tests that we had to pass with a grade of 90 percent or higher or we'd be sent home.

After we passed the written tests, we took practical tests. We went to an aircraft's mock-up and performed the emergency duties. Our instructors would ask each of us to locate the emergency equipment and then to perform the easiest task of arming and disarming the doors. Every passenger has heard the announcement for flight attendants to prepare doors for departure and landing. That means arming them for takeoff, which is engaging the emergency slide so that in case of an evacuation the slide will deploy and inflate when that door is opened; for landing, the door is disarmed, meaning the slide is disengaged, which allows the door to open normally. A lifting or lowering of a handle or the press of a button accomplished arming and disarming.

But most of our time in the mock-ups was spent practicing emergency procedures simulated by our flight instructor, who, with a control panel, could jam doors; simulate fire or water outside the aircraft window; produce airplane "rolls," missed runway approaches, emergency descents; and play tapes of screaming passengers. We were required to remove thirty-pound window exits, crawl out onto the wing, and assist "passengers" (our fellow trainees) in climbing down a rope off the wing to safety. On the 747, one evacuation method was via the cockpit window, over twenty feet high. We learned the safety instructions to give passengers before a potential crash (take off your shoes and glasses, remove sharp objects from your pockets, make sure your seat belts are fastened) and during ("Bend down and grab your ankles!"). As the simulator rocked and shook, everything went dark and a recording of screaming and crying played to give us an idea of what a crash might look and sound like so we were prepared in case it really happened.

"When they sent that smoke and fog through the cabin and shut off the lights, I was terrified," my friend Diane reminded me. "That was when I realized that this job was a lot of responsibility." Those emergency training sessions had the same effect on all of us. More than once, reenacting a crash or conducting an evacuation, the importance of the role of a flight attendant would hit me. Even though the chances of being in a plane crash were low, I had to know what to do if I was in one, and how to save lives. This was a sobering realization in a day that also had us taking classes on troubleshooting broken coffee makers, setting up liquor carts, and balancing meal trays.

Our job in an emergency landing was to find a safe exit and move passengers toward it and off the plane. Each aircraft had exits in different places—the DC-9's third exit was actually in the tail cone, which dropped off when it was armed—and it was essential that we learn how to find these exits in the dark. Once we located the nearest exit, before opening it we were to look out the window and check for fire or water—either one made that exit unusable. The instructor would set up these obstacles—blocking a window with red paper for fire or blue paper for water at some of the exits so we could practice the important step of looking before opening the door and then moving passengers to safer exits. In a practice section, there might be fire out my nearest exit, and fire out the next nearest, and I would be required to calmly and efficiently move to the safest exit. Staying calm in emergencies was of the utmost importance, and everything we were taught to do we were taught to do *calmly*. We then had to direct the passengers to the exit and open it. The door was armed, so upon opening it the slide inflated. "Jump and slide!" we shouted, calmly of course. "You do not leave the aircraft until the last passenger is off," we were reminded again and again. We heard a cautionary tale about a flight attendant who got so scared that she left the aircraft ahead of the passengers after a crash and was fired.

If there was a malfunction and the slide did not inflate, we practiced how to shimmy down an uninflated one. If our evacuation was in water, we had to be sure all the passengers had donned their life vests and then prepare to ditch. Slides weren't used in water ditches. Instead, life rafts were launched, if possible. If not possible to launch rafts, passengers were instructed to slide into the water, inflate their life vests, and hold their seat cushions for flotation devices. I never felt confident that in freezing or high seas, those flimsy seat cushions would actually keep us afloat. But I knew they were designed to float for at least a little while, and if help came quickly enough, they could save your life. So I practiced saying, "In the unlikely event of a water landing, your seat cushion can be used as a flotation device. . . ."

We also practiced water ditching from a mock-up plane into a swimming pool. In the dark. More than one trainee was sent home for her inability to execute a water ditching successfully, or for failure to learn how to swim. I would sometimes see trainees in the pool early in the morning taking swimming lessons, and I remembered that once perplexing question on all of the flight-attendant applications: *Can you swim?*

One of the hardest parts of emergency training was studying plane crashes: what caused them, how people were and weren't saved. We even heard those black box recordings with the voices of the cockpit in the moments before the plane crashed. Despite the seriousness and magnitude of emergency training, I was afraid only of failing and being sent home, not of actually crashing in a plane. During one written test on emergency equipment—its storage, usage, and troubleshooting for seven different types of aircraft—I actually broke into tears.

The correct PSI readings on oxygen bottles, how to find and use fire extinguishers on a 747, how to inflate and launch a raft in turbulent seas . . . all of it became an overwhelming amount of information. Information that I had to know perfectly in order to pass the test. If I failed, I'd never get on an aircraft to use what I'd learned. Paula, my instructor administering the test, led me out of the classroom and helped calm me down. "You just graduated from college," she reminded me. "You've taken tests a lot harder than this." Her soothing voice and calming nature—she made a great flight attendant—eventually relaxed me. I could see the PSI reading of 1250 on the oxygen bottle, picture all the places where there were fire extinguishers on 747s, and remember the safety rules to follow in an ocean ditching. "Ready?" she said. I nodded, went back in, and aced the test.

Still, my fear of flunking out stayed with me the whole time. For good reason. During my month training at Breech Academy, there were people sent home nearly every day because they

failed written tests, showed a bad attitude, got too frightened
during emergency procedures, or just got homesick. I wasn't the
only trainee who worried that I might be sent home too. Everyone at Breech had the experience of coming back to their living pod and finding a classmate gone, their bed stripped and
drawers and closets emptied. Rumors kept our fear alive too—
rumors of trainees caught cheating on tests, unable to swim,
gaining a few pounds, or acting rude or sassy and being sent
home. The slightest infraction could end our dream of graduat-
ing from trainee to flight attendant.

SEVERAL WEEKS INTO TRAINING, homesickness had set in for
most of us. I had never been away from home for this long. I
grew up in a big, close Italian American family in which every
Sunday was dedicated to doing family activities—church, Sunday supper with dozens of relatives, and Sunday evenings spent
playing cards together. Even in college I often dropped in to
see my parents for an afternoon or weekend. During training,
despite a weekly long-distance call home—waiting in line for
a phone booth to free up and then talking fast because long-
distance calls were so expensive—I missed my family. Maybe
that was why it especially struck me that in all the black box
recordings we listened to, so many last words were *I love you,
Mom.* I even had nightmares that something bad was happening
at home, that my mother or father was sick, or worse. Although
all of that emergency training didn't make me afraid to fly,
it showed me for the first time how fragile we all are, how
catastrophe could be right around the corner.

We were well aware that emergencies—hijackings and

crashes—were a real possibility and being prepared for one was our most important job. Sometimes during the safety announcements before takeoff, the flight attendant or pilot would remind passengers of that. "Our flight attendants' number one job is your safety..." In 1956, long before "Sully" famously landed a plane in the Hudson, one night Pan Am Flight 6 from Honolulu to San Francisco developed engine trouble that forced the Boeing 377 Stratocruiser into a descent. The pilot opted to circle until daybreak, at which point he began the planned water landing. During another ditching on Pan Am Flight 6, the tail had broken off, so all of the passengers in the rear were moved forward. As soon as the plane hit the water, its back end broke off too and the nose of the airliner sank. But the Coast Guard arrived quickly, the passengers were in the rafts, and remarkably there were no fatalities. A year later, Pan Am Flight 7, making the reverse trip, crashed into the Pacific for reasons still unknown and there were no survivors.

These were the statistics and stories we were told every day. Crashes caused by engine trouble, midair collisions, faulty electrical systems, flocks of birds, loss of altitude, damaged wings, lightning, pilot error. You can bet when we practiced ditching in that swimming pool, we were serious and especially careful to remain calm. The next time we evacuated an aircraft on land or sea, prepared passengers to brace, jump, and slide—would be for real.

It was sobering for me, the young woman who thought there was a parachute under airplane seats and that somehow passengers could all float gracefully to safety, to learn that although yes, my new job required me to smile, look well groomed, act professionally, and serve hundreds of drinks and meals, I was also responsible for all of these people's lives. When we studied plane crashes, we learned about one of the worst—Delta Flight 723, a DC-9 that crashed in fog after hitting a seawall during a landing at Boston's Logan Airport on July 31, 1973. I didn't remember it at the time, but the date made me gasp. That plane crashed exactly a month after my own first flight, on Delta, into Logan Airport.

·  ·  ·

OVER THAT MONTH at Breech, I learned to successfully evacuate seven kinds of aircraft, fix a broken coffeemaker, deliver a baby, mix proper cocktails, carve a chateaubriand, administer oxygen, demonstrate safety equipment, and make a baby's rattle out of two plastic cups and a couple of TWA propeller-shaped swizzle sticks. During one test, we had to correctly identify liquor miniatures without their labels because the labels often peeled off from the melting ice in the liquor carts. Amaretto, Galliano, Beefeater gin—I could recognize each one just by its shape. And I still can today.

To deal with drunk passengers, we role-played by speaking calmly and firmly, even when they grabbed at us or tried to steal minis from our liquor cart. It was hard not to laugh during these exercises, but it didn't take long on the job before I caught a tipsy passenger helping himself to a few Beefeater gin minis while my back was turned. We also practiced politely and delicately offering overweight passengers seat-belt extensions if they needed one. We'd say something like "Let me help you be more comfortable" while we buckled the extension onto the seat belt. "There!" delivered with a smile, of course. I found that usually any passenger who needed one asked for the extensions when they boarded, so I was spared from that duty. We were also taught how to politely brush off passes from male passengers—even though we were also taught to perch on the arms of first-class seats. Techniques varied from a flirty "Don't be naughty!" to "What would your wife say?" Anything was OK, as long as we said it with a smile.

Although I had hoped to be based somewhere far from Rhode Island, like Chicago or San Francisco, my class learned we would be based in Boston, a mere sixty-four miles from home and right in the shadow of my father's office in Government Center downtown. By this time, after living in my pod with twenty people and undergoing long days of training seven days a week, I'd formed many close friendships. Despite my initial disappointment of a domicile in my own backyard, I was eager to move into an apartment with my friends and start flying.

We had just one week of training to go before we'd be sent off for a week of working actual flights, then come back to Kansas City to debrief and graduate, and get our wings at last. I'd completed four years of college—a breeze compared to my four weeks of training and testing at Breech. As a KLM flight attendant recently blogged, "You don't get your wing. You earn it." Notice she said "wing," not "wings." Traditionally flight attendants wore just one wing; only pilots could wear a pair of wings. In 1936, the first TWA hostesses wore one gold wing affixed to a red circle with TWA in gold letters. Stewardesses, it was believed, weren't important enough to wear two wings. Those were reserved for the mostly male pilots.

A version of that one wing remained on TWA flight attendants' jackets until 1978. The red circle was replaced first in 1944 with an all-gold airplane with TWA on it, then with the white interlocking globe logo in the 1960s. But the wings I was earning were two silver ones with a small silver TWA above them, a victory in flight attendants' ongoing struggle to be respected and honored for their professionalism. During class, the flight-attendant wings on our instructors' jackets shined back at us, a reminder of what we were working so hard for.

But just as our own wings were in sight, American Airlines Flight 191, a DC-10 flying from O'Hare Airport in Chicago to Los Angeles, crashed on takeoff, killing all 273 people aboard. The news of such a devastating plane crash while in flight-attendant training was chilling, but by that time we were already thinking like flight attendants: a flight attendant wasn't afraid of flying and knew that no matter how catastrophic a plane crash might be, flying was still safer than driving. There was a long-standing debate between airlines who flew DC-10s and airlines like TWA who flew L-1011s over which aircraft was better. The mechanical problem that led to the crash of Flight 191 supported TWA's belief that DC-10s were flawed planes.

Shortly after news of the crash spread, we were called into the auditorium and told our training had just ended. With DC-10s being grounded, the airlines that flew L-1011s were in even greater demand. Our uniforms were hastily assembled—some people had to wear their own shirts or ties because not all of the uniform pieces had arrived yet. We would all fly from Kansas City to whatever airport our flight would leave from the next day.

I couldn't believe my luck. I was working a flight from Boston to Los Angeles, a transcontinental one with elaborate service in both coach and first class. I had never been to L.A., and

the naïve young woman I was then imagined seeing the Hollywood Walk of Fame and the Hollywood sign and maybe even
Laurel Canyon, where the singers from my teenage years lived.

Our instructors reminded us of the essentials. We always
had to have our safety and service manuals with us, easily accessible. These manuals were two doorstops of books filled with
everything we needed to know, one with a red cover, the other
with a blue cover. We jammed them into our uniform purses,
our service smock folded up beside them. Those purses were
big even when empty, with multiple pockets to fit everything
we were required to carry and Velcro to close it up so we could
access everything easily and quickly. Makeup, a hairbrush,
and a regulation flashlight (needed in case of emergencies or
on night flights to check seat belts) took up most of the other
pocket so that we hardly had room for our wallet and passport.
Somehow I always managed to squeeze in a paperback book,
too, but barely. The cover of the purse had a special place for
our employee IDs so that we only had to lift the cover and
flash it to go through security. All of this was reiterated to us
before we left Kansas City, as was a reminder to tip the hotel
shuttle driver a dollar. Remember, our instructors told us, you
can't chew gum or smoke cigarettes in uniform. Remember to
always smile and look approachable. Remember that when you
are wearing that uniform, you represent TWA. Have fun!

# 5

## *LADIES AND GENTLEMEN, WELCOME ABOARD TWA FLIGHT NUMBER . . .*

T HE NEXT DAY, our class dispersed at MCI, the three-letter code for Kansas City that was now second nature to us, to fly to the city our first official flight was departing from. I had an early departure out of Logan Airport that meant I had to spend the night at the Hilton Hotel there. I climbed into bed, excited, nervous, terrified, and studied the intricate services on the 1011. In coach, before takeoff, we walked through the aisles renting headsets for the movie and distributing menus with a choice of three entrees. We made sure everyone's seat belt was fastened, bags were stowed completely under the seats in front of them or in the overhead bin, seat backs and tray tables were in their full upright and locked positions. After takeoff, we started with a cocktail service, pushing the heavy beverage carts up and down the aisles as we pulled pop-top rings off soda cans, mixed drinks, and poured coffee and tea. That was followed by an appetizer service (skewers of salami, cherry tomatoes, and mozzarella balls); dinner (some kind of pasta, a beef dish, and a chicken dish); a coffee and tea service; an after-dinner drink service; and finally TWA pale green mints, embossed with the TWA logo and served on a silver tray.

I pored over my notes: "If there are any children on the flight, let them serve the mints. But keep a careful eye on them!" "Make sure you have a can opener in your smock pocket." "Make sure you have change in your smock pocket for cocktail purchases." "Make sure you remember who you owe change to if you run out." "The TWA cocktail napkin is always put on the tray table with the TWA logo at the bottom right."

First-class service required much more studying. We had to memorize all of the passengers' names and use them when we talked to them. Pre-takeoff, we offered orange juice, champagne, or mimosas passed on a tray, but passengers could order whatever they wanted and we had to make it for them, fast. Menus were handed out opened and headsets were given for free. As soon as we took off, we offered cocktails that we mixed at a bar we set up at the front of the cabin. Rolls had to be warmed, wine opened, and salad tossed while standing in the aisle.

Then there was that iconic chateaubriand that TWA first class was famous for. "The aristocrat of roasts," the menu description read. "A double tenderloin of beef, selected from choice Midwestern steers. Cooked to your liking in TWA's aircraft ovens and carved at tableside from the rolling cart." Remarkably, we did ask passengers how they wanted it cooked, and whoever was working galley had to approximate from rare to well done in our little ovens. The flight attendant working in the cabin carved the meat standing at the front of first class, a performance every passenger watched. When I talk to any of my flight-attendant friends about our days flying for TWA, the chateaubriand is always the first thing they mention.

For serving coffee, it was required to balance a small tray with cream and sugar and TWA's red, propeller-shaped stir rods in one hand, the coffee pot in the other. How many times had we rehearsed this: "Coffee? Please put your cup on my tray." The passenger was then supposed to put their coffee cup on the small tray, let you pour the coffee standing in the aisle, then remove the cup and add their cream and sugar. This was to prevent us from spilling hot coffee on anyone by having to lean across a row of passengers. In training, we had practiced this over and over—setting up the small tray and walking down the aisle of one of the mock-ups with it in one hand and a coffeepot with the TWA logo in the other. In coach, that tray was plastic; in first class it—and the creamer and sugar bowl—was heavy sterling silver.

That night, in my hotel room, all of these service rules—how to make a martini, how to carve a chateaubriand, how to place the cocktail napkin, and *Please put your cup on my tray*—mixed with the location of the emergency exits and life rafts and emergency equipment on the L-IOII, swirled around in my head, keeping me awake.

FLIGHT ATTENDANTS WERE required to arrive at the airport an hour before their flight's departure time to meet the crew, check the emergency equipment and service supplies on the airplane, set up the services—load and refill the beverage-cart drawers, set up the coffeemakers . . . anything that could be done ahead of time and safely stored during takeoff—and be ready at the boarding door or positioned in the aisles with uniform jackets, lipstick, and smiles on for the passengers.

But afraid to be late (even though the airport Hilton was literally in the airport) and also out of excitement, I showed up for my first flight much earlier than the required hour before departure. I punched the secret code into the keypad by the gate above crew scheduling, the room where the people who held our fate in their hands worked adjacent to the base's administrative offices and the crew lounge. Crew schedulers monitored the staffing on every flight arriving and departing from that airport, and made adjustments as needed. If a flight suddenly was overbooked, they'd add an X (extra flight attendant) to the crew. They knew who was supposed to be on which flights, who was sitting on reserve, and where we all lived. If a departing flight needed an X and you lived near the airport, crew scheduling knew to call you rather than someone who lived an hour away. In addition, crew schedulers collected our monthly schedule bids and awarded them by seniority. It was a very good idea to be extra nice to crew schedulers. That day, I made my way down the secret steps to the crew lounge at Logan Airport for the first time. Following the airlines' trend in hiring top designers like Oleg Cassini and Emilio Pucci, my TWA uniform was designed by Ralph Lauren. The uniform was one of the most important parts of being a flight attendant. Whenever I put mine on, I became a different person—professional, confident, knowledgeable, in charge.

Many decades after they've stopped flying, former flight attendants can still describe their uniform down to the smallest details. My old roommate Diane says that whenever she dressed for a flight and walked through an airport with her crew, she always felt special and professional. "I loved that uniform.

Eastern wore this polyester one. Ours was classy. I was so proud to be a TWA flight attendant."

She remembers how people in airports would come up to her and ask her questions, just because she had on a uniform. It was a sign that she could do just about anything.

A friend of mine flew for American Airlines for thirty-four years. When the coronavirus pandemic in 2020 forced airlines to offer early retirement in an effort to reduce furloughs, Matt spent weeks struggling with what to do—retire three years before he was supposed to? Or keep flying in a very changed landscape? As he grew closer to the decision to retire, his uniform became a painful symbol of the job he loved and had to give up. Our uniforms—even when the color was awful or the skirt unflattering—made us flight attendants. The sight of a full 747 back in the day, or 777 crew today in their uniforms walking across a terminal can still make heads turn.

But gone were the days of hot pants, paper uniforms and mini-skirts. My dark navy-blue uniform with maroon stripes at the wrist of the double-breasted jacket looked like a contemporary version of the original 1935 hostess uniform. We wore crisp white shirts, pants or a knee-length skirt, and a maroon-blue-and-white-striped scarf or necktie. Jackets had to be worn in the airport, during boarding, and for takeoff and landing. During the flight they were swapped out for a dark-blue serving smock with our names sewn across the top. There was a story, perhaps apocryphal, that instead of her name, one flight attendant had *Oh Miss* embroidered on her smock since that was what passengers always called out: "Oh, miss!"

Art Lujin, a former TWA air traffic controller who works at the TWA Museum in Kansas City, said that the Ralph Lauren was definitely everyone's favorite uniform. The tailored military style looked professional and sophisticated, and more than one former flight attendant I know still talks dreamily about what it felt like to walk through an airport with a crew dressed in that uniform. Introduced in 1978, it set the model for uniforms for years to come. Although Braniff Airlines had planes painted by Alexander Calder—"The Flying Colors of Braniff"—leather cabin seats, and ultrasuede flight-attendant uniforms designed by Halston, before long, most of the major airlines had switched to a similar military look.

· · ·

AS MUCH AS I loved finally wearing my TWA uniform, I was still more nervous the day of my first flight than I'd been for any of the interviews, or for any of the tests I'd taken during four years of college. The crew was based in Los Angeles, which meant that they were all very senior—L.A., Kansas City, and San Francisco bases only had the most senior flight attendants. When we landed in L.A., they would all go home and I would make my way alone to the hotel, as well as lay over on my own overnight. I had imagined margaritas and enchiladas with other flight attendants, not a room-service turkey club sandwich. But my disappointment turned to dread when we began bidding for what position we would work.

Everything in the airline industry is based on seniority, including which flights you work and where on the plane you work. Junior flight attendants got the flight schedules no one else really wanted because there were too many legs, or they were red-eyes, or the flights went to cities when it was too hot or snowy there, or the check-in times were too early in the morning or too late at night. Since where you worked on the plane was also determined by seniority, the most junior flight attendant on the crew—which was me on this flight—could count on getting the position that did the most work or covered the most passengers.

Every flight attendant was assigned a particular position with very particular duties. If you worked A on a 727, for example, you stood at the boarding door for boarding and deplaning, made all the announcements, and worked first class. B helped in first class and then assisted in coach. And C and D worked the main cabin. On wide bodies, there were eight or ten or even more positions, which determined which class and zone you worked in and what your specific duties were. Before the advent of business class, there was a gloriously quiet area between coach and first class called B Zone, where no children were allowed, which was populated by business-men. You can guess that senior flight attendants always took that position.

Before each flight, crews met in the crew lounge and bid on positions. Basically, the most junior flight attendant worked the position no one else wanted—for example, E on a wide body, which was the all-smoking section at the back of the plane; or, on the L-1011, something called GX, which set up the first class carts in the downstairs galley, sent all of the coach carts up the lift, took first-class orders, passed warm rolls and served drinks, picked up plates and stacked them in carts, brought those carts back down to the galley, passed more rolls, poured wine, and also helped in coach. In other words, GX worked harder than anyone else. Although later I would meet lots of flight attendants who liked working GX because they liked being busy or, ironically, did *not* want to interact with passengers much, for that first flight it loomed as the scariest position—too many things to do, too much organizing, and all of it done pretty much on your own.

My L.A. crew was not happy to have a new hire on her first flight working with them. When I introduced myself with a very eager *This is my first flight!*—they rolled their eyes, sighed, and then pretty much ignored me. When the bidding began, my nervousness made me not listen too closely as the nine flight attendants more senior than me claimed their positions. The next thing I knew, the room had grown quiet and the most senior one was looking at me. "That means you're GX. You know how to work GX, right?" I wasn't sure I did. But I was terrified that if I admitted I was overwhelmed by all the duties GX had, she would report me and I might be fired. For six months, we were on probation, and any infraction could get us terminated. I smiled and nodded, my head already pounding with all of the things I needed to remember to do.

BASICALLY, I DID everything wrong on that flight. I had imagined looking pretty, talking to passengers, effortlessly gliding down those beautiful twin aisles offering martinis and Manhattans. Instead, I had trouble opening and setting up the carts. I was forever running up and down the lift because I kept forgetting things below. I forgot the rolls altogether and another flight attendant threw them, cold, into the basket, growling over my incompetence. I couldn't keep the names of the wines straight, couldn't open the champagne bottle, couldn't remember where anything was stored.

Worst of all, I didn't know that I should have two pairs of shoes—the required high heels to be worn whenever we had our blazers on: in the airport, during boarding and deplaning; and a pair of flats for the rest of the flight, for the hours of standing and running up and down the aisles. That spare pair of flats also got jammed into your regulation purse. But I had only high heels, for seven hours straight. By about hour four, I was wincing with every step. My feet started to swell at hour five, at which point I took off my high heels and worked the rest of the flight in my stocking feet—something I could surely have been fired for had anyone noticed. I still can't believe that not one passenger said something to me or that another flight attendant didn't comment.

When we finally landed, a red-faced, angry flight attendant came marching up from coach to ask me where I'd been. I was supposed to help them, too, she reminded me. "I forgot," I admitted, mumbling an apology and trying to move my numb feet, which were now squeezed back into my high heels per our dress code: high heels, jackets, and lipstick must be worn in the airport and during boarding and deplaning.

The crew went off to the employee parking lot to retrieve their cars and drive home. I limped through LAX, trying to look like the polished person who belonged in her Ralph Lauren uniform. I retrieved the list of which hotel we stayed in at each city that was carefully folded up in my pocket. Almost in tears, I made my way outside and searched for the shuttle to the hotel, the dollar bill they'd told us to have at the ready for the driver's tip in my hand. Finally the van arrived. I got to the hotel, checked in, hobbled to my room, and took off my shoes and pantyhose. My uniform stank of smoke. My hair stank of smoke and something as yet unfamiliar but that I would soon recognize as "airplane smell." My hands smelled like all the food and liquor and Coke I'd spilled. But I didn't even bother to undress. I fell onto the bed and raised my legs, pressing my swollen, sore feet against the wall for relief. How could I have imagined I would actually go sightseeing? I was in Los Angeles—for the first time—but I could have been anywhere. It didn't matter.

Later I would soak my feet, and the rest of my body, in a hot bath. I would eat my room-service turkey club sandwich with a glass of chablis. And I would call my parents, who were giddy with excitement for me. While I talked to them, I lay down with my legs in the air and my sore feet pressed against the wall again.

"Tell us everything!" they said as soon as they heard my voice.

I was twenty-two years old, exhausted, and my whole body ached. I had never worked that hard in my life. Like me, my parents had imagined a life of glamour awaiting me. So I told them the only good thing that had happened: "I had someone famous on my flight."

They were beside themselves, no doubt imagining Al Pacino or Elizabeth Taylor. "You know the guy who played the teacher on *Room 222*?" I said. "Pete Dixon?"

There was the slightest pause, then my mother asked, "That old TV show?"

"Right," I said. "He was on my flight."

"In first class, I bet," my father said.

"No. In coach."

"Well, how about that," my dad said.

"So it was great?" my mom asked me.

"So great," I lied, wondering how I was ever going to put my feet back in those high heels and do it all again in the morning.

MY ALARM WENT OFF at five o'clock the next morning and I dragged myself out of bed. I had an eight a.m. flight, which meant I had to be at the airport at seven, which meant I had to leave the hotel at six thirty, which meant I had to be in the restaurant eating breakfast by six. I showered and put on my uniform that still smelled of stale smoke, put on my makeup, and went downstairs. The lobby and restaurant were empty, but it wasn't even six o'clock yet, so that didn't surprise me. The hostess seated me and I ordered coffee and an omelet without even looking at the menu. While I was eating, a man came over to my table.

"I'm a TWA flight attendant too," he said. "Are you OK?"

"Yes. Why?" I worried he was one of the spies I was always hearing about. Maybe he'd heard about me working a flight in my stocking feet or forgetting to go help in coach.

"Well, you're sitting here in your uniform in the middle of the night," he said.

"I'm on the eight o'clock flight," I told him.

"But it's three in the morning," he said.

I looked at my watch. "It's six," I said.

"On the East Coast," he said gently. "It's three hours earlier here."

Tears came to my eyes and I looked away so he wouldn't see them.

"It's OK," he said. "First flight out here?"

"First flight anywhere," I said.

"It gets easier," he said.

As soon as he was gone, I paid my check and went back to bed.

. . .

I ACTUALLY DON'T REMEMBER the flight back to Boston. Maybe I deadheaded—which means to fly as a passenger, albeit a passenger dressed in her full uniform—because surely I wouldn't forget how I managed to stand up for another six or eight hours on my sore, swollen feet, or if I'd had to manage working GX again.

After our first flights, my class was flown back to Kansas City for our debriefing and our graduation. I worried that I was the only one who'd forgotten some of my duties, wore the wrong shoes, and didn't like my crew. I worried, too, that my incompetence might get me fired. People were fired for wearing the wrong lipstick, looking sullen, having chipped nail polish, and scores of other reasons that seem archaic now. But even when I was a new hire, instructors popped up on our flights and quizzed us about safety and service. We often walked off the jetway to find a supervisor waiting there to weigh us.

It came as a great relief to hear that my nineteen classmates had a variety of good and bad experiences on their first flights. Joseph was one of the three men in our class. In his thirties and married to a flight attendant, he seemed so much older and more mature than the rest of us, as did Penelope, who had already had a career flying for Pan Am. Joseph had worked first class on his flight from JFK to L.A. when a passenger began to choke on a piece of steak. He immediately grabbed the man and performed the Heimlich maneuver, saving his life. Although part of our emergency training was learning CPR and the Heimlich maneuver, none of us had expected to have to actually do it on our first flight. Joseph seemed to take this in stride, but I was grateful that all I'd had was an unfriendly crew, an unmanageable position to work, and sore feet.

The rest of our uniform pieces had finally arrived, and we dressed in them for graduation the next day. We sat in the auditorium and heard a blur of speeches before a slide show of our time at training played on the big screen in front of us. There we were, sliding down the escape slide, practicing serving meals, mixing cocktails, ditching in the pool, smiling and smiling and smiling as the song "If My Friends Could See Me Now" played. At my college graduation, I'd barely listened as the opera conductor Sarah Caldwell gave the commencement speech. I was hot and bored and ready to leave the campus of the University of Rhode Island behind. But sitting in that auditorium at Breech Academy, I beamed as I watched that slide show. Look at what I'd learned and done and mastered! And look at me in this Ralph Lauren uniform, walking up to my instructors, Paula and Mike, and having my TWA wings pinned onto my double-breasted jacket.

The only other time I had such a feeling was the first time I saw my debut novel, *Somewhere Off the Coast of Maine*, in a bookstore window. To dream of doing something, of becoming something, since you were a little girl and then actually doing it is hard to describe. Let some people think I was just a glorified waitress, a sex kitten, an archaic symbol of women. I was a TWA flight attendant, and I was ready to gobble up the big, beautiful world.

# NEW HIRE

SINCE OUR TRAINING WAS cut short, we had to find apartments in Boston, fast. Alliances for roommates were formed quickly and I found myself one of six women agreeing to share an apartment together. I had just left college and the Alpha Xi Delta sorority house, so living with five other roommates sounded fine to me. One was Rebecca, my roommate in training who had shouted the airport codes in her sleep on our first night there. Tall and statuesque with honey-colored hair and enormous green eyes, at twenty she was not only the youngest among us, she was one of the youngest in our entire class. She seemed younger, too, with her wide-eyed innocence, frequent malapropisms, and boundless energy.

Another, Leslie, was a stunning Black woman who had worked as a telephone operator in Los Angeles. In those days, push-button phones were still kind of a novelty, so we found Leslie's prediction hilarious that someday those hashtag and asterisk buttons on either side of the zero would be used all the time. As ridiculous as the prediction by the mechanic who fixed Rebecca's always-broken-down Triumph Spitfire that soon it would be almost impossible to buy a car for under $10,000. At that time we could buy an adorable convertible

Bug for half that price, or a run-of-the-mill Ford Pinto for a little over $3,000.

Two of my roommates, Kim and Maureen, were from Long Island—the Five Towns, to be exact, which to their surprise I had never heard of. I quickly learned that when they said "the city," they meant Manhattan, not Boston. They also waited *on* line instead of *in* line, called pizza "pie," as in "Let's get a pie for dinner," and thought it was strange that at our favorite pizzeria in the North End, Regina's, we had to buy the whole pie instead of a slice. My other roommate was Diane, whom I had become good friends with during training. She'd been a journalism major at Bowling Green in Ohio, and we shared a love of reading and a desire to write. Diane had worked—and hated—a job in investments in Boston for the past year, so she already knew the city well and could tell us which T to take to Harvard Square, where the good bars and restaurants were, and where to get our hair cut.

All the six of us needed was a three-bedroom apartment with easy access to the airport. Which was not easy to find, especially in the notoriously expensive, crowded city of Boston. TWA put us up at the Hilton at Logan Airport for a week to give us time to find apartments. Even though I grew up only an hour away from Boston and had gone with my family to many Red Sox games and with my college friends to parties and bars there, I really didn't know the city well. Which neighborhoods were desirable? Which neighborhoods were safe? Which neighborhoods could we afford? We would be working that entire week, adding to the difficulty of searching for an apartment. When my father offered to find an apartment for us, we accepted gladly.

For six months, we would be on probation, which basically meant that we could be fired for the slightest infraction. Union representation didn't start until we were off probation, so we were subject to unannounced weight checks, safety quizzes, in-flight observations, and even having our earrings, heel heights, and hemlines measured. Any of these that did not meet regulations could get us fired, as could being late for a flight, missing a flight, crew complaints about our job performance, and passenger complaints. Passenger complaints were known as "onion letters" because they made you cry. Even one was enough to have you lose your job during probation. After probation, onion letters got placed in your file, and you were called in to a supervisor's office to discuss and explain your side. "CYA. Cover Your Ass," our instructors told us during training. "If a passenger is angry at you, write it up before that onion letter arrives." Three onion letters could get you fired post-probation. You were also called in for "orchid letters," which were compliments from passengers. Having an orchid letter or two in your file during probation was important because it could counter getting written up for a too-short skirt or lipstick-less lips. Every day on probation brought us closer to job security, but it also threatened one of those unannounced checks or the arrival of an onion letter and the possibility of dismissal.

From our rooms at the Hilton, we began flying on reserve, the unpredictable hell of not having a set schedule. All of the monthly bids for regular route pairings were typically taken by senior flight attendants. On the fifteenth of each month, we went to crew scheduling and picked up a fat bid package with every possible flight pairing for the following month. It took hours to pore over this thing, a pad and pencil in hand as you looked for pairings that allowed you to go to your mother's birthday party or have Tuesdays off or whatever you needed.

As a new hire, I looked longingly at trips with nice, long layovers or a lot of flight hours so I could make more money, knowing that if the trip was really good, senior flight attendants would get it. We listed our choices and returned the bid sheet to crew scheduling, then awaited our fate. The most junior flight attendants almost never held a line—that is, had a regular schedule for a month—and instead were on reserve, unless there was some horrible pairing that no one else wanted, like flying around the Ohio valley with four or five legs a day, for three days, in winter when there would surely be delays and canceled flights and angry passengers. Some new hires actually preferred that just so they'd have a regular schedule. Not me. I'd rather sit on reserve and hope for better flights.

On reserve, we waited for crew scheduling to call and put us on a flight, typically one leaving in the next hour or two. Before the days of cell phones, we all had pagers that we kept in our pockets, listening for the soon familiar buzz that meant we had a trip. To miss a flight was to get fired, no questions asked. To not answer when crew scheduling called was akin to missing a flight. It was easier to stay home by the phone, crew kit packed and uniform pressed and hanging on the outside of the closet, ready to go. But reserve could go on for days with no call and stir craziness would set in, forcing us out with our pagers clutched in our hands. We were required to be no more than an hour from the airport, as typically we might be needed because someone called in sick at the last minute or was delayed on an incoming flight or just failed to show up and we would have to get to the airport fast.

Delaying a plane was grounds for dismissal, so when crew scheduling called, I put on my uniform, grabbed my suitcase, and headed to the airport. Often I arrived and had to run onto a plane that was about to board or had already boarded. It was a strange feeling to be the last one on the plane, all of the passengers seated and the gate agent closing the boarding door before I even had a chance to stow my bag. As I got a quick briefing from the flight attendant working up front, it seemed like every passenger's head leaned into the aisle to see who had held up the flight, not realizing I was actually the one saving the day because someone else hadn't shown up.

While my roommates and I worked flights to Pittsburgh, Chicago, L.A., and Denver that first week, my father searched for a three-bedroom apartment near the airport that we could afford. One thing we had that many people our age in entry-level jobs didn't was a sizable paycheck that allowed us to live in nice apartments in nice neighborhoods. In 1946, flight attendants made less than file clerks, and were quick to point out that file clerks didn't also have the burden of having to look glamorous. Eventually, their pay did increase as a result of unionizing, rising 150 percent in ten years.

My college friends Susie and Donna, for example, had entry-level jobs in Boston's financial district with starting salaries of about $13,000 a year. With Boston rents high, they had to share a small one-bedroom at the edge of an iffy neighborhood. TWA flight attendants, on the other hand, were paid a $15,000 yearly salary, which was based on a minimum number of flying hours. If we flew more, we made overtime. If the plane was delayed on the runway, or if we had to fly more than our maximum daily flight hours due to weather or mechanical problems or airport delays, we received bonuses. Once a month we got an expense check with payment for all non-flight hours away from home, including time at the airport before and between flights and a per diem for days away from home. Our $15,000 a year easily became $20,000 or more, especially if we were willing to fly extra flights, which I always was.

Before our free week at the Hilton was up, Dad found that dream apartment in Harbor Towers, two twin skyscrapers designed by I. M. Pei that loomed over the Boston Harbor. The address—65 East India Row—sounded more romantic than the Commonwealth or Massachusetts Avenue addresses of some of our classmates. East India Row made me think of great ships sailing off to find spices and adventures, not unlike the six of us.

Harbor Towers and our apartment were fancier than we'd imagined. The two skyscrapers were all steel and concrete and glass, with four angled steel David von Schlegell sculptures that looked like solar panels dominating a concrete space in front and a uniformed doorman inside. Our apartment was enormous, with a long living room that had a wall of windows overlooking Boston Harbor and Logan Airport. We could actually watch each other's flights take off and land from that window. Our plan had been to put two of us in each bedroom, but it turned out that the rooms were uneven sizes. So Rebecca took the smallest room alone, Kim and Leslie shared the normal sized room, and Maureen, Diane, and I took the giant primary bedroom, our three twin beds lined up like the Seven Dwarfs' beds in *Snow White*.

Our neighborhood, however, was decidedly not nice. Newly gentrifying, the streets were mostly empty, with just a convenience store and dry cleaner on the corner. The New England Aquarium and the Aquarium T station—which was only one stop away from Logan Airport—were our nearest neighbors. But my father promised a lively nightlife across the busy highway, where Faneuil Hall, built by Peter Faneuil in 1742 as a marketplace for merchants, fishermen, butchers, and farmers, sat. In its former life, Faneuil Hall was a place for orators, such as Oliver Wendell Holmes and Susan B. Anthony, to give speeches and for patriots to protest and meet. A petition against the Stamp Act, which came with the now-famous cry of "No taxation without representation," was signed at Faneuil Hall, and Samuel Adams gathered colonists there to fight for independence.

In 1976, however, Faneuil Hall was mostly empty and about to be demolished until it was saved by Mayor Kevin White. Inspired by the renovation of Baltimore's Inner Harbor into a thriving complex of restaurants, hotels, shops, and tourist attractions, Faneuil Hall was being renovated similarly. When we six new-hire flight attendants moved to the waterfront, many of the stores at Faneuil Hall were still empty. There was a little shop filled with heart-themed things called Have a Heart, and another filled with hog-themed gifts called Hog Wild. Crickets, a restaurant/bar that attracted twentysomethings like us, sold chablis and Michelob to a wall-to-wall crowd. We could get overstuffed, overpriced sandwiches at one kiosk, enormous pickles at another, Boston souvenirs and T-shirts at several others. It seemed like a good backyard for us, and at $1,200 a month rent—just $200 each—with a wall of windows overlooking the lights of Boston Harbor and Logan Airport, we signed the lease, rented furniture, and moved in.

Our original apartment was on the sixteenth floor, with

grand, sweeping views. But we'd lived there for only a couple months before we were evicted for making too much noise. It was true that a lot of people came in and out of our apartment, the elevator constantly dinging and laughter and music going on until all hours. However, we appealed to management about how badly we needed an apartment and how we had no time to look elsewhere because we were always out of town working, which was also mostly true. Six flight attendants in distress must have worked, because he let us move into an identical apartment on the sixth floor. The view, though less majestic, was still breathtaking.

With six ordinary people in an apartment, even a big, swanky apartment, one would think there was no privacy. But with six flight attendants in an apartment, we were more likely to find ourselves alone or with just one other roommate when we weren't off flying somewhere. It was a special occasion if even three of us were there on the same night. Despite the unpredictability of our schedules, a routine quickly developed. We were either away working a trip, or at home waiting for the call that assigned a trip. In between, we did whatever it was other people did on weekends—slept late, watched television, talked on the phone, read, went out to eat and drink. Except our days off were almost never on weekends. Reserve meant flying when other, more senior flight attendants didn't want to. We flew Saturdays and Sundays, holidays and the Mondays of long weekends, early mornings and red-eyes.

The phone rang constantly—crew scheduling with flight assignments, families and friends in other cities, and men calling for dates. Rebecca kept a list by the phone of who got the most calls from guys, announcing your ranking on the list frequently. "Five guys called for Ann, four called for Diane, and I win because I got eight!" Like a French farce, the apartment door was forever opening and closing—one of us racing out with our crew kit bumping behind us to make a flight, one of us dragging her tired self in from days of flying; one of us dressed up for a steak dinner at the Rusty Scupper with a guy we'd met on a flight or with a guy we'd met at one of our hangouts. Nights out usually started at the new TGI Friday's on Exeter Street, where we shared glasses of chablis and nibbles of appetizers, ever fearful of the next weigh-in.

I liked the company of my friends but not the small talk with the guys who inevitably surrounded us at the bar as soon as they heard we were flight attendants. I was just bad at small talk and would watch fascinated as my roommates kept up a steady stream of chatter while the guys kept buying us drinks. Often, other flight attendant friends who were also off for the night would join us too, like Tavia, a former Playboy bunny who found TWA's restrictions almost lenient compared to the Playboy Club's. One night, some guys bought us all flaming shots, and when Kim lifted her glass, the nail polish on her pointer finger caught on fire, sending flames and screams into the air. The bartender doused it with water and a rag, and miraculously, although the nail polish was gone, she wasn't even burned.

When Friday's closed, the whole entourage of flight attendants and guys went to Daisy Buchanan's on nearby Newbury Street. Daisy's was a small, intimate bar with stiff drinks and a sign on the wall that read: DB, WHERE ANYTHING CAN HAPPEN. And anything did. Besides the men we'd met at Friday's who'd followed us there, more men—investment bankers in expensive suits, Red Sox players, MBA students—crowded around us too. Inevitably, people paired up and slowly disappeared into the night. I loved those nights out, but eventually, worn out from small talk, I would want to go home, get in bed, and read. Although I had my share of nights going off with someone to Chinatown for middle-of-the-night Chinese food or driving along the Charles River in someone's convertible with the top down and music playing loud, I also had a lot of nights when I walked home alone, oddly happy to be by myself for a time after days working crowded planes.

Put six attractive women in their early twenties in an apartment, and sometimes it did feel like a scene out of *Coffee, Tea or Me?* The doorman was always calling us with flower deliveries. Men showed up in their suits or jeans with cashmere sweaters, often with their friends, courting us. We went on their boats or zipped around in their Porsches or sat in their box seats at Fenway Park (sometimes we had even better seats, since Red Sox players seemed to love to date flight attendants). They took us to Anthony's Pier Four for fancy dinners and to fluorescent-lit dives in Chinatown after everything else had closed. Always our pagers sat on the table, ready to buzz and call us away to Vegas or Wichita.

It didn't take us long to figure out a way out of bad dates. We'd pretend to check our pager, send an SOS to whichever roommate was home, and she would then page us. "Oh no! It's crew scheduling. I've got a flight," we'd lie, and off we'd go, away from the boring guy and back to 65 East India Row, where someone really was heading out for a red-eye to L.A., someone else was entertaining a Brooks Brothers–suited bevy of guys, and someone else was kicking off her high heels and dropping into a chair in her uniform, exhausted from five days flying around the Ohio valley. Often, as soon as you escaped your bad date, crew scheduling really would call, and an hour later you had your lipstick and uniform on and you were standing at the boarding door of a 727, smiling and saying "Welcome to TWA" 189 times.

OTHER THAN MISSING A FLIGHT, the number-one reason new hires got fired during probation was for being overweight. Imagine a gaggle of tall, pretty, thin young women sitting in the sauna at the YMCA in Boston, trying to sweat off pounds. Ridiculous when you consider that by most people's standards, we were already underweight. But, scared of losing our jobs, that's exactly what we did. We also took diuretics; tried a crazy diet that called for eating nine bananas one day, nine eggs the next, and nine hot dogs on the third; and, sometimes, depending on the scale in Operations, we just drank water until a pound or two came off.

Part of being on probation was unannounced weigh-ins for male and female flight attendants. You'd walk off your flight and there would be a supervisor standing there, waiting for you. She'd check the length of your skirt, the dangle of your earrings, your lipstick and hair. She'd make sure you had on your uniform blazer and high heels and that your scarf was tied in one of the regulation ways. Then she'd lead you downstairs, where a scale stood ready to torment new hires.

I had dated a guy who was a college wrestler, and I remembered him having to "suck weight"—drop a lot of pounds—to qualify for his weight class. I used to think he was crazy, and the things he did to lose the weight crazier still. But here I was, five-seven and 120 pounds, downright skinny in my size-0 uniform skirt, sweating in a sauna at a YMCA.

Remember, we had to maintain our *hiring* weight, not the allowable weight on the weight charts. That weight, the one I wouldn't have even scored an interview with, was 135 pounds for me. Yet I could not gain fifteen pounds. I could not gain even one pound. I had to stay at my hiring weight. Thus the dieting and sweating and starving. I don't think I ever tipped the scale above my hiring weight, but the fear of getting "written up" loomed for those six months, and I continued to watch my weight obsessively. At TGI Friday's, three of us would share an appetizer called "steak on a stick": flank steak marinated in soy sauce and spices, served on three wooden skewers. We might also share loaded potato skins, which had cheese and sour cream and bacon, but we'd each only eat half of one. That was it for an entire day.

Some of us weren't as lucky or foolish as I was, and during weigh-ins they were found to be two or five or even seven pounds above their hiring weight. My roommate Rebecca's weight yo-yoed for most of the probationary six months. She was tall and what my mother used to call "big boned," and her hiring weight had actually been near the maximum allowed on the weight chart. Once she passed out while packing for a trip because she was so dehydrated from dieting. Somehow, she always managed to get back to her hiring weight before the next weigh-in, and she finished probation with a couple write-ups but her job intact.

My other roommate, Maureen, wasn't as lucky. At five-nine and 130 pounds, she was well below 145 pounds—the maximum allowed on the chart. But she could not go above her hiring weight of 130 pounds and keep her job. At one surprise weigh-in, she was a couple pounds over and got a warning. "I'm not going to write you up this time . . ." she was told. When she was five pounds over her hiring weight the next time, she did get written up. There was a three-strikes-and-you're-out policy, so we assured Maureen that she would lose the weight easily and the problem would be gone. Rumors always swirled about who was on weight watch with management, and it was humiliating to be one of those girls, so it was understood to not talk about it.

We gave Maureen our stash of diuretics, accompanied her to the steam room at the Y, but the truth was, she—like many of us—had starved herself for the interviews. Her normal weight was closer to that 145 pounds than 130, and it became harder and harder to keep the weight off. With our erratic flying schedules, we ate all kinds of food at strange hours when we were on trips. The airline provided us with crew meals on certain flights. We might eat our crew meal but then fly six or eight more hours and end up eating leftover first-class meals, the rolls off extra coach meals, bags and bags of peanuts, and the M&M's from the hotel minibar. Other days we might only have time to grab the famously delicious popcorn at the Dayton airport. No wonder our weight seesawed.

With Maureen on weight watch, my own paranoia grew and I started to eat even less, sometimes subsisting on just coffee and bags of peanuts for the three days of a hellish flight pairing through the Ohio valley. These flights were almost always crewed by new hires because no one wanted to fly three or four or five legs a day, performing all of those boarding and deplaning duties and serving hot meals to full planes only to get a nine-hour layover in Dayton with a six a.m. check-in the next day. Such were the joys of being a new hire.

I had my sights set on July, the day my six-month probation ended, my job was secure, and I got my free flying privileges. Flight attendants got free passes on TWA for themselves, their parents, their spouse, and their children. All we had to do was show up at the airport, go to crew scheduling, and put our name on a waitlist. Then we sat by the gate and waited for our name to be called. Unlike flights today, there were almost always empty seats on a plane and almost always one in first class. Even better, we had reciprocity with most other airlines. Although our status on the waitlist for them was lower than for their own employees, we still never had a problem getting on a flight.

But July was a long way off, and I had miles and lots of weigh-ins and surprise weight checks to go before I had those free passes.

BEING ON RESERVE during most of our probation not only meant not knowing our schedule ahead of time but also that we would fly almost every one of the seven types of aircraft (except for the 747, which was only used on international flights) without any notice. One day I would show up and have to work a DC-9, TWA's smallest plane, which required only two flight attendants. The next time I'd work an L-1011 with ten flight attendants and 256 passengers. Each aircraft had its own evacuation procedures, its own service procedures, and its own places to keep emergency equipment like oxygen and fire extinguishers.

One of the many things being a flight attendant taught me was how to think on my feet. I'd see that DC-9—or 727, 707, 1011— and have to immediately review all of those procedures, find and check the PSI on all the equipment, set up my bar cart and galley, and get to work.

Often, because on reserve you were covering for flight attendants who were stuck somewhere else or had called in sick, that meant walking on to the plane along with the passengers and therefore had no time to adjust. There were times I boarded planes and didn't even really know where we were going. Pittsburgh? St. Louis? Columbus? All three?

Passengers only see flight attendants in the aisle offering peanuts and cocktails. But during that hour before anyone boarded, we were already working, including going over any special details on the flight—wheelchairs, special meals, passengers with guns (like FBI or law enforcement agents), non-revenue passengers (family of an airline employee who were flying for free), and things like insulin we were storing on ice or even body parts for transplant—before we bid on which position to work.

On short-haul flights on narrow-body aircraft, there were two to five flight attendants: one at each exit and sometimes an extra—called X—if the flight was full. Most plane crashes happen during takeoff and landing, which is why you see a flight attendant on their jump seat at an exit during those times. But before we sat down and buckled in for takeoff, before the passengers even boarded, we got on the plane and did our safety checks—being sure the first-aid kits, oxygen and fire extinguishers were where they were supposed to be and were ready to use. We met the flight crew, which used to include a captain, first officer, and flight engineer (a position that doesn't exist anymore) and received not only the flight plan and weather in the city where we were headed but also what the cockpit liked to eat and drink; part of our job was serving food and beverages to them too.

After bringing the flight crew their coffee or Cokes, we counted how many meals were on board and contacted food services if there weren't enough. We set up the coffeemakers so they would start to brew as soon as we took off; set up our liquor carts and coffee-service trays; refilled our stash of magazines; and did a walk-through of the cabin, which, depending on the flight, might require putting pillows and blankets on each seat, straightening seat belts, and making sure the cabin looked neat and clean.

In between legs, cleaners came on and cleaned up. But sometimes things were missed or tucked into the seat pocket. One afternoon during boarding, I saw the corner of a napkin sticking out of a seat pocket in first class. When I reached in and took it out, a pile of toenail clippings fell into my hand. Another time I thought a passenger had left magazines, always considered a great find. But instead I pulled out a dirty diaper they had jammed deep into the seat pocket.

We were also not allowed to take trash bags in the aisles to pick up trash during the flight, especially in view of passengers. I cringe now when I see flight attendants wearing plastic gloves and hauling trash bags through the cabin. We could have been fired for doing that. Back in those days, part of our job was to always look professional—thus the rule about no chewing gum or smoking in uniform. Everything, even used paper cups or empty sugar packets, had to be picked up on trays. "TWA flight attendants do not touch trash," we were taught in training as we tried to juggle a tray full of stuff after a meal service. Because the plane would also be moving, and possibly even bumpy, in flight, trays were not stacked up our arms as waitresses do. We held on to them tight with our hands, allowing us to carry only two at once. Some flight attendants developed a way to stack them so they could carry four or even five, a useful technique to learn when you had to serve drinks and full meals in little more than an hour to a hundred or more passengers.

After everything was counted, checked, and in order, we notified the gate agent that passengers could board. Depending on your position, you placed yourself in the appropriate spot— boarding door, mid-cabin, rear of the plane—and assisted with boarding, which mostly meant directing people to their seats and telling them to put their bags in the overhead compartment or directly under the seat in front of them.

On short hauls, I loved working A, the position that stood at the boarding door and greeted passengers, made all the announcements, and worked first class. A was the one who said before the plane door closed, "You have boarded TWA Flight 62 to Detroit. If Detroit is not your final destination, this would be an excellent time to leave the aircraft." It wasn't uncommon for a passenger to jump up, grab their belongings, and race off the plane in search of the correct flight. What was worse was when the passenger realized they were on the wrong flight when A said after landing, "Welcome to Detroit!" Like the passenger who shouted, "Detroit? You told me we were going to DC!" Or the quiet man years later on my flight from Rome to JFK who sat the entire flight—nine hours—in his sweater and jacket, holding his fedora in his lap and refusing offers of beverages or dinner.

When we landed and the flight attendant announced, "Welcome to JFK, where the local time is three o'clock," he looked confused.

I sat on the jump seat diagonally across from him and asked if he was OK. "Palermo?" he said hopefully.

"Not Palermo," I told him. "New York."

"No!" he said, laughing. "Palermo."

It was the man's first flight, and he had no idea that a flight from Rome to Palermo in Sicily was only about an hour and ten minutes. No wonder he'd kept his coat on and his hat ready. He didn't even have a passport! So TWA put him right back on a flight to Rome.

ALTHOUGH I DID MY SHARE of those Ohio valley routes, I also worked a lot of nonstop flights to L.A. As a girl who grew up in a small town in Rhode Island, seeing celebrities never lost its thrill. During most of my years as a flight attendant, first-class passengers were predominantly male—businessmen, politicians, or celebrities. Female passengers in first class were usually movie stars, like Diana Ross or Barbra Streisand, both of whom I had on flights in my first months of flying. The time I had to stand in front of my first-class ice-cream cart— three kinds of ice cream ready to be scooped, silver bowls of hot fudge and butterscotch sauce, cherries, whipped cream, and candied walnuts—look Richard Gere in the eye after I'd scooped his ice cream and added the sauce and whipped cream, and ask: "Nuts?" still makes me blush.

On another flight to LAX, as I stood at the boarding door a TWA representative and two men in dark suits approached me, walkie-talkies in hand. "O. J. Simpson is about to board," the TWA rep said in a hushed voice. I only knew O. J. Simpson as the football player who runs through an airport to snag a Hertz rental in a television commercial. "The superstar in a rental car." Then Simpson appeared, not running but kind of slow-jogging down the runway, tall and handsome and smiling. By the time we landed, Ali, the cute, freckle-faced Southern strawberry blonde working first class with me, had a date with him for that night.

Not all famous people paid for first class, though when recognized sitting in coach could be embarrassed, even hostile, like the co-star of a TV sitcom who, when I called him by his character's name, said, "That's right. That's the only thing I've ever done in my whole goddamned life." Or the politician who always flew coach because he considered himself a regular guy, one of the people, a fact I'd read about him just the morning of my flight.

When I heard a "Psssst" on the other side of the curtain that separated coach and first class, I was surprised to see him there. "Do you need something?" I asked him.

He poked his head around the curtain, looked around, and said, "I see there's some empty seats up here. Can you move me up?"

"But you like to fly coach," I said. "You said so yourself in the newspaper."

"No one likes to fly coach," he told me.

Seeing my frown, he added, "Come on. The girls do it all the time for me."

"The girls?" I sputtered, trying to keep my TWA charm. "OK. I'll move you up. Get your credit card and I'll check how much the upgrade costs."

He shook his head. "You don't get it. They move me up for free."

"Sorry," I said, "not this girl." And I pulled the curtain closed.

ONE OF TWA'S RULES was that we had to call all first-class passengers by name. On one of my first flights to L.A., I had to practice what we were taught to say: "Hello, Mr. Jones. My name is Ann and I'll be one of your flight attendants today." I practiced it under my breath over and over as I struggled with those meal carts in the below galley. I had belted out an off-key "Matchmaker, Matchmaker" as Tzeitl in my high school production of *Fiddler on the Roof* and given speeches as the student body treasurer in college without feeling nervous. But introducing myself, dressed in that beautiful uniform on that luxurious jet, scared the hell out of me at first.

Eventually it became easier, though I managed to flub it more than once. We had been told to never call a woman traveling with a man in first class "*Mrs.*" Instead, we were to ask her what she'd like to be called. At twenty-two, this decorum puzzled me and one day in training, I asked why women were asked that question. "Because she may not be Mrs. Jones," our instructor said. Still puzzled, she added, "There may be a Mrs.

Jones back home." Slowly it dawned on me what she meant. Still, I did manage to call a few passengers Mrs. Jones, when the real Mrs. Jones was back home.

I KNEW SOME flight attendants who preferred working first class because they wanted to meet men. Rich ones. That made me uncomfortable, but I had gone to college in the days when some women still said they were there for their "MRS degree." My sorority had a ceremony for girls who got pinned, an archaic tradition that also made me uncomfortable. Pinning is a pre-engagement ritual for "Greek" couples (fraternity and sorority couples), in which the guy gives the girl his fraternity pin, which she then wears every day. It brings to mind the also archaic tradition of young women getting hope chests, as many of my high school friends did, for storing the linens they will need when they get married. Working first class to meet rich men harkens back to *How to Become an Airline Stewardess* and the promises of being whisked away by men who can afford to fly.

I liked working first class on short hauls because it was less hectic. When I would open the curtain that separated first class and coach, it was like opening the portal into a different, chaotic world. Whereas I had just served cocktails in glasses with TWA stamped on them in red, placed a linen tablecloth—the red TWA on the lower right—on tray tables, and served a meal on real china accompanied by wine in real wineglasses, cleared that and then made sundaes to order for six or eight people, back in coach three flight attendants were pushing heavy drink carts, sometimes uphill, and serving more than a hundred drinks and meals in the same amount of time, usually less than two hours.

Depending on my seniority, I was just as likely to be one of those three flight attendants working coach. As soon as the No Smoking sign went off, we leapt to our feet, turned on the coffee and the ovens, removed the liquor carts from their locked positions, put all the items we'd prepared during pre-flight— ice in a bucket, mixers, plastic cups, napkins, those red TWA propeller stir rods—and began our drinks service. TWA's policy was *galley out*, which meant you began service closest to the galley. We'd position the cart about ten rows from the galley, and start serving drinks, one of us moving from the last row to the row meeting the cart, the other working from the row closest to the cart on their side and progressing forward. Even with limited time, when we placed the cocktail napkin on the tray table, that red TWA was supposed to be in the lower right corner. Every detail mattered, we were taught. That was part of what made me so proud to be a TWA flight attendant—every special detail. Even today when I'm setting the table for dinner with just my husband and kids, I remember the difference those small details make.

Of course, in the hectic moments of serving an entire plane, executing those details sometimes seemed impossible. I can remember slapping cocktail napkins down crookedly on tray tables, and hastily adjusting them so the TWA was where it was supposed to be. All of those empty cups and napkins had to be picked up on trays, fast. *Galley out* also meant that once you started serving meals from the row closest to the galley, as you made your way back down the aisle you could pick up the cups and napkins. One flight attendant manned the ovens in the galley while the other two took meal orders, asking "Chicken or beef?" a hundred or more times, then telling the flight attendant in the galley, "Three beefs, two chickens" (if you could carry five trays).

That flight attendant working in the galley was so rushed that she would grab those hot, foil-wrapped meals out of the ovens barehanded. Then she'd rip the foil off—red stripes for beef, blue for chicken—and place the meal in the center of the meal tray, between the salad and the napkin-wrapped silverware with its red TWA logo on the napkin holder. If any foil stuck to the plate—which it would, a lot, thanks to spilled gravy or marinara sauce or faulty overheated ovens—it had to be removed. TWA did not tolerate strips of foil on its meal trays. If I worked galley enough, my fingertips became numb from burns by the end of a three-day trip. Worse than prying foil off a hot plate was when, on a breakfast flight, the foil was removed only to reveal that the eggs—powdered—had turned green from too much heat. In that case, I could only hold my breath and hope that enough passengers chose the cereal option or passed on breakfast so we'd have enough meals—there was no way to fix those green eggs.

Once the meals were served, eaten, and cleared, it was time for the coffee service. Out with the tray that had a pitcher of cream, a cup of sugars, and another of Sweet'N Low. Coffee cups were provided on the meal tray, but extra ones were also placed on the serving tray. Then it was down the aisle with that coffeepot and tray in hand. If a passenger wanted coffee, and it seemed like they all did, I'd say, "Please put your cup on my tray" and hold my tray out to them. So many passengers didn't understand that request and instead tried to take the tray from me, or the coffeepot, that there were T-shirts that read PLEASE PUT YOUR CUP ON MY TRAY. There were also T-shirts that read MARRY ME, FLY FOR FREE.

When the No Smoking sign came on (it used to be right there beside the seat-belt sign), we knew we were on our initial descent and had to finish service, fast. That meant not only finishing caffeinating the passengers but cleaning up the cabin and the galley, locking everything down, checking that seat belts were buckled, seat backs and tray tables returned to their original upright and locked positions, and passengers' items used during flight were stowed under the seat in front of them or the overhead bin. It was not uncommon to get to the jump seat just as the plane was making its final approach. On short-haul flights, no sooner did we land and thank the passengers for flying TWA than the catering and cleaning crews arrived, the gate agent brought on the new manifest, and we did everything all over again.

Long-haul flights—transcontinental or international—required the same duties: the meeting in the crew lounge, the pre-flight safety and service checks, boarding, and in-flight services. But the reason I loved them more was that you only did those things once, and over the course of six or eight or ten hours. No hastily served drinks or picking up half-eaten meals as the plane prepared to land. No "Welcome to TWA" a hundred times, and then another hundred, and then another and even another. When I dreamed of being a flight attendant, although I did not know it then, I imagined the twilight boarding, the leisurely meal service, the time to talk to passengers, and the long layovers once we landed.

That's why one of the plum flights to land on reserve was

the nonstop to L.A. with a layover and a nonstop back to Boston the next morning. I loved when I got the call from crew scheduling to work that flight. Not only did it have its share of celebrities and sports stars—everyone from Charles Bronson, the tough-guy actor who boarded the plane holding a delicate little plant, to the seven-foot-tall Harlem Globetrotters—but it was fun handing out the menus and taking meal orders, mixing cocktails and talking to passengers in coach or first class. TWA even had signature cocktails: the Royal Ambassador, which was a mimosa with Grand Marnier, and the Bocce Ball, which was orange juice, vodka, amaretto, and a splash of club soda.

I was fresh out of college, and pretty naïve. Little did I know the kinds of human behavior I'd see up close being a flight attendant. One day a woman boarded in first class in Los Angeles, her cat tucked into its carrying case. It was very unusual to see women in first class, especially one wearing a flowing caftan and beaded sandals. Even in coach in 1979, people still dressed up to fly. We served drinks and were in the galley getting the meals ready when I did a walk-through to refill beverages. There in 4F sat the woman, breastfeeding her cat. At least, she had the cat to her breast and it was sucking or licking. I stood, frozen in the aisle between rows 2 and 3, trying to think of what I should do. We'd been taught how to deflect a passenger coming on to us, how to politely stop serving intoxicated passengers, how to get someone to change seats. But not what to do when a passenger pretended to breastfeed a cat.

I turned and went back to the galley for help. One by one, my fellow flight attendants went to see this for themselves. But no one could figure out what to do. By the time the chateaubriand was ready, the cat was back in its carrying case, where it stayed for the rest of the flight. We kept checking, but that was it.

A chief hostess for TWA told author Kathleen M. Barry in *Femininity in Flight* that a stewardess had to be able to "spill a cup of coffee in a man's lap and get away with it." It wasn't coffee, however, that I spilled in a man's lap, and unfortunately I didn't get away with it. One of the features of our transcontinental first-class service was to serve individual salads that were tossed in front of the passengers. We rolled a salad cart to the front of each aisle and added cherry tomatoes, sliced cucumbers, and croutons to the lettuce waiting in a big crystal bowl. Two silver gravy boats of different dressings sat on the cart, too, as did a bowl of crumbled blue cheese. These two special features— the dressings and the blue cheese—were how we individualized each order. "Would you like blue cheese on your salad, Mr. Franklin?" "Would you prefer creamy Italian or ranch dressing?" Once the ingredients had been added to the lettuce, we picked up our silver salad servers and tossed, with as much dignity and flair as we could muster.

Most of the businessmen, bent over their paperwork with a martini in hand, ignored us completely. But a few liked to watch the show and the high-school theater star in me always liked to have fun doing it. That was the case with 2C, a middle-aged businessman sitting next to his wife, who was dressed in a Chanel suit and pearls, her ash-blond hair cut into a neat bob. 2C's rheumy blue eyes twinkled as I set about the salad service. His wife's gaze remained steely, unnerving me. I added the tomatoes and cucumbers and croutons, picked up the silver salad servers, and *tossed*, sending cherry tomatoes and bits of lettuce flying right into 2C's lap.

"I'm so sorry!" I blurted, then reached for the tomatoes resting in his gray-flanneled lap.

"Oh no you don't," the wife said. She grabbed my wrist, hard. "Do. Not. Touch. My. Husband."

Our eyes met over the top of her husband's balding head. There was no use trying to convince her that balding, middle-aged men weren't my type. I just smiled and apologized. She paused a moment before letting go of my wrist, but not before she added a little twist for punctuation.

I cleared my throat, smiled some more, and asked, "Which dressing do you prefer, creamy Italian or ranch?"

Only a decade after Betty Friedan and Gloria Steinem helped start the women's movement, many women—including me—found ourselves with one foot in the idea of change for women and the other still stuck in typical women's roles, like 2C's wife in first class. This became clear to me on a layover in Chicago at a now-forgotten fancy hotel with a gorgeous restaurant on the top floor, complete with panoramic views. Like the flight to LAX where the whole crew was based there and I was on my own, this crew was based in Chicago, so I made my way to the hotel alone. Finding the airport shuttle and getting to my hotel became second nature pretty quickly, not at all intimidating, as it was that first night in L.A. However, at this point in my life, I had never eaten in a restaurant alone. At twenty-two, the thought terrified me. But I was hungry, and I'd been eating a lot of room-service club sandwiches, and I wanted to take in that view of the city.

I did what I always did when I needed advice: I called my father. He told me to put on that nice outfit I kept in my crew kit and go right to that restaurant. "Order yourself a steak and a baked potato and a glass of red wine," he told me. "Get some dessert. And be sure to leave a 10 percent tip." I took a deep breath, changed into that good outfit, grabbed a book, and took the elevator up to the restaurant.

A very officious maître d' greeted me.

"You're meeting someone?" he said.

"No. Just me."

He stared. "Table for one?" he said with disdain.

"Yes." I tried to sound braver than I felt, but that man's stare and tone made me shrink as he walked me to a table right by the kitchen and dropped the enormous leather-bound menu on the table.

Tuxedoed waiters floated past me, but not one stopped. I opened my book and began to read, glancing up from time to time to try to catch someone's attention. My water glass remained empty, no rolls appeared on my table as they did at the table for two across from me. No one seemed to realize I was even there. Finally, fifteen or twenty minutes later, I flagged down a waiter, who looked as put out and disgusted as the maître d' had.

"I'd like some water? And rolls?" I began, and he started to walk away. "And a steak and baked potato and a glass of red wine," I called after him.

Everything arrived at the same time. He didn't return to see how my meal was or if I wanted another glass of wine or dessert. In fact, the next time I saw him he placed the check on the table and walked away without even looking at me.

Although I'd never eaten at such a fancy restaurant alone, I'd eaten in plenty just as fancy with my parents, friends, or dates. I was, I realized, being treated this way because I was a woman alone. In the days before ATM machines, when the crew arrived at our hotel, we wrote a check that the front desk would cash for us, so I took out my fresh stack of twenty-dollar bills and left the exact amount of the bill. *Don't forget to tip 10 percent*, my father had told me. But weren't tips for good service? I turned the bill over and wrote: *My tip for you is to treat women eating alone better and you'll get a monetary tip.* Then I practically ran out of there and back down to my room, where I called my father and told him the whole story, including the "tip" I'd left. "You did that?" he said. "I am so proud of you! Never take that kind of treatment from anyone ever! Good for you."

The next time I ate alone at a fancy restaurant, I requested a seat away from the kitchen. And I never had to leave that kind of tip again. But the experience was a strong reminder about how far women still had to go. A single man eating alone would not have raised any eyebrows.

Of course, the '70s brought some significant changes too: *Roe v Wade* legalized abortion in 1973, the Equal Rights Amendment to the Constitution was passed by both the House and the Senate (although failed to be ratified by the states), and doors of opportunity in law, science, business, and politics were beginning to open. In 1979, women surpassed men in college enrollments in the United States for the first time.

However, change was slow and the women's rights movement, despite these advances, also met with great setbacks. The wage gap remained; women were still paid 45 percent less than men. Perhaps more significantly, many people's attitudes were not changing. An Old Gold cigarette ad showed a man stepping on a tiger-fur rug that had the head of a pretty woman, with the tagline: "It's nice to have a girl around the house." But some women also were slow to change. This duality was expressed well on a Fiat ad on a bulletin board that read over a picture of a Fiat: "If it were a lady, it would get its bottom pinched." Beneath it someone spray-painted: "Or she'd run you down!"

For stewardesses, some of that change was even slower. There had long been a standing rule that flight attendants had to be single. "The job simply would not be compatible with married life," Hugh Flynn of United Airlines said in 1965. "A wife would have to be away from home days at a time . . ." Some of the stewardesses agreed with the policy. "Having married stewardesses would take some of the fun out of the job for the single girls—and the male passengers," retired hostess Esther Sievers told the *Dayton Daily News* that same year. A 1967 United Airlines ad featured a pretty brunette woman with the words "Old Maid" beneath her picture. "That's what the other stewardesses call her," the ad went on to say, "because she's been flying three years now." At the time, the average tenure for stewardesses was about twenty-one months before they quit to get married. The ad ends on this hopeful note: "Everyone gets warmth, friendliness and extra care. And someone may get a wife." Not only did the airlines impose marriage restrictions, they even advertised to marry off their stewardesses.

That same year, advertising executive Mary Wells said of her ad campaign for Braniff, "When a tired businessman gets on an airplane, we think he ought to be allowed to look at a pretty girl." A mere seven years before I was hired by TWA, a TWA executive was asked, "What is a TWA Hostess?" His reply included: "She is a woman who always looks as though she has just stepped out of a bandbox and is, among other pleasures, a feast for the eyes." And: "To attract the attention she inevitably does, she must first look the person she so charmingly is. To hold attention, she must be the person she so charmingly looks." Of course, he continues, "The personal result of this success creates a rapid turnover of the title 'Miss TWA' to the tile of 'Mrs.,' but we are proud of this success too." Finally, in 1968, the marriage restriction was lifted. But it would be another two years before stewardesses could have children and still keep their jobs.

American Airlines, with an age limit of thirty-two, argued that a stewardess's basic requirement of attractiveness was found in *young* women. Northwest Orient and most other airlines also had an age limit of thirty-two, though TWA stewardesses had an age restriction of thirty-five. (Male flight attendants, however, had a retirement age of somewhere in their sixties.) Even into the 1960s, the stereotype of young stewardesses dating and even marrying pilots was real. But when I started flying with TWA, that had become outdated. TWA had a hiring freeze on pilots, so our cockpits were made up of older, mostly married men, and very few women. In 1978, Lynn Ripplemeyer, a former flight attendant, was the second female whom TWA hired as a pilot and one of just twenty-five female airline pilots. Many of our pilots had flown in Vietnam during the war, but those dashing young pilots were twenty years older by the time I began and ranged from paternal to sexist to standoffish to nice guy.

I heard a lot of stories from the more senior flight attendants about the days when international trips lasted a week or more, and the crew flew through Europe and Asia and Africa together, touring foreign cities, eating and drinking together, and sometimes falling in love. "Luxury was how the airlines competed . . ." the TWA Museum says of the 1960s. "Frills included in-flight movies, free cocktails, and nubile steward-esses in leggy uniforms . . ."

. . .

THE END OF MY probation period neared, but summer travel had begun and that meant more flying hours. Traditionally, that's when families took vacations, and TWA offered free compan-ion tickets, reduced rates for kids, and added flights to popular destinations. I found myself on a lot of nonstops to L.A. with families headed to Disneyland. On the flights back to Boston, when I looked down the aisle in coach on the 1011, I'd see a sea of Mickey Mouse ears on kids' heads.

On one flight to L.A., blue-blazered businessmen took the seats in first class as usual. Then a woman boarded and sat in 2C, the lone female up front. She was dressed in business attire too, with a briefcase that she slid under her seat. After takeoff and cocktails, she left her seat and went into the bathroom. A moment later, the man in 1A went into the same bathroom. People were always curious about the "mile-high club." Did it really exist? How often did people "join" it? Until that morn-ing, I had rarely seen couples slip into the lav together, presum-ably to join the mile-high club. And usually that happened on night flights, when the dim lights made it easy to go unnoticed.

But this was a bright, sunny morning. 1A came out, and 1B went in. I told my flying buddy, and together we watched 1B come out and 1C go in. In fact, one by one, every guy in first class visited the woman from 2C in the bathroom. She finally came out, looking as cool and professional as she had when she boarded. No one acknowledged her, and she ignored all of them.

"How did they know she would go along with that?" I asked a male flight attendant over margaritas that night.

He laughed. "They hired her," he said.

"What?"

"She was a prostitute."

I've told this story for years, and everyone who hears it immediately comes to that same conclusion—the men had hired a prostitute to do this. But at twenty-two, fresh out of college, I would never have concluded that, ever.

USUALLY THE SHORT-HAUL FLIGHTS had many legs and very short layovers of only ten or eleven hours, spread out over three or four days. Long-haul flights typically had one leg and at least a full day and overnight layover. Many flight attendants preferred the short hauls—they didn't like to battle jet lag or work those long hours, or they wanted to get in all their flight hours and spend more time at home. Some flight attendants who were mothers or juggled other careers preferred flying turnarounds—flights that flew to Miami or Chicago or Las Vegas and back in one day.

Hall and Oates had a 1973 hit song, "Las Vegas Turnaround (The Stewardess Song)"—*"Sara's off, half hiding, far above the clouds, high she flies"*—that was written for stewardess Sara Allen. The story goes that John Oates was living in New York City when he struck up a conversation with two flight attendants on the street on the Upper East Side. He introduced one of them, Sara, to his singing partner, Daryl Hall, and their relationship lasted more than thirty years and inspired many of their songs. (Hall also wrote the song "Sara Smile" for her.)

Despite my terrible first flight from Boston to Los Angeles, I quickly fell in love with long-haul flights. Too often reserve sent me on days-long trips to small cities with short layovers. So desperate was I for adventures that I squeezed in visits to BBQ joints, offbeat museums, presidents' birthplaces, anything at all—if I could muster the energy.

Short haul or long haul, there was no way of avoiding the mess of being a flight attendant. By the time we landed, I was sticky from splashed sodas and smelled like cigarette smoke. Cigarette smoking on airplanes wasn't banned until 1990. In a 2015 *New York Times* article, Joe Sharkey describes what it was like before that ban. "It was a routine chore to get the cigarette smell out of uniforms during hotel layovers," he writes. The flight attendant union fought for a smoking ban for decades before the federal government enforced one. In the article, Tracy Sear describes working for PSA—"the world's friendliest airline"—in the late '60s, wearing polyester hot pants: "Passengers would have their elbows on the armrest and then plop their hand out into the aisle with a lighted cigarette in it. So we would have to dodge it," or risk getting a burn in those hot pants or pantyhose. "I remember getting off the airplane," former flight attendant and international president of the Association of Flight Attendants Sara Nelson told Sharkey, "and feeling like I had to scrape off layers and layers of ick . . ."

But despite those layers of ick, I still felt special when I put on my uniform blazer and walked through the final airport toward the shuttle that would take us to our hotel. Even now, all these years later, when I am in a hotel and a flight crew walks in, I get a strong feeling of nostalgia. How well I remember walking across lobbies from San Francisco to London, part of a crew who had just flown hundreds or thousands of miles, and getting those heavy brass room keys. As my roommate Diane told me, "I just remember how proud I felt when I looked around at all of us in our uniforms, ready to fly." Good thing, too, because as a new hire on probation, you had to be ready all the time.

UNBELIEVABLY, the final sexist restriction for flight attendants—weight—was not lifted until 1991, twenty-three years after the age ceiling was removed. In 1979, we were all very afraid of that scale waiting for us in crew scheduling. One day, a month before our probation ended, I worked a nonstop flight from San Francisco to Boston, which meant the full transcontinental service. By the time we landed late that afternoon, I wanted nothing more than to kick off my shoes, take off my stinky uniform, and plop down somewhere with a good book. I walked in the door of our Harbor Towers apartment to find all of my roommates standing around Maureen, crying. Maureen's crew kit and boxes of her belongings were piled up in the hallway.

"What's going on?" I asked.

"They fired me," Maureen managed to say. "For five pounds."

"No!" I said. "They wouldn't do that."

"Well, they did," she said.

She wanted nothing more than to go home, and who could

blame her? Here we all were with our pagers and our trips and our uniforms—with our jobs. Home would be its own source of embarrassment. Like all of us, she had long dreamed of being a flight attendant, and she had survived the most difficult interview and training processes in the business. She had flown for months, with her big smile and big blue eyes, loving the passengers and the travel.

Once she'd come home all excited. "I had a movie star on my flight," she said.

"Who?" we wanted to know.

When you worked a Boston-to-L.A. flight you almost always had a celebrity on board. I'd served Diana Ross, Richard Gere, F. Lee Bailey, Ryan O'Neal, and countless others.

"Benji!" she said. "The dog!"

Benji was a golden mixed-breed dog who starred in five films throughout the '70s, with titles like *Benji: Off the Leash!* and *Benji the Hunted.*

"He was in first class!" Maureen said, falling into uncontrollable laughter.

Now she was fired and going home.

The first weight-discrimination suit had been filed by the union against American Airlines just five years earlier, in 1974. That was followed by another in 1988, and still another in 1990, when the EEOC (Equal Employment Opportunity Commission) joined the union's discrimination suit and finally won. San Francisco attorney Kathleen S. King told the *Chicago Tribune*, "This is a victory for all working women. Weight is a ridiculous standard that has nothing to do with job performance." When Maureen got fired from TWA, we were still almost fifteen years from airlines finally agreeing to abandon weight charts and substitute a performance test requiring flight attendants to show that they can move comfortably down the aisle and fit quickly through the cabin emergency windows.

Nancy Segal, attorney on behalf of the Association of Flight Attendants told the *New York Times*, "A lot of women went through indescribable psychological agony knowing that if they gained a pound, they could lose their jobs." Even flight attendants returning from maternity leave as recently as 1986 had to weigh in before every flight and lose one and a half pounds a week to meet their hiring weight within twenty weeks or get fired. Speaking of the years of weight restrictions, Segal said, "It caused a lot of eating disorders and a lot of grief."

We all saw that grief firsthand when Maureen got fired. It sent us back to the sauna, swallowing diuretics, afraid we might be next, even with just weeks to go before we were finally off probation.

# HOLDING A LINE

IN JUNE, a miracle happened. I was able to hold a line and have a regular schedule for two whole months, with a long layover in San Francisco. In fact, almost the whole crew were new hires. Part of that crew was a flight attendant named Maisie who had been in my training class. Maisie was from San Francisco, and she was eager to show us all her hometown. We would take a quick nap and then get dressed and meet her in the lobby. If it was a Sunday, we'd have eggs Benedict and Ramos gin fizzes for brunch at Perry's on Union Street. Or crab Louis on Fisherman's Wharf, followed by Irish coffees at the Buena Vista. We went to Alcatraz, climbed Coit Tower, and took the ferry to Sausalito, where we ate at the Valhalla, a restaurant owned by a famous madam named Sally Stanford.

I've always felt that those two months of long layovers in San Francisco transformed me from that young woman afraid of a snobby maître d' to someone who felt confident and sophisticated. Even when Maisie wasn't on the flight, there was always another flight attendant or passenger willing to share places to go for brunch, or which stores to shop in.

A flight attendant told me that the best breakfast in town was the sourdough French toast at Sears Fine Foods; a passenger told me where to find City Lights Bookstore and Caffe Trieste in North Beach, where he frequently saw Allen Ginsberg.

Sometimes on a layover I would spend the afternoon at City Lights, feeding that secret side of me that wanted to be a writer. I would walk down Jack Kerouac Alley and copy the Lawrence Ferlinghetti quote on a plaque there into one of the composition notebooks I always carried. *Poetry is the shadow cast by our streetlight imaginations.* I had that, I used to think, a streetlight imagination. My notebooks were full of lines of poetry, ideas for stories, observations of odd passengers, or new things that seemed writerly.

I would write stories when I was alone in my crowded apartment, which wasn't often. But I wrote them all the time in my mind, even as I served dozens of trays of chicken or beef or stood in the galley mixing lemonade. A few hours in a bookstore, especially a legendary one, fed that streetlight imagination of mine. Then I would walk to Caffe Trieste, order a café macchiato, and watch Ginsberg write at a corner table in the back. At night I'd join the rest of the crew for cheap pasta at Basta Pasta on Grant or Café Sport on Green Street, my new copies of *Howl* or *A Coney Island of the Mind* tucked into my purse. How easily in those days I shifted between my introverted, literary self and my fun-loving, adventurous self.

My dream of being a writer didn't fade, but jet lag and an irregular schedule kept me from starting that vague, unformed novel I dreamed of writing. At least as long as I was a new hire, I had to be satisfied with jotting my thoughts in my notebooks.

WE QUICKLY LEARNED why senior flight attendants didn't want to work this flight with the gloriously long layover: they knew

that SFO was notoriously fogged in, a lot, during that time of
year. About a quarter of the time, we never left LAX because
the fog at SFO showed no intention of lifting. More reliably,
we'd take off and be unable to land at SFO and get rerouted
to San Jose. For the passengers whose cars were parked at SFO,
this did not go over very well, even though TWA bused all the
passengers—and the crew—from San Jose to San Francisco.
The first time that happened, a more senior flight attendant
who had flown the same trip during the foggy season the year
before, grabbed my arm just as I was about to board the bus to
San Francisco.

"No!" he told me, holding me back. "Wait for the next one."

"Are you kidding me? I want to get to bed."

"That bus"—he pointed to the one passengers were boarding—"is full of people who are pissed off because they're in
San Jose. Wait for the third bus. Fewer passengers."

Sometimes, the nearest city we could land in was Bakersfield,
almost three hundred miles from San Francisco. When that
happened, TWA actually bused everyone four and half hours
to San Francisco. You can bet I waited for the third bus on
those trips. One night we sat on the ground so long in LAX
waiting for the fog to lift at SFO that the pilot sent a gate agent
for McDonald's burgers and fries for us to serve the hundred
passengers on board. "Give them free drinks too," the captain
told us when the McDonald's arrived. "These poor people have
been sitting here all night."

We left Boston in the evening and flew the short flight to
Newark, doing a beverage and snack service en route. From
Newark to L.A., we did a full service—the Caesar salad/
chateaubriand one up front, and a beverage service followed

by appetizers followed by dinner with a choice of three entrees in coach. By the time we got to L.A., it was about two in the morning West Coast time. We sat at the gate for an hour or so before boarding passengers for the ninety-minute flight to San Francisco. For the passengers who boarded in L.A. at three a.m., they were ready to keep partying. For the Boston-based crew, however, it was six a.m. and we'd been working for over twelve hours. Unfortunately, it was the flight out of L.A. where something almost always went wrong.

That flight attracted people who didn't mind showing up at an airport after midnight for a cheap ticket. They arrived in glitter and boas, drunk and stoned, dirty and newly in love. Anything could and did happen on that flight. People threw up, danced in the aisles, sang, kissed, and more than kissed. Some flight attendants broke up whatever two people were doing beneath the red TWA blankets, others ignored it. When we finally landed in San Francisco, all the delays and service and craziness of the last leg immediately vanished. I fell in love with that city, a love that has lasted ever since. We would check into our rooms at the dazzling Mark Hopkins Hotel at the top of Nob Hill, nap, then head out to explore.

More than once an ambulance had to meet the plane upon landing because someone had overdosed. One night when the flight was almost but not quite full, a group of partying people traveling up to San Francisco together kept changing seats to sit near different friends. They drank a lot and made a lot of trips to the bathroom, which I had learned usually meant they were in there doing drugs. Part of our job was to knock on the lavatory door if someone was in there too long to make sure they were all right. We were even taught how to open the locked door if the person didn't reply: by using the can opener we kept in our apron pocket for the beverage service. (Pop tops on cans weren't standard until a few years later.)

Although we weren't required to know which seats were occupied and by whom, on longer flights you developed a sense for where people were seated—the family with the crying baby, the couple in love, the college student studying—because you not only served them but you walked up and down the aisles so often that the seating became a pattern in your mind. But this flight was less than an hour, and it was a busy one with people moving around a lot, so none of us noticed if someone wasn't in her correct seat for landing. I was working, as usual, in E Zone, the all-smoking section in the back of the plane. After everyone had deplaned, I rolled my crew kit up the aisle of the L-1011 toward the open door in first class.

Midway, two other flight attendants were standing in the aisle, holding an oversized handbag, a pair of shoes, and a denim jacket, looking puzzled. "What's up?" I asked them. "Either someone forgot her stuff and walked off the plane barefoot, or she's still on board somewhere." We knew that more than one passenger had overdosed on this flight before, and although none of us said it out loud, we were all thinking it. By this time, other flight attendants had come to see what the holdup was. We were all exhausted and wanted to get to our hotel. Instead, we started to search for the missing passenger while the purser informed the pilot about what was happening. Not sure where to look, I walked back the way I'd come, peeking under the rows of seats where I'd seen people stretch out for naps before. I walked all the way back to E Zone and then up the other aisle. I didn't get too far before I heard a commotion near the center bathrooms.

As I moved toward the bathrooms, someone shouted for me to go back and sit down. "You don't need to see this," he said. The passenger had overdosed and was dead. The crew joined me in the back of the plane to wait for an ambulance. It seems terrible to say that some of us, so tired, lifted the armrests on the seats in a row so we could lay across them and sleep. Eventually the EMTs arrived and the pilot and the flight attendant who found the woman dead in the bathroom gave them a statement. After that, I tried to make a mental map of my section, even though that was impossible on short, full flights when we hardly had the time to complete service, never mind memorizing who was sitting where.

ONE NIGHT, the EWR–LAX leg of the flight was especially quiet, except for a strange intermittent rattling coming from the middle section of the L-1011 in C Zone, which was where I was working.

"You think you can make that stop?" a guy growled at me.

The food had been served and the lights had been dimmed. People wanted to watch the movie or go to sleep. I made my way toward the noise and found a man and woman playing Boggle. The rattling was the plastic letters getting shaken in a plastic cube, but now I was more interested in the game than the noise.

The guy glanced up at me. "Want to play?" he asked.

I love word games, and I took the empty seat beside him for a few minutes and joined in. His companion, however, seemed to not like me interrupting their game.

"This has been fun," I said as I slid out of the row. "I'll have to get a game of Boggle when I get back to Boston."

"When will that be?" the man asked.

"Saturday."

The woman narrowed her eyes at me.

"I'll be back on Sunday," he said, cocking his head toward her. "I'm just going to help my sister move."

Ah! Sister!

I wasn't surprised when he found me after the plane landed and asked me out.

"Is it OK with your sister?" I asked him, teasing.

"She's my big sister, so she's overprotective," he said.

We made a date for the next week. When he arrived at Harbor Towers, the doorman buzzed him up. I heard the elevator ping, and then the unmistakable rattling of Boggle letters in their little plastic cube. I opened the door and there he stood with a Boggle game topped with a big red bow. I wish I could say that this was the beginning of something special, but by the end of the night, despite several rounds of the game, I knew he wasn't my type. A benefit of being a flight attendant is that it's very easy to avoid someone, so after a few calls when my roommates told him I was on a flight, he stopped calling. But all these years later, I still have that very same Boggle game.

The other guy I met on that red-eye was a tall, handsome representative for a ski company. He fit the part too; with his longish dark hair and tanned cheeks he looked like he'd just come in from the slopes. He hung out for most of the flight in the galley talking to me, and when it was time for landing he asked if I'd like to have dinner the next time I was in San Francisco, which was just five days later. Boy, would I!

He picked me up in a little sports car that was dominated by a black Lab with a red kerchief tied around his neck. We ate at an outdoor restaurant overlooking the Bay, the dog snoozing at our feet. This guy, I liked. He was thoughtful and smart and very cute. His job took him to Europe every month, and I liked listening to him talk about what he saw and ate on those trips. When he dropped me off at my hotel, he asked me out for the next time I had a layover there, which was in another five days. "Call me when you arrive and we'll make a plan," he said.

I bought a new dress for the layover and could hardly wait to see him again. But when I called, he stammered a bit before blurting out that he had gotten back together with his ex. In five days? I thought, but I wished him well and got off the phone quickly. I passed the dress on, unworn, to one of my roommates.

THE FOG OVER San Francisco lifted and I was ready to be back on reserve for my final month of probation. Instead, to my surprise and delight, we junior flight attendants could now hold flights to Las Vegas. I quickly learned why new hires could hold Vegas flights all summer—with temperatures around 105 degrees or higher, it was too hot there to even sit for long by the hotel pool. While more senior flight attendants were enjoying that long layover in San Francisco, we were sweating in Vegas. Still, once again, I was happy to have a regular schedule— Boston–Chicago–Las Vegas, with a long layover and the same trip in reverse the next day, two or three times a week. The flight from Chicago to Las Vegas was like a big party. The passengers were eager to hit the slot machines or poker tables and started celebrating as soon as we took off. When we landed in Vegas, the flight attendant doing the announcements always said, "Good luck!" But on the way back, we were told to not mention anything about luck or gambling. Most of the passengers had not won big, and the flight from Las Vegas to Chicago was always very quiet.

This was the old Vegas, with hotels like the Stardust, the Tropicana, and the Flamingo, which was built by Bugsy Siegel and his fellow mob boss Meyer Lansky. The Strip didn't have colorful fountains and pyramids then, just lots of neon, expensive cars, and women in fur coats and diamonds. As soon as I stepped off the plane and into the airport, I heard the sound of slot machines and the ringing of bells announcing someone had just won a jackpot. Famous Vegas performers taped recordings giving directions to Baggage Claim over the PA. "Hi, this is Shecky Green. Welcome to Las Vegas." Out into the scorching desert heat and onto the shuttle to the hotel, where we slipped into our bathing suits and stretched out by the pool with sweet cocktails, sweating, until it was time for dinner and a show.

This was also the Las Vegas of Liberace, Wayne Newton (who married a Pan Am stewardess that he met on a flight), Paul Anka, and Glen Campbell. All we had to do was flash our TWA ID card and we were ushered to the best seats in the house, gratis. Flight attendants were ornaments for Vegas shows and, as I'd learn, live audiences for television shows in L.A. I am not a Paul Anka fan or a gambler, but that Las Vegas with the fingerprints of the Rat Pack and all that flash was intoxicating. I'd allow myself $20 to spend in the casino, usually losing it all in about twenty minutes. The first time I walked into a hotel casino, I was so dazzled by noise, bright lights, and the crazy assortment of people that I took out my camera and started trying to capture what I was seeing. Immediately a large hairy hand reached in front of me and grabbed the camera.

"Hey!" I said before realizing the guy attached to the hand worked for the casino.

"There are people in here," he said slowly in a thick New York accent as he opened the camera and removed the film, "who do not want their picture taken."

He handed me the camera, the back flopping open. "Have a good evening."

On the flight the next day, I shared the story with my fellow flight attendants.

"Why wouldn't someone want to be in a picture of a person they'll never even see again?" I wondered.

They all laughed.

"Mobsters," one said.

"A guy with a woman other than his wife," another one added.

"A person who is supposed to be somewhere other than a casino in Vegas," said a third.

"Shall we go on?"

I shook my head. "I get it," I said, marveling yet again at the big world and the crazy players in it.

Summer came to an end, Vegas temperatures cooled down, and even though I was off probation, I was back on reserve.

One night, an old college boyfriend and I went out to dinner at Legal Sea Foods in Boston. At the time, Legal Sea Foods on the waterfront was famous not only for fresh, delicious seafood but also for their no-reservations policy, which resulted in an hour or two of waiting in a very long line—a rite of passage. As we waited, he was looking at me like he was seeing me for the first time.

"You've changed," he said.

He had always seemed erudite and worldly to me. A piano player and singer, he'd traveled around Europe on his own for a year after college, sending me postcards from Heidelberg and Vienna. He'd gone to law school in a city out west, then got a job in the Senate. Dashing, I used to think, impressed.

"No, I haven't," I said, laughing.

"You have," he insisted. "It's like you've grown up. Become sophisticated."

When we had dated, I was a dreamy teenager in khaki pants and Izod shirts, trying to fit in.

"Well, I am a flight attendant," I said.

He looked at me thoughtfully. "But it's more than that," he said.

I knew that he was right. I was no longer the small-town girl he had dated in college. In just six months, I'd flown thousands of miles, fixed countless mistakes, helped thousands of people, and navigated new cities—often by myself. I'd learned how to make decisions, dine alone in elegant restaurants, solve problems. Being a flight attendant had turned me into a confident, worldly young woman.

"You know," I said, "it actually is being a flight attendant that's made me different."

Glorified waitress? Not at all. I had the best job in the world.

# "IF YOU TAKE OUR HAND, WE'LL TAKE YOUR DREAM ACROSS THE SKY . . ."*

I WANTED TO BE a flight attendant to see the world, and once I was off probation I had those free passes to do just that. Almost immediately, Diane and I visited her sister Kate, who flew for Eastern Airlines and was based in San Juan. We took the T out to Logan, went to the Eastern check-in desk, flashed our TWA IDs, and got handed boarding passes to San Juan. It was so easy that we flew there anytime we both had the same days off in a row.

Kate and her roommates lived in a condo on the beach in Isla Verde, and there was nothing like leaving the rain or chill of Boston behind to lounge on a white-sand beach with a fruity rum drink in hand for a few days. At night we'd wander Old San Juan, eating dinner at La Mallorquina, the oldest restaurant in Puerto Rico. With its Old World charm and décor, tuxedoed waiters, and the buzz of Spanish that filled the air, La Mallorquina seemed to me to be the height of sophistication. It was there that I had my first tastes of gazpacho, paella, and

* TWA theme song, 1968.

flan, rocketing me into a newfound culinary awakening that has never left me. In Boston I ate mostly Italian food in the North End, American bistro food at the bar/restaurants we all frequented, or cheap Chinese food late at night in Chinatown. I wasn't a fussy eater, just an uninformed one. But those nights in Old San Juan changed that.

FOR MY MOM'S BIRTHDAY that September, I flew my parents in first class for a long weekend in San Francisco. I was excited to share my newfound independence with them and to show them this city I had fallen in love with. Although my father had happily been around the world many times during his twenty years in the navy, Mom was not a very good or eager traveler. My parents had lived in Italy from 1952 to 1955, and during their time there went on vacations to Germany, Austria, and England, as well as exploring most of Italy. I still have black-and-white slides of them with my toddler brother watching excavations at Pompeii, on a boat near Capri, and climbing Mt. Vesuvius. Although my mother cherished their time there, she was quick to point out all of the horrors of traveling—foreign smells and languages and customs all scared her.

But when my parents and I boarded the TWA L-1011 for San Francisco and took our seats in first class, any trepidation Mom held vanished. She had dressed up for the flight, the way most people did then, and sitting beside my father—he in a pinstripe suit and a blue tie, she in a smart camel-colored skirt and sweater—Mom beamed as she took the pre-takeoff champagne the flight attendant offered. I don't think she stopped smiling for the entire flight. Through the warm nuts, shrimp cocktail, salad tossed in full view in the aisle, perfectly cooked chateaubriand, and made-to-order ice-cream sundaes, Mom kept looking over at me and grinning. "I love this, Ann," she said as each new course arrived.

For the next five days, I led my parents around San Francisco on city buses, ferries, taxis, and cable cars. We did all the touristy things, like visiting Alcatraz, wandering Fisherman's Wharf, and climbing the Coit Tower. But we also ate that sourdough French toast at Sears Fine Food and Thai food at a place in the Sunset that a passenger had told me about. We took a bus out to Ocean Beach for brunch at the Cliff House and a ferry to Sausalito and a tour of vineyards in Napa Valley.

This was so different from our annual car trips to Indiana or Mom's other travel back in the '50s aboard a navy cargo plane. That flight had been cramped and cold, and the plane stopped frequently to pick up and drop off passengers and cargo, making the trip last more than twenty hours. At one point she and my toddler brother Skip had to deplane for several hours somewhere—Tangiers or Morocco, perhaps, as she recalled a crowded bazaar and minarets. All of it was scary to a twenty-two-year-old with a baby who had never been farther from her home in Rhode Island than her honeymoon road trip to Indiana. All the ups and downs on that long-ago flight kept her and Skip airsick for most of the trip. Other than our annual summer family car trips in our station wagon, without air conditioning, that was Mom's only experience of traveling. This one flight changed that forever. After that, all I had to do was suggest a trip anywhere and Mom packed her bag.

My comfort with new places and growing familiarity with different cities had come gradually those first six months of

flying. Though there were days when I was gripped by loneliness or homesickness, mostly I ate up each new sight and
restaurant and city map. During that trip to San Francisco with
my parents, they saw this new side of me—confident, mature,
sophisticated—and they were both impressed and stunned.
Their dreamy, long-haired, blue-jeaned daughter was making
dinner reservations, navigating city streets, and ordering wine,
all with ease.

After that trip, my parents and I frequently used my passes.
We went to Amsterdam, Rome, and Paris together, and they
traveled on their own to Germany, Brussels, Las Vegas, and
even for a long winter weekend in Sarasota. As a kid, I never
would have imagined that my mother would agree to join me
on whatever flight I got next on reserve. But she loved the idea,
and years after that first trip to San Francisco, she and my
father drove to my apartment on Bleecker Street in Greenwich
Village, suitcases packed, and waited for me to call crew scheduling and get my flight assignment. I hung up, looked at them,
and said, "We're going to Paris!" And off we went.

For the rest of her life, long after I stopped flying, my mother
would talk happily about that first trip to San Francisco, and
how my own wanderlust and job as a flight attendant had
changed her life too. It seems almost impossible looking back
that my mother had turned just forty-eight that September. She
lived almost another forty years. The last trip I took with Mom
was for my Italian book tour. She was eighty and suffered from
a botched hip replacement, so I splurged on first class tickets
on Alitalia. With each course set before us, Mom looked at
me sadly and said, "It's not as nice as it used to be, is it?" She
meant the quality of the food and the service, I think. But it

feels to me now that she was talking about so much more—life without my father, the three of us young and healthy enough to walk the hilly streets of San Francisco, hop on and off a cable car, and stay up late talking in our hotel room.

ONE DAY THAT AUTUMN after we got off probation, Diane and I decided, on a lark, to go to London. We had these free passes, didn't we? We had four days off, so why not? Looking back, we probably chose London from all those possibilities in TWA's flight schedule because it wasn't too far away, English was spoken, and it was just different enough. If someone handed me a free ticket to anywhere today, I'd choose a far-flung city— Saint Petersburg or Istanbul or Cape Town. But that fall I was a twenty-two-year-old with little foreign travel behind me. Sure, I wanted to go everywhere. But actually going, with just my equally untraveled roommate, was daunting. So we packed our little crew kits and headed for Logan, where we put our names on the waitlist for the next London flight. Eight hours later, tipsy and drowsy from first-class wine, we arrived at Heathrow.

I can still remember standing beneath the clicking Arrivals board as a woman with a clipped British accent made flight announcements to Dakar, Baghdad, and Rio de Janeiro. I had spent plenty of time waiting for the hotel shuttle outside LAX by then, listening to a robotic voice say over and over, "The white zone is for loading and unloading passengers only. No parking." It drove me mad. But these announcements in Heathrow were thrilling and exotic, made even more so by the people who passed us: a group of men in kilts, the first teenagers I saw in full punk regalia with bright-blue Mohawk haircuts, and a Gucci-suited man followed by a dozen women wearing niqabs—long black clothing that covered their entire body, including most of their faces, with just slits at their eyes so they could look outward.

I could have stood there all day people-watching, but we had come to see London. Other than vague ideas to see a play and go to the Tower of London, we hadn't thought much about what we were going to do when we were actually in the city. For example, we hadn't booked a hotel, or even bothered to get the name of one. One of us remembered from training that there were kiosks in airports specifically to find rooms for travelers.

Sure enough, such a kiosk was right there, centrally located. We asked for a room, and in the thickest accent I'd ever heard the man began asking us questions, presumably about price range and location. Neither of us understood him, at all, so we just told him we wanted to see a play and maybe go to the Tower of London and a museum. We had no idea what the exchange rate for pounds was, so we couldn't tell him how much we wanted to spend. He mumbled and shook his head, gave us an address, and pointed us toward the Underground.

"But where do we get off?" I asked. I remembered how my father had told me and my friend Nancy when we went to Bermuda that as long as we could find someone who spoke English, we'd be fine. But here was a man who spoke English— real English—and we could not communicate because his British accent was so thick.

We managed to understand that we were to take the Piccadilly Line to somewhere. But where? He repeated it at least four times before Diane and I agreed our stop was Ascot. Somehow we bought tickets and even managed to get on the train going in the right direction, but the map hanging on the subway car wall did not have Ascot on it. Or anything that sounded like Ascot. We studied the crisscrossing green and yellow and blue lines. In Boston, we took the T everywhere. We were used to subways. But this one was huge, and even as I traced my finger along the Piccadilly Line, our stop did not seem to exist.

"Leicester Square?" I read out loud.

Diane shook her head. It didn't start with an *L*.

"Kings Cross? Arsenal?"

No. Nothing sounded like Ascot.

The train kept barreling toward central London, and each time it stopped and the doors opened, we asked anyone, "Ascot?" The answer was always no.

Finally, desperately, we showed the address the man had scrawled on the scrap of paper to a guy sitting across from us.

"Oh," he said, nodding, "that's in Earl's Court. Two more stops."

Diane and I looked at each other and fell into a jet-lagged laughter of relief. Ascot was Earl's Court!

Everything went wrong on that trip. The room was in a rundown B & B, the man probably assuming we were college kids and low on funds, instead of two flight attendants with brand-new Mastercards and fat bank accounts. In order to get heat in our room, we had to feed pence into a small heater. We arrived on a Sunday, and back then most London restaurants were closed on Sundays. Figuring out which way to look while crossing the street made us nervous. And the breakfast of fatty bacon, blood sausage, baked beans, and soggy tomatoes was awful. Yet on the flight back to Boston, I remember feeling like

I'd done something important. I had, I suppose. I'd dipped my toes for the first time in a foreign country, alone.

I RETURNED OFTEN to London after that trip. It was a short flight and the security of knowing the language (for the most part!) made it easy to fly there for a weekend. On one of those weekends in March, Diane and I realized we were in London on St. Patrick's Day. Why not hop a British Airways or Aer Lingus flight to Dublin? In Boston, St. Patrick's Day meant drinking too much green beer at a local bar, dancing, and participating in drunken sing-alongs of "My Wild Irish Rose." St. Patrick's Day in Dublin would be even better, we decided. All those pubs, all that Irish music, all that Guinness.

But when we landed in Dublin, we found a rainy, somber city with the pubs closed. Although there had been a parade earlier, back then the Feast of St. Patrick was more of a holy day in Ireland, a recognition of their patron saint. There were even Lenten restrictions on eating and drinking, and most people celebrated at home with family.

Unfortunately, this twenty-three-year-old American and her friend wanted an American celebration, so we turned right around and flew back to London without even taking in any of the sights. I don't remember feeling bad at all about our brief three hours in Dublin. Rather, the freedom to hop planes and go anywhere, anytime, for free, made the trip special—perhaps more special than if we'd drunk beer in a crowded pub.

I visit Dublin often now. One recent summer, as I stared at the Bog Man in the National Museum and wandered the library at Trinity College, I tried to imagine that young woman who left this remarkable city without even walking around it. Despite all the freedom and independence she had acquired, I realized that she was still a little afraid of the world at her feet. It would take years of flying before she resembled the middle-aged woman standing in front of the Book of Kells.

. . .

DESPITE AN ERRATIC, ever changing work schedule, my life settled into its own routine. I went out on dates, barhopped with my roommates, took long weekend trips, and kept scribbling notes in my notebooks. Maybe I would write a novel about a flight attendant, I thought. Not like *Coffee, Tea or Me?*, but a serious novel with a young protagonist out on her own for the first time. Or maybe I would write an exposé about what it was really like to be a flight attendant. Neither of these ideas grew into anything but more notes, but at night if I was alone in my room in Harbor Towers, I jotted down ideas.

What that new flight attendant rushing to her flight or fresh-out-of-college me didn't realize was that at the exact time I was putting on my black polyester suit and telling airlines I loved people and I loved to travel, major changes were happening in the aviation industry. Changes that would turn my life upside down as well as change the way we flew. Because of those changes, there are now seats on airplanes without windows, no in-flight meals, and underpaid employees who work more hours for less money. And it all began with the Airline Deregulation Act of 1978, the year I graduated from college and got hired as a flight attendant.

The Airline Deregulation Act, written by Stephen Breyer and Ted Kennedy, was created to regulate airline routes, control airlines' entry and exit into various markets, and mandate fares, which would allow more airlines to fly more places and more people to afford flying. In 1974, the cheapest flight from New York to Los Angeles was the inflation equivalent of $1,442. This was why flights were often not full; people couldn't afford the cost of flying. According to *Forbes*, 45 percent of Americans flew commercially in 2015, compared to 21 percent in pre-deregulation 1971. That same year, less than half of all Americans had flown at all. Now over 80 percent of Americans have traveled by plane. The Airline Deregulation Act removed government control over fares, routes, and markets. As a result, the number of flights increased, fares decreased (New York–Los Angeles flights today can be found for as low $300), and more passengers flew more miles.

One of the major changes brought on by deregulation was the airlines' movement from the point-to-point system to the hub-and-spoke system that we are all familiar with today. Before deregulation, all American airlines used the point-to-point system, which allowed them to fly direct routes between small cities and also reduced the travel time associated with having to connect through a hub airport. There were no long layovers waiting for connecting flights and no risk of delayed flights leading to missed connections. However, since demand on some of these routes was small, planes were often not full, which drove up ticket costs. During my first year, I worked many, many nearly empty planes to Wichita or Tucson or Oklahoma City.

It took a while for deregulation to take effect, but as soon as it did American airlines switched to the hub-and-spoke system. An airline selected airports as its hubs, as American did with Charlotte and United did with Denver, for example—and flights left from those hubs to other destinations, the spokes or cities that radiated from the hub. With this system, my passengers going to Wichita or Tucson or Oklahoma City would have to connect through one of TWA's hubs, like Chicago or St. Louis.

What had once been nonstop flights were now often two flights that connected through a hub, adding that connecting time to flights. As a passenger these days, I have run through the Charlotte airport more times than I can count, trying to make my connection to Providence on American Airlines. Shouting "Excuse me!" with my suitcase bumping along behind me, shoving past people on the people mover, sprinting through the food court and then down the long arm of whichever terminal my plane was leaving from, and hopefully arriving before it took off. Gone are the days when I could get on a plane in Miami and land in Providence two and half hours later. Instead, it takes me at least five hours—and that's if I can run fast enough to make the connection. Otherwise, it can be six or more hours, most of them waiting in Charlotte to connect. That's thanks to deregulation.

A transcontinental nonstop like I used to work from San Francisco to Boston took five hours; a connecting one takes seven or eight hours of travel time, including waiting for connections or racing to make them. For example, these days I can fly one-way from my home in Providence, Rhode Island, to Los Angeles for $161 on Southwest. My first leg would leave at six a.m. from Providence to Baltimore, one of their hubs. I would fly from there to Phoenix, then arrive in Los Angeles ten hours later. Even the most direct route I could fly would go from Providence to the hub in Baltimore and then on to Los Angeles. That flight is $204 and would still take almost nine hours. I could travel to Boston, a hub for some airlines, and take a non-stop, but that adds at least an hour of driving time to the trip each way, resulting in eight hours of travel.

The Airline Deregulation Act also phased out the CAB— the Civil Aeronautics Board—which used to regulate airline schedules. Under the CAB, it could take as long as eight years to approve new routes. Without the CAB setting fare prices, the average fare today is about 97 percent lower than it was in 1978. With cheaper flights, more people fly; in 1978, passengers flew 250 million miles, compared to 750 million miles in 2005. But it can also be argued that the Airline Deregulation Act is responsible for many of the things flyers complain about today, such as poor service, cramped planes, and unhappy crew members who have experienced pay cuts, increased work hours, and losses in pensions and benefits.

Even the changes to in-flight service can be traced back to deregulation. Cutbacks, like substituting powdered creamers for real milk or cream and eliminating or decreasing multi-course meals in first class, began with deregulation. As Daniel L. Rust notes in *Flying Across America: The Airline Passenger Experience*, seemingly small things, like American Airlines' decision to remove the olives from their salads, became prevalent until finally, in the late '90s airlines began to charge for meals, or not offer them at all. Instead, passengers are offered an endless rotation of pretzels, chips, or cookies.

During TWA training, our instructors told us that deregulation was coming. But I either didn't listen hard enough or didn't pay enough attention, because I had no idea how drastically things were going to change, or how quickly. My early flight announcements still included CAB regulations as well as FAA regulations. (We also used to notify passengers when the No Smoking sign came on or went off, and tell them that only cigarettes were allowed, no cigars or pipes.) They explained the new hub-and-spoke system to us, too, but without having even worked on an airplane yet it didn't seem very important. So what if everyone had to travel through Chicago or New York?

We were also told that TWA was going to open a hub in St. Louis. That seemed as ridiculous as United having a base in Cleveland. St. Louis, Missouri, was going to be one of our hubs? To most of us, that sounded like one of the rumors that constantly circulated among crews. But in just a few years, St. Louis's Lambert Field Airport—known by the airport code STL—accounted for 20 percent of TWA's domestic flights, and added nonstop flights to Paris, London, and Frankfurt. TWA had to build an entire new concourse, and soon new hires were getting based there.

Dizzy with having to learn so many things, I didn't really absorb what deregulation was about to do to the airline industry, TWA, and my livelihood. Many of the changes were gradual, but the expansion of some airlines, the drop in the cost of flying, and the general chaos that descended on airlines struggling to figure out how to operate in a deregulated industry led to extensive furloughs of flight attendants throughout the industry and, eventually, even the bankruptcy of the majority of major airlines during my years as a flight attendant. Just in my first year, there were transfers, opening of new routes, closing of old routes, mergers and sales of airlines, and wild expansion at airports like Denver for United and St. Louis for us.

Rumors swirled constantly. We were getting furloughed. TWA was going out of business. They were closing the Boston base. Or the opposite: TWA was hiring another thousand flight attendants, flying international flights out of St. Louis, buying more aircraft. The only place that felt secure was on the airplane itself, where passengers still wanted to get fed and our routines remained unchanged. But in the crew lounge or on layovers or even when my roommates and I were sharing a glass of chablis at Friday's, talk centered on how precarious our jobs were. TWA, infamous for weak management and bad business decisions, seemed especially vulnerable to the problems deregulation created.

BETWEEN 1978—the year I was hired—and 2001, seven major airlines ultimately went bankrupt as a result of deregulation—Eastern, Braniff, Pan Am, Midway, Continental, Northwest, and TWA—as did over one hundred smaller airlines. Today, only four airlines control 90 percent of the market: United, Delta, American, and Southwest. Richard Finger, a business analyst and trader, pointed out in *Forbes* the example of United Airlines, which controls over 90 percent of domestic travel in and out of Houston. "Many flights have been consolidated so travelers have fewer choices," Finger writes. Therefore, there is actually less competition, increasing fares, decreasing employee pay, and a monopoly that was not what Stephen Breyer and Ted Kennedy wanted when they co-wrote the bill for deregulation.

In 2011, Stephen Breyer, now a Supreme Court Justice, wrote in "Airline Deregulation Revisited," an article for *BusinessWeek*: "No one foresaw the spectacular growth, with the number of passengers increasing from 207.5 million in 1974 to 721.1 million in 2010 . . . no one foresaw a flight-choked Northeast corridor, overcrowded airports, and delays making air travel increasingly more difficult. Nor did anyone foresee the extent to which change might unfairly harm workers . . ."

If this sounds like he had any regrets for pushing deregulation forward, he does not. "So we all sit in crowded planes, munch potato chips, flare up when the loudspeaker announces yet another flight delay. But how many now would vote to go back to the 'good old days' of paying high, regulated prices for better service?" He concludes with a reference to the FTC official who pointed out that before deregulation, a business traveler almost always had an empty seat beside him where he could put his briefcase but did not realize his high fare was actually paying for that seat. Breyer writes in defense of deregulation, "Even among business travelers, who wants to pay full fare for the briefcase?"

DESPITE ALL OF THE RUMORS and chaos in the airline industry, I still believed what I'd believed back when my college friend told me how unstable TWA was—it would never actually go out of business. There would be some rocky years as TWA—and every airline—adjusted to deregulation, and then we would all settle into a new normal.

But when I walked into our apartment from a flight one afternoon, I found my roommates in the living room looking stunned, open letters in their laps.

"Oh no," I said, dropping my crew kit and racing to take the letter Rebecca was holding out for me. I immediately recognized the familiar red-and-white logo, the very one that had appeared on the letter telling me I was hired.

Instead of opening it, I said, "We're furloughed?"

Outside our window, Boston Harbor glistened. I had a date that night for dinner at the Rusty Scupper with another flight attendant, a guy I'd just started seeing. If we were furloughed, we'd have to give up this apartment. Maybe leave Boston altogether. What the hell would I do for a job?

But then I saw that they were shaking their heads, even laughing.

"Not furloughed," Kim said. "*Transferred.*"

"What? We're all transferred?" I said, confused. Maybe, I thought hopefully, TWA was increasing international flights—another rumor that was circulating—and we were all transferred to JFK. Suddenly, things didn't seem so bad.

"Yup," Rebecca said. Then she added with a groan, "To St. Louis."

Relief that I still had my wonderful job flooded through me, but just as quickly reality hit. I would be leaving the new beau, this cosmopolitan city, our gorgeous apartment, for St. Louis? Missouri?

"Saint Lousy in the state of Misery," Kim said. "We start there on the first."

I flopped onto the couch, my transfer letter still unopened in my hand. The first was just two weeks away. We had to break this lease, pack up, get cars, drive to St. Louis, find apartments—all in two weeks. Thanks to deregulation and the new hub-and-spoke system, I was headed for TWA's newest, biggest hub.

# ST. LOUIS BLUES

SINCE ALL OF OUR FURNITURE was rented, we had to pack up only our kitchen stuff and personal belongings and then hit the road. Diane and I took the bus to my parents' house in Rhode Island to pick up their second car, then off we went to Fremont, Ohio, to pick up her car. From there, each in our separate cars, we headed west. The farther we got from the East Coast, the more the realization that I was going to live smack in the middle of the country hit me. St. Louis, from everything I'd been told—which was a lot, because so many flight attendants were getting transferred there and, of course, rumors about it abounded—was not so much a city as it was a provincial town.

"I heard people are nicer there," my beau offered optimistically that night at the Rusty Scupper when I'd first learned I was transferred.

Easy for him to say. The most junior flight attendants were the ones getting transferred out of Boston. None of us were very happy about leaving Harbor Towers or Boston for a small Midwestern city. One of the reasons I'd chosen TWA over United was because I would probably be based in Cleveland with United, and now here I was heading to St. Louis. This guy was three years senior to me, so there was no way he'd end up in St. Louis. Or so I thought then. In fact, he too got transferred there eventually as TWA kept growing the St. Louis hub and shrinking Boston, which would become a mere spoke in no time.

"I don't need nice people," I muttered. "I need a city. A real city."

As we drove across Interstate 70 west out of Ohio and into Indiana, with tractor-trailer trucks whizzing past us and cornfields in the distance, I tried to embrace the excitement and I'll-do-anything attitude I'd had when I boarded the plane to Breech Academy. *What an experience!* I told myself, hoping it would stick. *An adventure!*

OUR ROOMMATE SITUATION had shifted, and now we were four: Rebecca, Diane, me, and our friend Tavia, the former bunny. Many of the transferees moved to apartment complexes with names like Pheasant Run or Quail Ridge out in the suburbs. These were sprawling, multilevel apartments with shiny new kitchens and big bedrooms. But they were on empty, treeless lots with nothing much around them except more apartment complexes. After living right downtown in Boston, they didn't appeal to us. However, there didn't appear to *be* a downtown in St. Louis. With just a week left before we had to start flying and our temporary TWA paid hotel rooms ended, we plucked a Townhouse for Rent sign off the bulletin board in crew scheduling and called the number on it. As it turned out, the married couple subletting it had been transferred to JFK.

The duplex townhouse, with two bedrooms and two bathrooms, was right near the airport in a bleak, mostly empty landscape. We could see cornfields out the windows and hear planes taking off and landing.

"It's pretty grim here," the guy told us. "So it's good to be near the airport so you can leave on your days off."

"Great," I mumbled. I was moving to a place whose best attribute was that you could leave it easily.

"There is a bright spot," his wife said cheerfully. "They've been sending new hires here for months, so you won't be on reserve."

Diane, Rebecca, Tavia, and I looked at one another. Why not? It was better than being stuck in Quail Ridge in the middle of a different kind of nowhere.

"We'll take it," we said.

Once again we went to a furniture-rental place and got enough to fill the apartment. Our first night in our new place, we sat, miserable, in the living room. The smell of new furniture and Mr. Clean filled the air.

"Something's really weird," Rebecca said.

We agreed.

Then I started to laugh. "It's so quiet," I said. "There's no noise at all."

"This sucks," Tavia said.

Once again, we agreed.

The very next day, Tavia presented us with a list of bars and restaurants in a neighborhood called the Central West End, near Washington University.

"Here is where we need to go," Tavia told us.

We piled into my red car and drove down Highway 270 to Culpeppers. The CWE made us feel a lot better about living in St. Louis. In no time Tavia also told us about Tony's in Clayton for fine Italian food, and eventually Laclede's Landing, which sat on the Mississippi River in the shadow of the Arch and reminded us of Faneuil Hall with all of its shops and restaurants, opened. Although St. Louis was full of strip malls and chain restaurants back in 1980, we did quickly find our favorite spots and soon enough had a similar routine to our Friday's/Daisy Buchanan nights out. My brother was living in Houston at the time and frequently had business in St. Louis. Skip was five years older than me, so that by the time I was old enough to be even vaguely interesting to him, he was already in college. Then he got married as soon as he graduated and had a daughter just a year later, again sending our lives into different orbits. But now, at twenty-three and twenty-eight, we were actually able to spend a lot of time together and grew as close, or even closer, as we'd been as kids. We would go to Laclede's Landing and drink martinis and marvel that two kids from West Warwick were sitting at a bar looking out at the Mississippi River.

THE AIRPORT ITSELF was a mess of temporary terminals and mobile lounges as Concourse D grew around us. The first day I showed up for work, while I sat at the gate waiting for my flight, I was written up for not wearing lipstick and because I did not look "approachable." I was reading a book. "In uniform, you must always look approachable," the stern supervisor told me. The rumors about how strict they were in St. Louis were apparently true. I immediately put in a transfer request for every other base, with JFK as my first choice.

The guy we sublet our townhouse from had been right—we weren't on reserve here. All the new hires were getting based in St. Louis, moving us up the seniority ladder. But since we were smack in the middle of the country, flights to L.A. and San Francisco were turnarounds, so we held lines with short layovers in Pittsburgh or Albuquerque. For a few months I laid over in Houston and instead of staying at the hotel, I stayed with my brother. He took me out for tacos al carbon and margaritas, or country-western dancing. Before too long, the new things that living in St. Louis brought me started to kick in. Time with Skip, the Gateway Arch shining in the sun, blues bars in East St. Louis, fireflies, and magnificent thunderstorms.

That winter, however, in St. Louis was brutal. The sky was always gray, temperatures were frigid, and it snowed seemingly constantly. I used to carry a small hammer to break the ice that enveloped my car in the distant employee parking lot while I was off on a trip. I'd stand in my high heels in a foot of snow chipping ice off my windshield, exhausted after flying around the Ohio valley for three days.

As brutal as winter was in St. Louis, summer was not much better. Despite a brief, lovely spring, in May heat and humidity seemed to settle over the entire city. Added to the weather were the tornado warnings that went off more often than I liked. Once, while we stood in the doorways of our apartment as the sirens wailed, a tornado tore the roof off the apartment building directly across from ours.

Too often I popped into crew scheduling to check the status of transfers.

"Why don't you just try and make it work here?" my supervisor scolded me.

I was trying. I went out with my friends and dated guys. As promised, TWA started flying international trips out of STL, and every chance we got my roommates and I hopped a flight to London or Paris. But I missed the busy city life that Boston gave me, and I missed being just an hour away from my family. I also still pined a bit for the guy I'd started to date just before we got transferred, even though he had clearly moved on—why have a girlfriend eleven hundred miles away, even if you do have free plane tickets?

· · ·

WHEN TWA STARTED a route to Providence, I bid for it immediately. For a few months I worked a DC-9 trip from St. Louis to Cincinnati to Pittsburgh to Providence, laid over in Providence, and then flew the reverse the next day. That took care of my homesickness. Twice a week I landed at PVD, my parents picked me up, and I went home for the night, eating my mother's spaghetti and meatballs and sleeping in my childhood room. On one flight out of Providence, we had a mechanical problem that prevented the cabin from being pressurized. So we had to fly to Pittsburgh at under 10,000 feet. Everyone had to stay seated with our seat belts fastened, even the two of us flight attendants. I moved to an empty window seat and watched the landscape unfold below me—trees and swimming pools and rivers. This was what the reporter Jane Eads saw back in 1927 on her twenty-four-hour flight, the ground so close and so beautiful.

Baseball season had begun, so I was able to watch the Cardinals play at Busch Stadium. One morning after I'd been at a game where the Cardinals played the Phillies, I went to work on my flight to Philadelphia and the gate agent came on board as soon as the whole crew had arrived.

"You've got the Phillies on this morning," he said. "They're going to take up most of the plane, but there will be some regular passengers too. Treat everyone nice. The star players will be up front."

My three other crew members weren't baseball fans like I was. I'd grown up going to Fenway Park with my family to watch the Red Sox, and my father and I spent many Friday nights going to watch the Pawtucket Red Sox, their triple-A team, play at McCoy Stadium in Pawtucket. Having the Philadelphia Phillies on board was as exciting to me as when I'd had Diana Ross or Ryan O'Neal. I hadn't asked anyone for an autograph before, but this time I would ask the star players and give them as a birthday gift for my baseball-fan father.

The team boarded with a lot of ruckus. The players were loud and rowdy, crowding the aisles and switching seats, acting like a bunch of middle schoolers on a class trip without a chaperone. Before I knew they'd be on board, I'd already bid to work in first class, which meant I had the bad luck of serving the team's stars. When I did the safety demonstration, two of them stood in the aisle and imitated me, swaying their hips and pursing their lips and grabbing their crotches. That went on pretty much the whole flight, grown men making sexist comments, burping loudly, not sitting down when the seat-belt sign came on, blocking the aisle. When we finally landed two hours later, I didn't bother to ask for any autographs. I stood at the door and thanked them each for flying TWA—one mimicked me and the others cracked up. As they disappeared down the jetway, I muttered, "Good riddance."

Although celebrities usually showed up on transcontinental flights, mostly to or from L.A., the Phillies weren't the only famous people who surprised me on one of my flights from one small city to another. One night I handed a meal to a young, blond woman in a middle seat in coach and when she looked up to take it from me, I recognized her as Jodi Foster, best known then for her provocative role in *Taxi Driver*. On an early morning flight to Detroit, Bill Cosby bounded on board. Although I knew him from his comedy records that my brother used to play repeatedly, he was especially visible as the spokesperson for Jell-O Pudding Pops. It's hard to reconcile the sex offender with the guy who took the microphone away from me and riffed over the intercom about flying and Pudding Pops, to the delight of the whole plane.

Ted Kennedy was running for president, and lots of Kennedy family members were out campaigning for him. I'd had Ethel (Bobby's wife) and Joan (Ted's wife) on flights frequently out of Boston, their hometown. But that year I often was surprised by having as a passenger a niece or nephew sporting buttons with their uncle's face on them: KENNEDY KNOWS WHAT AMERICA NEEDS or just TED KENNEDY FOR PRESIDENT. In no time, I had about a dozen of those buttons in my crew purse.

If the flight was on a DC-9, there was no first class, and although everyone had always been polite, smiling their big Kennedy smiles and handing out buttons, once one of the family boarded and threw a loud fit because she had to sit in coach—even though I showed her that everyone on the plane was in coach. She got into her seat noisily and gruffly. I saw a lot of passengers rolling their eyes as I went down the aisle to my jump seat. We had just reached our cruising altitude when she started to ring her call button. Although the seat-belt sign was on, we could get up and start preparing our service, though walking through the aisle was like climbing a steep hill. I made my way to her seat and she pointed at her tray table, which she'd put down before the announcement that it was safe to do that.

"Clean. It."

All that role-playing for difficult passengers back in training came in handy as I cleaned her tray table. During the beverage service, she demanded a Fresca.

"We don't have Fresca, just Tab for diet soda," I said.

"Just find me a Fresca, OK?"

"I'm really sorry. We only have Tab. There's no place to go and get something different," I said.

She narrowed her eyes. "I will never fly TWA again," she roared.

*If only*, I thought as I handed her a Tab.

DELAYED FLIGHTS, bad weather, no Fresca, even running out of a passenger's first choice for dinner—anything and everything could make someone threaten to never fly TWA again. Of course, our job was to convince them that they *should* fly us again. So we apologized for their lost luggage, for the blizzard, for anything that had gone wrong, even though it usually wasn't TWA's fault and almost never the flight attendant's fault. We had so many things available to help make them feel happy again. We could rebook them the flights they missed, get messages to people on the ground, give them free drink coupons or even a bottle of wine from first class to take home with them. But one of the most valuable things we had on flights was a stack of dry-cleaning vouchers.

At the smallest spill, we whipped out a dry-cleaning voucher, scribbled what had been spilled on, signed it, and the passenger got it cleaned and paid for by TWA. I've had enough red wine spilled on me during flights to wish they still handed these things out. But alas, they, too, are a thing of the past. I used to be hyper-aware of passengers wearing white, as if they were almost begging me to spill something on them. Most of the time, the passenger was quickly mollified after a spill when handed that voucher. But a nun in an all-white habit was not.

She sat in a middle seat in coach, like a snowcapped mountain. The guy at the window ordered a Bloody Mary. As I reached across the guy in the aisle, I kept repeating to myself *Don't spill, don't spill. Don't spill* . . . And as my hand holding the Bloody Mary passed the nun, I spilled it. All of it. Right down the front of her habit, the lime wedge landing in her lap.

"I am so sorry!" I said, handing her napkins and club soda, our go-to for immediate stain removal (it never seemed to actually work, though throwing coffee grounds on vomit really did remove the smell).

"I cannot believe this!" she fumed. "How clumsy can a person be?"

I was already filling out the dry-cleaning voucher. "TWA will pay for the cleaning of your suit," I said.

"My suit?" she said.

"Sorry! Your habit!"

"I don't want TWA to pay for anything. I never want to fly TWA again," she said, and shooed me away.

Once, when I picked up a passenger's meal tray, he said, "Now I know what TWA stands for."

Confused, I said, "Oh?"

"Yeah," he growled. "That Was Awful."

· · ·

WHEN I'D BEEN FLYING out of St. Louis for several months and gotten used to how much stricter supervisors were there, we all got memos on ways to improve our service. They had been getting complaints about TWA flight attendants not being friendly enough, so we were directed to speak *meaningfully* to at least three passengers per flight. Supervisors would do surprise checks, showing up on flights unannounced, to be sure we complied. On a long haul, talking to three, or even more, passengers would be easy. I'd even played games of Boggle on that red-eye to San Francisco. But that flight had been six hours long. This month I was flying short hauls, two hours or less with full beverage and meal services on packed flights. Still, when given an order by TWA, I followed it.

The next day as I stood at the boarding door welcoming passengers aboard, I noticed four people traveling together, dressed alike in black pants and turtlenecks. Eventually, I would come to realize that many people dress in black, and when I moved to New York City, I was one of those people. But these were the days when people took a quiz to find out what "season" they were so they'd know what colors to wear. There was lots of baby blue and pale pink, moss green and maroon, lemon yellow and coral.

When I saw four people all dressed alike and in all black, I thought: folk singers. I thought of Joan Baez or the New Christy Minstrels, dark smoky clubs in Greenwich Village, guitars and harmonicas.

I made a point of finding them after takeoff and with my brightest smile said, "Are you a folk group? I noticed you're all dressed alike in black!"

As soon as the words *dressed alike in black* came out of my mouth, I realized why most people dressed in black. And it wasn't to sing "Blowin' in the Wind."

One of them looked up at me with red, puffy eyes. "Our mother died," she said, "and we're on our way to her funeral."

"Of course," I said softly, wishing I could get off the plane and hide.

The very next day, a group of people boarded in Atlanta for a flight to Washington, DC, all of them with blue and black ribbons pinned to their jackets. In my sorority, we wore "happy ribbons" in double blue and gold—our sorority colors—pinned to our jackets or sweaters when something good happened, like graduation or pinnings.

"Happy ribbons!" I said, well, happily. "What are you celebrating?"

I don't think I'll ever forget the look in the eyes of the woman who stared at me hard and said, "We are on our way to Washington, DC, to protest the disappearance and murder of our children in Atlanta."

They filed past me, rightfully shaking their heads. What was I thinking? Why would adults ever wear something called happy ribbons? I pulled back on the forced effort to find three passengers to talk to meaningfully on every flight and stuck with the basic chitchat as I took and served their drink orders—*What an adorable baby! How are you liking that book? Is DC home for you?*

. . .

MORE AND MORE I came to realize that a flight attendant's job involved doing a lot of damage control. When you flew as much as I did and interacted with so many people, problems happened. A lot. And it was the flight attendant who had to fix them. On a flight from St. Louis to San Francisco, I complimented the pretty white suit a passenger sitting in the middle seat had on. (Why did things always happen to the people in the middle seat?)

"Thank you," she said, smoothing the wool pencil skirt. "I'm so nervous. I have a big job interview in San Francisco, and I really want this job."

"Well, you look great," I said. "I bet you're going to knock them out."

She smiled and slid her big leather purse under the seat in front of her. "They're picking me up at the airport and taking me to lunch," she said.

I made a mental note to wish her luck when we landed.

Just as we announced our initial descent, a shriek came from her row. I rushed down the aisle and there she sat, staring at her pretty white wool pencil skirt and crying.

"What's the matter?" I asked her.

But all she could do was point to her skirt, which I now saw had strange brown streaks all over it. Her bag was upside down on the floor.

"Look," she finally managed.

I bent down to investigate. "Oh no," I said, reaching under the seat and pulling out a dirty diaper, left there from the previous flight, opened and full. Her bag had been sitting right on the diaper the entire flight. When she'd heard that we were getting ready to land, she pulled out the bag and put it on her lap so she could apply fresh lipstick. Now her skirt was covered in baby poop.

"Let me get you some napkins and club soda," I said. "And a dry-cleaning voucher."

"That's not going to help!" she cried. "They're picking me up *now* and I'm covered in *shit*."

Since then, I always peek under the seat in front of me before sliding my bag there. I also wonder what happened to that woman. We never got to know the end of the stories we saw begin. Did she manage to clean the skirt at all, maybe in the airport bathroom? Did she get the job? Did she even go on the interview?

I wonder, too, about the bridal party I had on a flight to Oklahoma City. They arrived with their bridesmaids' gowns in ruffles and satin in plastic travel bags that they put in the overhead. They had all gone to college together. This was the first of their friends to get married. I heard the couple's love story and details about the wedding, which was at six o'clock that evening. Hmmm, I thought, I would never fly the day of a wedding. What if something went wrong?

Well, something didn't go wrong that day. *Everything* went wrong. A mechanical delay. Bad weather. The flight diverted.

Another mechanical. The hours ticked away and the group of friends—the entire bridal party—grew quieter and quieter with each delay, until there was no way they were going to make that wedding. They ran off the plane when we finally got to Oklahoma City, dragging their gowns behind them. (Did they change into them in the bathroom?) I had the pilot radio OKC to try to get a message to the bride. But did she get that message? Did they hold the wedding until the bridal party arrived? Or did the bride get married without her maid of honor and bridesmaids?

And what about the sad man that Christmas who boarded during a snowstorm in Chicago with bags of beautifully wrapped presents? Although he never told me why he was so sad, he did tell me this was the first Christmas he'd be home in a long time, that he hadn't seen his kids in years. He showed me their school pictures. "Beautiful," I said. The snow fell and continued to fall and, of course, we couldn't take off. Once we finally got cleared to leave, we had to get de-iced. Then de-iced again on the runway. Then the pilot came on the PA and announced that we had to go back to the gate. We, all of us who fly, have been there before. "There's a light on that we need to get checked," the pilot said. Then we sat at the gate for what seemed a very long time, waiting for maintenance.

Finally the captain told us that passengers could either sit and wait on the plane or get off and the gate agent would rebook them. I pulled out the OAG (the Official Airline Guide, a book that listed information such as flight schedules and connection times for most airlines) and found alternate flights for passengers who wanted to leave, including the man who desperately wanted to see his estranged kids for Christmas. Passengers deplaned. We sat a bit more at the gate. The snow stopped. And eventually we took off.

When we landed and the overhead compartments were opened, I saw the bags of exquisitely wrapped gifts. The estranged father had forgotten them in his haste to get home. When did he realize he didn't have the gifts? Did his children care that he showed up empty-handed? Or were they so happy to finally see him again that all was forgiven? Or at least some things were forgiven? I hoped his Christmas was what he'd imagined it would be, that his family welcomed him back in, that the Marshall Field's bags left behind on the TWA plane didn't ultimately matter.

EVERYONE KNOWS that you have to remain seated with your seat belt fastened until the captain turns off the Fasten Seat Belt sign. We were told in training about incidents when passengers or flight attendants were badly hurt trying to walk on an ascending or descending aircraft. Once, I landed at Logan Airport in Boston to find an ambulance at the terminal and a Delta flight attendant on a stretcher. Trying to complete the food service during turbulence, she was thrown against the wall and the cart smashed into her, breaking her legs. I had a beverage cart get away from me on an L-1011 when we hit unexpected turbulence as I was loading the cart onto the lift to send it up to first class. Lucky for me, I wasn't trapped behind it or hit by it.

Even worse for possible injuries was moving about the cabin during taxiing on an active runway. Shortly after takeoff on a flight from St. Louis to Miami, an older woman got up and tried to make her way to the lavatory, which is kind of like trying to climb a very steep hill. That's why you have to wait for the seat-belt sign to go off, an indication that the plane has leveled off and it's safe to move. But also, most plane crashes happen during the time right after takeoff or on landing, and you have a better chance of survival if you're in your seat with your seat belt fastened.

The woman had the soft, styled curls of someone who went to the beauty parlor weekly, pink lipstick, and a flowered shirt dress that came to just below the knee. She reminded me of my older aunts and great-aunts, dressed up for a special occasion.

From my jump seat, I called out for the woman to please take her seat. She just kept slowly and with considerable effort moving up the aisle, a hand gripping the aisle seat backs as she walked.

"The seat-belt sign is still on," I told her.

She kept right on walking.

I noticed an empty aisle seat a few rows from her, so I unbuckled my own seat belt and moved to meet her.

"It's not safe for you or me to be up right now," I said, motioning to the empty seat.

"I've got go to the bathroom," she whispered.

"The seat-belt sign will be off in a few minutes, I promise. Just sit here until it's off and then come on back."

She hesitated. The lav was only another five or six rows from us. But it was even more dangerous to be in there on the toilet.

I patted the seat. She pursed her lips into a tight line and sat.

When the seat belt sign went off, I went straight to her and told her it was safe to get up now.

I'll never forget how she looked at me with equal parts anger, resignation, and humiliation as she unbuckled and stood up. The seat was soaked with urine, the acrid ammonia smell filling the air as she pushed past me, the back of her flowered dress also soaked.

I rushed after her and put my hand on her shoulder. "I'm so sorry," I said softly.

I saw she had retrieved lemon scented wet wipes from her brown purse.

"I told you I had to go," she said, her voice shaking.

Never again did I so strongly enforce that particular rule. Instead, I reminded the passenger that the seat belt sign was still on and cautioned them that they were up at their own risk. I never wanted to humiliate another person again. I grew into my authority, confidently telling passengers to extinguish their cigarettes, place their bags under the seats in front of them, return their tray tables and seat backs to their original upright and locked positions. I learned how to defuse trouble, or how to reroute people onto missed flights, how to . . . well, be a flight attendant, which meant a person in charge.

• • •

FLYING SO MANY short haul flights out of STL that stretched for three or four days kept me away from writing that novel I dreamed of writing even more. I was always too tired when I came home from a trip, and just wanted bed or a night out with someone serving me instead of me serving hundreds of people. On a six a.m. flight from Chicago to Philadelphia, on the fourth day of a hellish five-day trip working four or five legs a day, I held the coffeepot up to a passenger and asked him, "May I warm up your car?" "Well," he said, "it's back in Chicago but sure." I groaned. "Coffee! I mean may I warm up your coffee?" "Long day already, huh?" he said. But even though I wasn't flying to glamorous cities like San Francisco or Las Vegas, and even though I was working harder, I still loved being a flight attendant.

I had that OAG, the *Official Airline Guide*—at my fingertips. The OAG was first published in 1929, when there were thirty-five airlines and three hundred flights in the United States. A fat paperback book, it listed every flight on every airline world-wide. An OAG was stored in a first-class compartment, and almost every flight required checking it. For example, when a flight was late we would take out the OAG and walk down the aisle offering rerouting options. We could also check to see if a passenger could leave on an earlier or later flight, which airlines flew where they wanted to go, and even which type of aircraft would get them there. I liked to browse the OAG the way I'd studied maps in *The Golden Book Encyclopedia* in my childhood bed-room, reveling in how accessible the world seemed. *The Golden Book Encyclopedia*, with its different-colored spines for each vol-ume, had vivid illustrations of the pyramids, the Great Wall of China, the Taj Mahal. Although the OAG was just pages and pages of small type, filled with flight numbers, arrival and departure cities, takeoff and arrival times, and airlines that flew the routes, I could sit on the jump seat with it and entertain myself while passengers ate their dinner or in the times between cleaning up and landing.

It may seem strange that I had time to sit on my jump seat and flip through the OAG, time to fantasize about taking the different flights listed there, to Tokyo or Nairobi or Buenos Aires. Of course, on short-haul flights, to LaGuardia from Dulles or Pittsburgh to Boston, with full beverage and meal services, downtime was indeed minimal. But if flights weren't full, or on flights over three hours, there was always time to fill. A great find was discovering that a passenger on the last leg had left behind a pile of magazines in the seat pocket, providing us with hours of reading. There were the crossword puzzles in the *Ambassador* magazines tucked into seat pockets to fill in, the Sky Mall magazine to peruse, or quick dips into a paperback. How I wish I had known how to knit back then! I would have knit miles of scarves.

IN TRAINING we were taught how to be gracious no matter what: when angry businessmen yelled and swore at us because our flight was delayed; when drunken men tried to pull us onto their laps; when a mother placed a dirty diaper right into our hand. Being gracious was especially hard for me when a passenger made assumptions about who the woman wearing that Ralph Lauren uniform actually was. Once, as I made my way down the aisle, I noticed a man reading a book I had just finished. I told him I'd recently read it and asked if he liked it.

Like a cartoon character, his mouth dropped open and his eyes grew wide. "You *read?*" he said.

I did read. A lot. But the stereotypes of flight attendants as dumb sexpots were still common.

Despite the few passengers who were angry or just plain jerks, most people were nice and easygoing. I heard their love stories, their child-rearing stories, their childhood stories. I wasn't actually writing, but I was listening to people, the way they talked and looked and felt. I put in another transfer request, adding St. Louis International to my list. Eventually, I would either get transferred to another base or at least get to fly international if I had to stay in St. Louis. Slowly, flight attendants not too much more senior than I were getting those transfers. My turn was surely soon.

# WHEN THE WORST HAPPENS

ALTHOUGH FIRST AID had been a big part of my flight-attendant training, most of the first aid we needed to do was handing out airsick bags or Band-Aids. Sometimes a passenger needed oxygen because he felt faint, and once I had a passenger go into labor about twenty minutes before we landed in St. Louis. I gave her oxygen, too, and held her hand, and assured her an ambulance would be waiting for her. Of course she never knew that I was praying she didn't have the baby on that DC-9. In the training room at Breech, having to perform CPR seemed as remote as having to evacuate a 747 out of the cockpit window. Sure, it might happen. But probably it wouldn't.

But then one evening, it did.

I was working D position on a 727 from Pittsburgh to St. Louis. During boarding, D stood at the rear of the aircraft, around the last four rows. A man came on who reminded me of my dad. People often told my father he looked like the actor Carroll O'Connor, and he did—the same round, jowly face and big blue eyes. This passenger had that same look, and maybe that's why I felt compelled to talk to him. He had on a business suit, and an old-fashioned fedora with a small feather in the band.

"Nice hat!" I said as I put the hat and his London Fog overcoat—just like my father's—in the overhead compartment for him.

"On your way home?" I asked him.

"Business," he said wearily, dropping into the aisle seat. "But back home in Pittsburgh tomorrow."

"That's not too bad," I said, noticing how flushed his cheeks were. He was slightly out of breath, too, but like my father he was carrying extra weight, mostly in the stomach, and he'd had to rush to the gate, he'd told me.

I didn't give him another thought as we went through the usual hectic boarding of an almost full 727. Before I knew it, the captain was announcing, "Flight attendants, please take your seats," and I had to rush into my jump seat beside C and buckle up.

Right then, on takeoff, I saw the passenger who reminded me of my father trying to get up, his body jerking slightly and his hands reaching forward awkwardly.

Before I could call to him or even nudge C, the man in the window seat in his row (the middle seat was empty) twisted his body around to face us and began to shout for help. We were still actively taking off, but C and I unbuckled and pulled ourselves uphill to that row where the man was clearly in distress. C and I went into first-aid mode immediately. We got him out of his seat belt and flat onto the floor. I heard myself say loudly and firmly, "Sir, sir, are you OK?" He couldn't talk, and his eyes struggled to focus. But when I cleared his airway we could see that he was breathing. C ran to tell the pilot and I started him on oxygen. At least I don't have to do CPR, I thought as I watched the oxygen bag inflate and deflate with each breath.

C was on the PA asking if there was a doctor on board.

There wasn't. She returned with the flight attendant working B, who was the most senior.

"It looks like you've got everything under control," he said. "You two stay here and keep an eye on him. I'll see if the captain is diverting to a closer airport."

As he was talking, I stared at the oxygen bag. It wasn't inflating. The man had stopped breathing.

"He's not breathing," I told them, and B took off to tell the captain we had to land.

Without wasting a moment, we had the oxygen mask off and I was breathing a hard rescue breath into the man's mouth, watching to see if his chest rose. Nothing. I breathed a second and a third time—that last time a geyser of vomit rose up in him and into my mouth—then C began the chest compressions, counting off the way we'd been taught.

At one point, the man actually pushed us away and tried to sit up before falling back down. This time when I lifted his head it seemed to have grown even heavier. I'm not sure if that was the exact moment when he died, but I always thought so. It was as if the last bit of life in him surged through him and then was gone. The air filled with the smell of feces, and the plane grew eerily quiet, only the sounds of counting punctuating the still, stale air.

B ran back to tell us we were landing, and to relieve C with the chest compressions. I heard A make an announcement explaining we had a medical emergency and were landing. All the while, I kept trying to fill the man with air. Even if it's clear that the person has died, we were taught that we could not stop CPR until medical personnel arrived and took over.

We landed and EMTs rushed on board and down the aisle. I stood up for the first time in I don't know how long and watched as they examined him and lifted him onto a gurney. One of the EMTs looked at me and shook his head to let me know the man had indeed died.

"You all did great," one of them said. "Sometimes nothing works."

I stood there and watched them until they were off the plane, then I collapsed onto the jump seat. I'll never forget how quiet that plane was. Even after we took off again and flew on to St. Louis, the plane remained silent.

After everyone had deplaned, as I took my own coat and roller bag out of the overhead, something caught my eye across the aisle. There in the overhead compartment was the man's London Fog coat and his hat with the little feather tucked in the brim. I took them down and thought of how just a few hours earlier I had stood right there and complimented him on his hat. Now he was dead. Did his family back in Pittsburgh know yet?

I gave the coat and hat to the gate agent. "So sad," she said, and I agreed, then headed away from the gate, numb.

"Oh, miss!" a man called to me. "Were you on this flight from Pittsburgh?"

I nodded.

"Is everyone off the plane?" he asked.

"Yes."

He looked confused. "I'm supposed to pick up a guy coming in for business," he said. "I didn't see him get off."

I stared up at him, unable to tell him the man he was waiting for had died. To my great relief, the gate agent had overheard and came over to us.

"Sir, please follow me over here," she said. To me she said softly, "You go home."

Home. If I had one, that would have been just the thing I needed.

I drove the ten minutes to our apartment and walked across the ice and snow in my high heels, still numb from what had happened. I kept seeing the man's face, his eyes wild as he struggled to breathe. Inside, the apartment was empty. Everyone was on a flight. How often I'd come home wishing for some solitude instead of talking about passengers and dates and layovers. But that night I was disappointed. Company and normal life would feel good, I thought. I brushed my teeth and took a hot shower and then I brushed my teeth again. That guy had thrown up in my mouth. He'd soiled himself. He'd died. By the time I'd climbed into bed, I realized that being alone was exactly what I needed after all. I lay there, slowly absorbing the enormity of what had happened. A man had died while I was doing CPR on him. Back in Pittsburgh, a family was getting the news, falling apart, crying.

I dozed off and then heard one of my roommates coming home. She climbed the stairs and outside my room, in the dark, she said hello.

"A guy died on my flight," I said.

"I heard about that. You were on that flight?"

She couldn't see me nod, but she said softly, "You OK?"

"I think so," I said.

And then, finally, I started to cry.

TWA GAVE OUR CREW a leave for the next two flights, then we were all back together doing the same trip. On our way from Pittsburgh to St. Louis on the second day, a call bell started ringing right after the seat-belt sign had gone on for landing. We couldn't believe it, but a man sitting mid-cabin was having a heart attack. Again. This time, we were only about fifteen minutes from landing and the captain called for an ambulance to meet the plane. We gave the man oxygen, all of us silently willing him to please keep breathing. He'd torn the top button off his shirt and loosened his tie in an effort to breathe before we were administering oxygen to him, and he sat, scared and wild-eyed and ashen, his shirt ripped open and his tie all crooked. But he kept breathing.

The ambulance arrived and everyone was told to remain seated until the passenger was safely off the plane.

"They're here," I told him as I watched the EMTs rush onboard.

I straightened his tie and patted his hand.

"Thank you," he said, tears falling down his cheeks. He held on to my hand tight until the EMTs told me to move.

The next day, I called crew scheduling to ask if they knew how the passenger was doing.

"It was a heart attack, but he's alive and well," they told me.

I cried when I heard the news, with such great relief and gratitude. Then the next day, I went back to the airport and worked the same flight again.

# FURLOUGH

I WAS HOME WITH three of my roommates, reading magazines and drinking coffee and sharing stories about weird passengers and cute passengers and what to bid for the next month, when Rebecca burst in the door, home from a three-day trip.

Before we could ask her how her trip was, she said, "I've got big news!"

Her eyes were shining and she had the look of someone who did indeed have big news.

"Our transfers went through!" I said.

"Thank God! To JFK? Please say it's JFK," Tavia said.

Rebecca shook her head. "Nope." She paused for dramatic effect.

"Are we on international here?" I asked. That would be fine. London and Paris instead of Cincinnati and Pittsburgh? I'd take it happily.

"Nope." She paused again. "We're furloughed!"

Instead of the excited energy that had filled the room a moment earlier, the air went flat and quiet.

"Furloughed?" one of us finally managed to repeat.

"Yup," Rebecca said. She told us that we were getting letters in the mail any day, but she'd stopped to check on our transfer status after her flight and her supervisor told her. We were all furloughed. Jobless. Effective in just two weeks.

Thanks to deregulation and a continued oil crisis, all airlines were laying off flight attendants, so there were no jobs to be had. Diane and I decided to wait out the furlough back east, in a rented house in a beach town on the North Shore of Massachusetts. The owner's wife had died, and he'd moved into the basement apartment and rented out the house. With its knick-knacks and fussy curtains and braided rugs, it looked like someone's grandmother's house. But the rent was cheap, and since we were jobless and furniture-less, it suited us fine. The town, Nahant, and its neighboring town of Marblehead, were about forty miles from Boston and attracted flight attendants from every airline who needed to be close to the airport but wanted to be out of the city. There were beautiful rocky beaches, plenty of bars and restaurants, and a cinema that showed old movies. A lot of flight attendants were buying up old colonial houses and restoring them, and it seemed like there was always a party to go to. With a built-in social life filled with flight attendants we knew—some furloughed like us and some still flying—and lots to do, it was the perfect place to collect unemployment and wait for TWA to call us back.

With my future frozen in place, I decided it was time to finally write the novel I'd always dreamed of writing. *The Betrayal of Sam Pepper* was a roman à clef about the people I lived near and socialized with, a terrible, typical first novel. Sprawling and imitative, I made every new novelist's first-novel mistakes—I sought revenge on real people who had hurt or slighted me, I made people I liked heroic, I overwrote, I told instead of showing. But bored after so much time spent always on the go, racing to and from airports and up and down airplane aisles, I threw myself into writing that novel, longhand, in my notebooks.

Eventually unemployment ran out, there was no news from TWA, and we realized we needed to get jobs. Diane took one at a hotel in Boston, and I started waitressing at the Landing, a popular spot on the water in Marblehead. I moved into the first floor of a Victorian in Marblehead that a married flight attendant couple had bought and renovated, right off the main street, and got a springer spaniel puppy I named Molly. When I wasn't working or meeting up with friends for oversized Cape Codders at Mattie's up the street, I walked Molly along the shore or sat at my kitchen table and wrote my novel.

But I wasn't making any real money sitting at that kitchen table. My fellow furloughed flight attendants and I shared any news or gossip we heard, but most of it was bad—Pan Am, Delta, United . . . everyone laying off more and more people. A Saudi Arabian airline hired flight attendants, and some of my friends went off to live in the Middle East and fly for them, but I didn't want to be in Saudi Arabia when TWA called me back.

Eventually word spread that Capitol Air, based out of JFK, was hiring. They were holding interviews in Boston, and furloughed flight attendants from TWA and Pan Am and everywhere else flocked to the interviews. Before deregulation, Capitol had operated as a charter airline. Charter airlines, like Capitol, World, and Transamerica, offered low, all-economy fares on airplanes that were configured to fit more passengers than scheduled airlines carried. They didn't fly scheduled routes, and were often literally chartered, such as back during the Vietnam War, when they were chartered to take soldiers to Vietnam. Post-deregulation, charter airlines could enter the scheduled-airline market.

In college, my friend Jane and I had flown to Rio on Capitol, giddy with how cheap the flight was and with the excitement of going somewhere so exotic and far away. Ten hours in cramped seats with terrible food made us wonder if it was worth it, even at such a low cost. But the sweep of white-sand beaches in Ipanema and Copacabana, the cheap lobster dinners at fancy restaurants and the discovery of feijoada, the hearty meat-and-bean stew that is the Brazilian national dish, made us forget the dreadful flight. Until it was time to leave.

Charter airlines did not provide the benefits at airports that scheduled airlines could, so flight delays were common. After hours waiting in the Rio de Janeiro airport, we were quickly shuttled onto the plane, only to land a few hours later with no explanation, and taken to a crummy hotel in what looked to us like a jungle. Monkeys and birds screeched outside. We were given meal vouchers for the bad hotel food and ordered not to leave. The next morning our phone woke us and we were told to be in the lobby right away to catch our flight back to New York—on that horribly cramped plane for another ten hours. Jane and I vowed never to fly them again. Just a few years later, there I was, hoping to work for them.

Taking advantage of deregulation, Capitol was starting regularly scheduled flights to Zurich, Frankfurt, Brussels, Puerto Plata in the Dominican Republic, and San Juan, as well as domestic flights to L.A. and San Francisco. I loved those long-haul flights, and except for the shorter flights to Puerta Plata and San Juan, that was all I would be flying. More than one of my TWA flight attendant buddies thought I was crazy to take the job—the pay was terrible and the work hours long. But I wanted to work as a flight attendant.

Unlike my interviews when I was in college, the interview for Capitol was simple. Basically, I had experience as a flight attendant and they needed flight attendants. In no time, I was living in a motel in Smyrna, Tennessee, with nineteen other new hires learning to work on a DC-8, a plane similar to TWA's 707s but with almost 300 passengers crammed into it instead of 190. Many of us were laid off from other airlines and, though I hate to admit it, we never stopped believing that our airlines were far better than this one. Of course, our "better" airlines were laying off flight attendants at a rapid rate, and this one was hiring just as fast. Many sentences in the galley began with "At Pan Am we were taught . . ." or "We would never do it this way at TWA . . ." Flight attendants with common names were differentiated by their "real" airlines—Pan Am Bob or United Ron. Our uniforms were beige polyester with rust accents, a big change from my sleek Ralph Lauren one or Pan Am's Galaxy Gold. But the truth was, at a time when the airline industry was going crazy and those "better" airlines were collapsing, Capitol gave us jobs.

With Capitol, I always had long layovers, mostly in Brussels and Frankfurt. Sometimes I even took my parents along with me. They loved Germany, having spent time there on weekend trips from Italy as a young married couple. We ate wursts and drank beer together, and I bought them their first moules-frites when they joined me on a Brussels trip. I loved the shaggy mixed crews I worked with, some first-time flight attendants, some Capitol lifers, and others furloughed like me from other airlines. I had fun talking and laughing with them and with the passengers on board—that is, when I wasn't working myself to death running up and down that one long, skinny aisle serving hundreds of passengers. There was no first class on Capitol, just a seemingly endless DC-8—nicknamed a Stretch—of coach seats jammed in close together.

Although they flew scheduled flights, Capitol still did charters, and it wasn't unusual to find myself on a flight to Rome or Paris or somewhere completely unexpected. Once I showed up for a flight to Brussels and was moved instead to a charter to Majorca. Another time, I was put on a charter trip to Lourdes, the small town in the French Pyrenees that is one of the world's most famous pilgrimage sites. With Capitol Air, you could end up flying anywhere.

Flights on Capitol were dirt-cheap, and many of the passengers would not have been able to afford tickets on the bigger, commercial airlines. Gone were the linen napkins embossed with the TWA logo and the pale-green mints served on heavy silver trays. Instead we shared stories of passengers showing up on board with live chickens, trying to eat the hot towels we passed after takeoff on international flights, and even one passenger who had a garment bag with a dead grandmother in it instead of clothes. Perhaps some of these stories were apocryphal, but as a flight attendant I saw enough shocking, bizarre, and just bad behavior to believe anything.

On a flight from San Juan to JFK, I was working the bar cart.

"May I get you something to drink?" I asked the guy in the aisle seat.

"Coke," he said.

As I went to open the can of Coke, I saw that although he had on a nice white dress shirt, that was all he had on, except for his tighty-whiteys.

"Where are your pants?" I shrieked.

He pointed to the overhead compartment.

I opened it, and sure enough there was a neatly folded pair of suit pants, which I took down and handed him.

"Put these on," I whispered.

He shook his head.

"Now!"

"But they'll wrinkle," he said.

He was being so polite that I hesitated.

"So what if they wrinkle?"

"I have a job interview as soon as we land, and I won't have time to have them pressed," he explained.

"OK," I said, refolding his pants and handing him a blanket. "Just keep this over you."

He did, for the rest of the flight. Although I didn't see him put the pants back on, he gave me a big, smiley goodbye as he deplaned—fully clothed.

·   ·   ·

AT FIRST, I kept my apartment in Marblehead and commuted with a lot of other flight attendants to JFK, by plane. This wasn't that unusual. At TWA, I knew flight attendants who lived in Phoenix, Miami, Denver—anyplace where TWA flew out of and into their home base. I'd always thought it would be too stressful for me to do that. After all, flying non-rev (non-revenue, or free) meant being on standby and possibly not getting a seat, thereby missing the flight you had to work out of hundreds or thousands of miles away. But Capitol paid us so little, and NYC was so expensive that I was hesitant to lay out all that money for first month's rent, last month's rent, and a security deposit on an apartment. Besides, I still held on to the hope that at any minute TWA would call me back and I'd have to move to St. Louis again, meaning I'd lose my last month's rent and my security deposit.

An airline called New York Air had started up to compete with the longtime Eastern Shuttle, which flew between Boston, New York, and Washington, DC, hourly. New York Air hired furloughed flight attendants and some first-time ones and undersold Eastern by offering flights for as low as $19 each way. Although Capitol didn't share reciprocity with other airlines like TWA did, I could get to work from Boston to JFK for less than it would cost me to fill my gas tank. New York Air flight attendants wore khaki cargo shorts and red Hawaiian print shirts, and instead of doing a meal service they handed out bags stamped with the I Love New York logo and filled with New York bagels, cream cheese, and an apple—for the Big Apple. Like Southwest does today, New York Air urged their flight attendants to make jokes, sing songs, and have fun.

I rented what was called a commuter apartment in Kew Gardens in Queens with a dozen or more other Capitol flight attendants, all of us furloughed from other airlines like United, Pan Am, and TWA and expecting to get our real jobs back soon. Like me, they didn't want to drop a lot of money on an NYC apartment just to have to move again to Chicago or Miami. Commuter apartments were close enough to JFK that we could get to work for early check-ins or back there after late arrivals for just a cheap shuttle ride. The problem with commuting to work by plane is at off hours there aren't any flights, so I would go to the apartment in the fake Tudor building and reminisce with whoever else was there about the airlines and jobs we all missed.

When my lovely ground-floor apartment in the Victorian in Marblehead became infested with rats, I decided that it was time to find a real apartment in New York City. For months I camped out with flight attendants in their apartments—in a grand building in the Bronx with a marble foyer and sweeping staircase, in a tiny one-bedroom converted with drywall and a Japanese screen into a three bedroom on the Upper East Side, and in an empty apartment in my cousin's building on West Fourth Street in Greenwich Village. It didn't take me long to realize that the Village felt like the place I was meant to live, had maybe always been meant to live, and I set about spending my days off apartment hunting. In the early '80s in New York City, this meant a lot of apartments above "shooting galleries," where heroin was bought, sold, and taken; fifth-floor walk-ups in dingy buildings; apartments with the bathtub in the kitchen, roach-infested apartments, or all of the above.

At that time, I was flying a lot of L.A. trips. Our layover there was at a hotel near the airport, and without a car there was no way to explore the sprawling city. Often, the crew would chip in for a cheap car from Rent-A-Wreck and get tickets to *The Tonight Show* or rent roller blades at Venice Beach, usually followed by dinner at Marie Callender's or the Cheesecake Factory, which had not yet popped up at every shopping mall in the country. But usually the crew just met up in the hotel lobby and walked to the Mexican restaurant down the street. Somewhere beyond this nondescript neighborhood was the L.A. I'd seen on TV and in movies, I knew. But even driving around in our Rent-A-Wreck didn't look like that L.A.

On one flight to L.A. a passenger invited me out to dinner that night. He had the shaggy blond hair and big blue eyes of a stereotypical surfer boy, but he was instead the president of a natural shampoo company. "Jojoba," he told me, "is the secret to everything." Apparently jojoba was the ingredient in the shampoo that made his company so successful. Happy to not have frozen margaritas and burritos for the third time in ten days, I accepted. He picked me up that night in a zippy convertible sports car and drove me along the curving mountain roads of Laurel Canyon, pointing out the Hollywood sign and the Canyon Country Store where Joni Mitchell used to buy groceries and that Jim Morrison famously called the store where the creatures meet in the song "Love Street." Finally I felt like I was seeing L.A. I was riding on the very roads that the Mamas & the Papas and Crosby, Stills & Nash had driven on.

I don't remember where we ate dinner, but I do remember that the shampoo executive was a vegetarian and a wine connoisseur. At twenty-four, I was still drinking cheap chablis and thinking it was good. But the wine that night changed that. Dazzled by those blond locks and sleepy blue eyes, and the stories about all the celebrities who bought his jojoba shampoo, not to mention all the wine I drank, I stupidly agreed to go back to his house with him. We went on those winding roads again, climbing higher still until we arrived at a house made of redwood and glass, filled with contemporary art and furniture covered in batik. It didn't take long for me to realize what the shampoo guy had in mind when he invited me, which I did not want to do.

After a bit of a struggle to peel him off me, he angrily asked me what the hell I thought we were there for. I honestly didn't have an answer. I had been feeling so happy, so grown-up sitting in a restaurant in Laurel Canyon, a place I'd dreamed about as a kid in love with all the music that came out of it. I think I started to cry. For sure I wondered how I would find my way back to my hotel, wherever that was, down these dark, winding roads.

Eventually he did take me to my hotel, the air in the zippy sports car angry now. He didn't even bother to turn off the car when we finally reached the lobby door, although, oddly, he did give me several bottles of shampoo and conditioner with jojoba.

"Thank you," I said, awkwardly holding the hair-care products in my arms. But he was already speeding off.

Every flight attendant I knew seemed to be meeting interesting men on flights and dating a lot, but somehow I kept meeting the absolute wrong guys. Then, in 1982, flying international out of JFK, I met a guy on a flight from Rome to New York who I liked. Really liked. I'd stayed out way too late in Rome the night before, and the other flight attendants and I all asked the captain for the best hangover cure—a hit of the oxygen hooked up in the cockpit. This guy with the greenest eyes I'd ever seen asked me what we were all doing in the cockpit, and I told him. His laugh was so nice I thought he should bottle it, which I also told him. Something went wrong on the flight and we were forced to land in Shannon for a mechanical problem, and that gave me a few hours to drink tea with him in the little restaurant in the terminal. I told him about my apartment hunting and, a native Brooklynite, he gave me a rundown on all the different neighborhoods. We discovered that we were both Italian American, and our family stories were so familiar that it was clear we had to go out on a date when we got back.

I arranged to stay at my cousin's on West Fourth Street the night of the date, then met the green-eyed guy at a play. He'd asked me to choose, and when I picked a drama instead of a musical, he'd acted surprised. Maybe that was the first sign that this wasn't such a great match. After the show, we went to Caramba!, a popular Mexican restaurant that made their margaritas in a Slushie machine.

"These," he said, holding up the enormous glass, "are deadly."

Deadly and delicious, I learned when I ended up in the bathroom throwing up less than an hour later. Three women in there made jokes with me about how strong the margaritas were and they'd ended up in there before too. I was happy when they left so I could throw up some more in peace. Imagine my embarrassment when I finally went back to our table and the same three women were sitting there, talking to my date about the poor girl puking in the bathroom.

"That would be me," I said.

Even worse, they worked at *Mademoiselle* magazine as junior editors, which meant, I thought, that they were actually writers. They got paid for writing! I hated them. I hated the green-eyed guy who knew them in some vague, fun way. I hated myself.

I apologized to that guy for weeks, hoping we could try a margarita-less date. But he wasn't interested. It was over as quickly as it had begun.


UNLIKE TWA, on Capitol domestic and international flights were mixed together in our bid package. In a month, I might fly JFK to Brussels, three San Juan turnarounds, a couple trips to Frankfurt, and an L.A. or San Francisco trip. The San Juan and

Puerto Plata turnarounds were my least favorite trips. The crew had to be at JFK by five in the morning, which meant flagging a taxi at three thirty or four. The taxi would pull over, the door would fly open, and a group of drunk, happy partyers would spill out on their way to another bar. After Daylight Saving, it was still dark when I set off to work. I'd work a full flight to San Juan or Puerto Plata, then sit sweating on the plane for several hours with the air conditioning turned off, waiting to head back to JFK. Outside, the tropical sun burned bright. I could glimpse palm trees in the distance, and the humid air filled the plane.

At three o'clock, we'd board another full aircraft and land back at JFK at seven. By the time I was in a taxi back home, it was dark again. After flying these turnarounds for an entire month, I actually called in sick with light deprivation. The most daylight I saw was outside the airplane window as we sat sweating at the gate.

. . .

THERE WAS NO WAY to know that the things I was learning as a flight attendant would also teach me about living my own life. And no way to know how seemingly small interactions could become so meaningful and unforgettable. I know that in my eight years as a flight attendant, I walked over a million miles up and down those aisles. But I don't know how many people I met and had conversations with and traded stories and travel tips with. Certainly all of these experiences helped me become a writer—the overheard conversations taught me the cadences of dialogue, and the way people reacted to delays and problems big and small gave me insight into human nature. So many particulars though are lost to time. The ones that remain proved so influential that they can't be forgotten.

Freed of San Juan turnarounds in December, I held a line with a mishmash of mostly Europe trips, including a surprise trip to Paris. Paris wasn't one of our scheduled cities, but there it was on my schedule just before Christmas. I spent my layover shopping for bargain Christmas gifts at Printemps and Le Bon Marche, and browsing the kiosks along the Seine. I walked through the Latin Quarter, eating a crêpe Suzette from one of the crêpe vendors, then made my way to the bookstore Shakespeare and Company. Unlike when I flew for TWA and made my good salary plus per diem and overtime pay, I made so little with Capitol that buying even one book was extravagant. But I browsed the shelves for a couple hours, vowing to come back and buy armfuls of books once I was flying with TWA again.

On the flight back to JFK the next day, a man came into the galley. We had finished the meal service and shown the movie, and I had dimmed the lights so the passengers could sleep. Most passengers had followed our request to lower their window shades so everyone could see the movie. He was maybe forty-five, he hadn't shaved, and it was clear from his red, swollen eyes that he had been crying. He asked for a scotch, and I opened the little miniature Dewar's and poured it into a cup for him. But he didn't leave. He stood and sipped his scotch.

It was common for passengers to come and hang out in the galley, mostly just for something to do on long flights. I asked him some banal questions, made small talk. Then just like that he began to weep.

"My brother," he said. "My baby brother. He died this morning."

"Oh no," I said. "I'm so sorry." I knew nothing of a loss like that then. I didn't know my own losses were right around the corner and would pummel me soon enough.

He told me what had happened, something sudden and quick with no chance of saving him. He told me how they'd grown up outside of Detroit, how close they'd been as children but then he went off to college and eventually moved to France with his French wife, and he and his brother only saw each other once or twice a year. That made me think of my own brother, Skip, and how we'd grown so close when I was based in St. Louis. Now that I was flying out of JFK, we didn't see each other as much. In this year or so, he and his wife had split up and he'd been transferred by Merck to Pittsburgh.

I was proud of Skip. He was a chemical engineer and often assigned to clean up catastrophic environmental disasters. He was working on Love Canal in upstate New York, a landfill that had been used as an industrial dump for a chemical company for more than two decades, leading to a public health catastrophe. He had a new girlfriend too. She was about my age and came from New Orleans. They were both coming to Rhode Island the following week for Christmas.

I listened to the guy talk, knowing how in the dim light and quiet of an airplane, people confided in us flight attendants. It was easier sometimes, I think, to tell your secrets and deepest feelings to a stranger, and flight attendants were taught how to listen.

"He was coming with his family for Christmas," the man said, which set off a new wave of sobbing.

Christmas was just a week away, and now the brother was

dead. The enormity of that took my breath away. I gave the man more scotch and let him talk and cry until the movie ended and the cabin lights came on. Passengers lifted their window shades, flooding the plane with light. The man went back to his seat. But before he left the galley, I hugged him. I was twenty-five years old and I did not know what else to do. He held on tight during that hug.

Just six months later, I was on a layover in Los Angeles. The crew had gone out for Mexican food and we were back at the hotel, all of us staying on the same floor, laughing as we walked down the hall. My room was at the far end of the hallway, so eventually I was the only one still in the hall and I heard a phone ringing. Some part of me knew something very bad was at the other end of that phone call, and that part of me made my feet and legs grow leaden so that I could hardly walk. The phone stopped ringing, then started again. Yes, it was coming from behind my door.

I fumbled with the room key. The phone stopped ringing, then started yet again.

I sat on the bed and I answered the phone, and a male flight attendant I had dated was on the other end saying, "I have very bad news."

Only a few months earlier this same guy had been dog sitting for Molly and he let her off the leash and she ran into the street and got hit by a car and killed. I was at this same hotel when he called to tell me. And here he was again with more bad news. Very bad news.

I hung up.

If I didn't hear the news, then something very bad had not happened.

But he called right back, and I picked up again, and he said something that people say when they are about to crush you, something about sitting down or being sorry.

I hung up, this time for a moment to imagine who it was that I was going to have to live without for the rest of my life. My mother? She had high blood pressure, female problems, a heart murmur. My father? His brother had just died of a massive heart attack last Christmas. Another had diabetes. Who else? Various aunts and uncles moved through my mind and the phone rang again.

My hand was shaking. *I* was shaking.

"Don't hang up! Your brother Skip is dead and there's only one flight out tonight and you have to go right now."

*Skip?* I hadn't even considered him when I tried to imagine my life without my mother or father or favorite aunt. Skip was thirty years old. He'd just had corrective surgery on his eyes so that for the first time since he was eight he didn't need to wear glasses. He was getting married, in New Orleans; the pale-green moiré silk fabric for my bridesmaid's dress had just arrived. I had just spent Memorial Day weekend with him and his fiancée and he'd grilled chicken and showed me how to doctor canned beans using barbecue sauce and onions.

Now I was being told that Skip hadn't shown up for work and someone went to his house, the details confusing me because I thought if my thirty-year-old brother died then it must have been in a car accident, not from a fall in his bathroom.

But there was no time for questions. I had to get to LAX, and somehow I did, and somehow I boarded the plane, but at some point I got up to use the bathroom and when I was done I couldn't remember where my seat was.

A flight attendant poked her head around the galley curtain and said, "Need some help, hon?"

I started to cry and I blurted, "My brother is dead."

She wrapped her arms around me and very gently led me into the galley, sitting me beside her on the jump seat and keeping her arm around my shoulder as I cried. Not that night, but soon afterward, I remembered the man on my flight, how death had seemed so far away from me then, when in no time really I was the one crying in the galley, a flight attendant offering comfort, my brother dead, as the plane flew through the night toward home.

．．．

LIFE UNFOLDS ON AIRPLANES. People are flying to funerals and weddings, they are on their honeymoon or leaving a partner, they are carrying a newborn on their first flight to meet grandparents or taking a kid to college or on their way to adopt a baby. And they fall in love.

In November 1982, just a couple months after my disastrous date at Caramba!, I was flying JFK-to-SFO trips with nice long layovers in San Francisco. I laid over on Saturday nights, and I liked taking the *San Francisco Chronicle* with its pink Arts section with me early the next morning to Caffe Trieste in North Beach to read over a cappuccino (and still sometimes glimpse the poet Allen Ginsberg there).

It was a strange time for me. My brother had died five months earlier, and after a summer on leave at home with my broken parents, I'd finally started flying again and was still squatting at an apartment in my cousin's building on West Fourth Street in Greenwich Village. On off days I'd stay with various friends, hoping to find roommates or a cheap apartment with an actual lease. I felt alone and at sea, yet oddly content with that. Maybe it was processing grief, or maybe it was that old idea of how you have epiphanies after someone dies and you realize how precious life is. I'm not sure. But I had decided I was moving to New York City and I was going to finish *The Betrayal of Sam Pepper*, the novel I'd started that was now well over four hundred pages.

I was working in the back of the plane, and during boarding I noticed a curly-haired guy with beautiful brown eyes take a seat in 47F, a window seat. A pilot from another airline, who was deadheading on the flight, had already started coming on to me. Not my type—too aggressive and full of himself, but he wouldn't take a hint. Just my luck, I thought, a guy who does look like my type is on board and this pilot is going to scare him away. No sooner did I have that thought than 47F took out the pink Arts section of the *San Francisco Chronicle* and started reading it. To say I swooned would not be hyperbole.

At one point during the flight, I saw 47F looking out the window, where the sunset was spilling swaths of violet and pink across the sky.

"Beautiful, isn't it?" I said.

He turned, surprised. "I was going to invite you to come and look at it, but I figured you were so used to it that it would seem ridiculous."

"I never get used to something like that," I said.

Yes, over the beverage cart, sparks flew.

The meals that day were short ribs and lasagna. Inevitably, we'd run out of one of the options and sometimes a passenger got truly angry when that happened. I admit that as often as I could, I found ways to be around row 47. But the flight was a full one, I was trying to avoid the pilot, and it was time to serve dinner.

When I reached row 45, I had run out of lasagna. Usually what we did in that case was simply slide the short-rib dinner onto the tray table without explanation. If the passenger said he wanted the other option, you politely apologized and explained you were all out of the lasagna. If they made a fuss, you could offer a complimentary cocktail. But there really wasn't much more to be done since there we all were, up in the sky.

At 45C, I slid the tray with short ribs onto the tray table and asked what he would like to drink.

He stared at the short ribs. Then he stared at me.

"I want the lasagna," he said.

"I'm so sorry," I said. "We've run out of the lasagna. But the short ribs are really good."

He leveled a steely stare at me.

"I. Want. The. Lasagna."

"I'm so sorry, sir. We're out of lasagna. But I'd love to give you a wine or cocktail on the house?"

Just like that he was banging the overhead lighting unit and screaming: "I want the lasagna! I want the lasagna!"

He banged so hard that the overhead compartment above his seat popped open and the lighting unit broke off, dangling by a few wires.

"You've given all of the lasagna to your friends!" he yelled, pointing at me now.

I saw 47F jump up, along with other passengers, everyone ready to restrain the guy. Two male flight attendants reached

us first, one of them with the restraints we kept on board—
another item I never thought I'd actually have to use. The
captain arrived next. He opted not to divert and have the guy
removed, but rather to continue on to JFK and have the police
meet our flight.

"Really?" the captain said when I told him what had happened. "All of that over the lasagna?"

They moved the restrained passenger and I was ordered not
to go below row 30, leaving me for the rest of the flight in
the back, near row 47. 47F came and stood with me for the
last hour of the flight. He was an actor, moving to New York
City on this very flight. He had a sublet in the East Village, on
First Avenue at Second Street, an agent, and a bartending job
all lined up. Could there be anything more perfect for aspiring-
writer me, just moving to Manhattan, than to meet an aspiring
actor who was just moving to Manhattan? I imagined a heady
parting upon landing as he asked for my phone number or even
offered to share a taxi into the city with me.

But right before we landed, one of the flight attendants from
the front came back and told me the captain wanted me up
front to meet the police and give them a statement.

"I can't!" I said, eyeing 47F. What if he deplaned while I was
talking to the police? What if he walked out of my life?

"You have to," she said.

We were on our final descent and so I had to hurry to the
front jump seat, all the while trying to figure out how I could
keep from losing 47F. By the time we were taxiing to the gate, I
had a plan. I scribbled a note on a cocktail napkin:

*Dear 47F, if you ever want someone to explore the city with, call me?*
*Your flight attendant*

I wrote my phone number on the bottom and stuffed the napkin in my pocket. Now all I had to do was be sure 47F didn't walk past me unnoticed.

All passengers had to stay on board until the lasagna passenger was removed. Then the police came on and I stood in the jetway with them as the passengers filed out, looking up every few seconds. I was signing my statement when I realized that 47F had just walked past me.

"Wait!" I called. "47F!"

He stopped and turned around, a wide smile on his face.

"This is for you," I said, and placed the napkin in his hand.

"It is?" he said, smiling even more.

The policeman said, "We're not done here."

"Got to go," I told 47F.

By the time I got home that night, my brand-new answering machine was already glowing green with a message.

"Hi, this is 47F . . ."

That was the beginning of one of the biggest love stories of my life, begun at 35,000 feet with a sunset so vivid, I still remember it almost forty years later.

# UP, UP, AND AWAY

$47F$ LIVED IN A sublet apartment in the East Village, right around the corner from the Hells Angels headquarters. New York City was dirty and dangerous in those days, but I fell in love with it, and him, as we explored the city together. We got spicy, hot Szechuan food delivered, ate at the cheap Indian restaurants on East Sixth Street, went to off-off Broadway plays, and listened to old Lenny Bruce records. 47F went on auditions and took acting classes while bartending at a yuppie bar on the Upper East Side. I wrote late at night, waiting for him to get home. With perpetual jet lag, I had no problem staying up late. One night I was working on *The Betrayal of Sam Pepper* and I realized that I was sick of flying so many hours, being away from the guy I loved so much, feeling constantly exhausted, all for no money. TWA would call me back eventually. Once again I'd be working on one of those gorgeous planes and having money in my bank account. The very next day I called Capitol crew scheduling and quit.

As it turned out, Capitol Air's success was short-lived—they went bankrupt in 1984, one more victim of overexpansion due to deregulation—but for a brief time they allowed me, and others like me, to return to the job we loved. As soon as I stopped

flying for them, I got a job as a waitress at a Tony Roma's: A
Place for Ribs on Sixth Avenue in the Village. My boyfriend
had moved from his sublet to a railroad flat with the bathtub in
the kitchen on East Twelfth Street, right down the block from
none other than Allen Ginsberg, and I moved into a tiny studio
sublet in a pink former convent on Sullivan Street with a courtyard and gurgling fountain.

Tony Roma's had opened in Miami a few years earlier and
was starting to franchise. Those of us hired to open their flagship Manhattan restaurant got trained in their service procedures and menus, most notably enormous racks of glistening
baby-back ribs and onion rings baked into loaves. Our vaguely
Bavarian uniforms were brown flowered polyester mini dresses
and oversized, ruffled white panties. The ruffles peeked out
from the hems when we walked and came into full view when
we bent over. We were all waiting for something—me to be
called back to TWA, many for breaks in acting, some for life
to start properly. After work, we would go to Café Central
on the Upper West Side, where everyone had a crush on the
bartender—Bruce Willis. Some nights Christopher Reeve or
Robin Williams was there. It didn't escape me that once again
I was in a sexist job, serving people and in the shadow of celebrity, except all I did in this one was sling ribs without the benefit of ending up in Paris or L.A.

MY SUBLET WAS UP and I took over one of the other waitress's
apartment on West Twenty-First Street in Chelsea while she
traveled. I acquired a couple cats and, restless, eventually quit
Tony Roma's, first to teach fifth grade—without a license or

any experience—in Bed Stuy and then to work at a bookstore on Spring Street in Soho. This was the perfect job for me— reasonable hours and a 60 percent discount on books. I still remember the excitement and crowds that came into the store the day *Bright Lights, Big City* was released in a new line of original paperbacks called Vintage Contemporaries. I couldn't imagine that day as I watched people line up at the cash register that in a little more than a year, my own first novel, *Somewhere Off the Coast of Maine*, would launch another original paperback series, Bantam New Fiction. I took a writing workshop at NYU with Bill Decker, a retired Viking editor teaching there. I'd ditched *Sam Pepper* and started something new about women who went to college together in the '60s, inspired by Skip's death and what had happened to him and his '60s-era friends. But it was just a bunch of stories at that point, and I felt that I was frozen in place, moving from job to job and sublet to sublet.

After the semester ended, Bill called his friend Bob Pack, the director of the esteemed Bread Loaf Writers' Conference, and recommended me to attend that August. The next thing I knew I was in Vermont for two weeks with real writers, getting my stories workshopped, hearing readings, and drinking wine on the porch of Cherry, the little house where I stayed with five other women. I couldn't believe there were so many people like me, people who thought about POV and character development, who could spend hours analyzing a short story. Just like when I flew to Kansas City to start flight-attendant training, I once again felt like I finally belonged in my own skin.

My parents, worried about the bad neighborhoods and tiny apartments I was living in, helped me buy a one-bedroom on

Bleecker Street. Although it was newly renovated and had a doorman, the neighborhood wasn't much better than any of the others I'd lived in. Now called NoHo, it didn't even have a name then, straddling the East and West Villages in a desolate area. But I loved it. And no sooner had I moved in than my mother called with wonderful news.

"A letter from TWA just arrived," she said.

"Open it!" I screamed, knowing the only reason TWA would be writing to me.

The furlough was over. I had to report to two weeks of retraining at JFK in a month.

. . .

THERE WE WERE AGAIN, those of us who had survived Breech Training Academy together and so many others I'd met being based in Boston and St. Louis, flying together and laying over together, now back in our uniforms practicing arming and disarming doors, learning new service procedures, giddy to be back. There we were, almost half a century since Ellen Church became the first flight attendant, ready to get back to work on a TWA jet. Like me, most of the returning flight attendants had flown for small or charter airlines, worked odd jobs, bided their time. Some were now married and some, like Maisie, who had shown me around San Francisco on those long layovers, were pregnant. Seeing them made me realize how hard flight attendants had fought for basic rights, like eliminating age, marriage, and pregnancy restrictions.

We were living examples of winning those struggles for

equality and professionalism. Yet another reason to feel proud to be a TWA flight attendant.

. . .

SINCE I HAD MADE a life in New York City, I was pleased and relieved that I was finally based out of JFK. Although I was put on domestic, I got my transfer to international in right away. The rumor was that, come spring, TWA would need a lot of international flight attendants and I'd most likely get transferred. For the time being, I happily walked from my apartment on Bleecker Street to the West Fourth Street subway station, dressed in my uniform and rolling my crew kit behind me. I'd board the "Train to the Plane," which took people all the way out to JFK, then board a shuttle bus to the TWA terminal. The ride took about an hour, and I'd spend it working on my novel, so lost in writing that I was often surprised when I had to be told that we'd reached JFK and I needed to get off.

I was the happiest flight attendant, working mostly transcontinental flights on my beloved L-1011s. Now that everyone had been called back and TWA had started hiring again, I even got to hold a line every month. We had started to fly to Seattle, and I flew three-day trips there, laying over in Chicago one night and Seattle the next, with a Seattle nonstop on the way home. I had never been to the Pacific Northwest, and quickly fell in love with wandering the Pike Place Market and taking drizzly ferry rides to Bainbridge Island, once even spotting a whale. But best of all was discovering Elliott Bay Book Company in Pioneer Square. With thousands of books on cedar bookshelves, a café, and a schedule of writers coming to give readings and do book signings, Elliott Bay was what I'd always imagined a local bookstore to be. I bought a signed copy of Frederick Barthelme's *Second Marriage* and Louise Erdrich's *Love Medicine* there.

Standing among all those books, the smell of wet wool and strong coffee in the air, I couldn't imagine that in just three years my name would be on the Events board and I would be standing at the podium reading from my book. That seemed remote, impossible.

47F AND I BROKE UP that fall, just after I started flying again, and I was heartbroken. I had started feeling restless and uncertain about where our relationship was going and decided I needed a break, time to think. Deep down I harbored a fantasy that we would reunite after a year or two, desperately missing each other and getting back together. Meanwhile, I started dating a writer I met at Bread Loaf, and my life soon became filled with lavish book parties thrown by publishers and magazines and smaller house parties where writers I'd read in *The New Yorker* drank red wine. At one party I glimpsed Jay McInerney, whose book *Bright Lights, Big City* had been such a big seller when I worked at Spring Street Books. I could never bring myself to say I was a writer too when someone asked. But when I said I was a flight attendant, people always wanted to hear about my job.

Even after I signed with an agent, I still didn't feel like a writer yet. Writers had books on the shelves at Elliott Bay and City Lights. All I had was ninety pages of connected short stories. But one evening I came home from a flight and my answering machine was glowing red. I hit Play, and the agent's booming voice filled my apartment. I had met her only once, in an awkward half hour in her gorgeous apartment with original Expressionist paintings staring down at me. She seated me in a chair that faced the long bank of windows, and I could barely see in the bright sunlight that streamed through them. At the end of the meeting, she announced that "pretty sells," and I'd do just fine. She would sell my book. And as I stood listening to her message, my heart pounding, she was telling me that she had done just that.

The novel, *Somewhere Off the Coast of Maine*, sold to Bantam Books as one of the two launch books in their Bantam New Fiction series—a rival to those Vintage Contemporaries I'd sold at Spring Street Books—and was scheduled to be published in summer of 1987. Until then, I would keep working as a flight attendant, of course. I had no desire to stop flying. I was finally back with TWA and I loved my job more than ever. I imagined years ahead of writing books and being a flight attendant.

One day shortly after I sold my novel, I was working first class to Tucson. A man boarded and began opening and closing the overhead compartments, pushing the buttons above him, and in general acting like someone who had never set foot on an airplane before—unusual for a passenger in first class. After takeoff, I asked him what he would like to drink.

"How do I know?" he said angrily. "I don't know what you have."

I listed everything on board—the juices, the sodas, the beers and wines and liquor—before he shook his head and waved me away. When it was time for dessert, I wheeled out my cart with all the fixings for ice-cream sundaes.

"Hot fudge sundae?" I offered him. "Or butterscotch?"

His face grew red with anger. "What? You think I'm a child? Only children eat ice-cream sundaes!"

I couldn't stand it any longer. Who was this guy? I had to find out.

"What are you doing in Tucson?" I asked him later.

He told me that he was a best-selling writer and he was going to Tucson to give a talk.

"How about that?" I said. "I'm a writer too." I still felt funny calling myself that. After all, the book hadn't even come out yet. But I was trying to get used to saying it out loud.

"Oh, you are?" he said, amused.

I told him about my book sale and he scrunched up his face and studied mine carefully.

"You look too dumb to be a writer," he said finally.

Oh, that TWA training kicked in, thankfully.

"I think you mean you don't expect a flight attendant to also be a writer," I suggested.

He scrunched up his face again, studied me even more, then declared, "No. You look too dumb to be a writer."

A few years later, after my first novel was published, I did a book signing at the ABA—American Booksellers Association—Convention and Trade Show (now called Book Expo) in Washington, DC. The ABA is the trade association that promotes independent booksellers, and during the convention thousands of booksellers come to hear writers talk about their books and to get signed galleys of upcoming books. For a first-time novelist, the sight of a line of people waiting for you to sign their galleys is overwhelming and about as exciting as something can be. Seeing a passenger who called you dumb just a few years earlier waiting in that line is downright thrilling.

"I bet you don't remember me," he said.

"Oh, I will never forget you," I told him with a big smile, channeling my inner flight attendant.

. . .

SPRING CAME and the rumors proved to be true—I was transferred to international. As a young girl who had dreamed of the glamorous life of being a flight attendant, flying out of Terminal 5 at JFK epitomized that dream. Its white wing-shaped roof, designed by Eero Saarinen, was supposed to evoke a bird about to take flight, and to me it did. Although the building was over twenty years old, it still looked modern, like a glimpse of the future. Inside was all deep blue and red—TWA's colors—multi-leveled with enormous windows that showed the planes taking off and landing. A concrete balcony allowed you to look down at the people coming and going. A Departures board clickety-clacked in the center of all the action, and two hushed, red-carpeted passageways—we called them "tubes"—led to the departure lounges and the jetways where jets stood waiting. To walk through that terminal in my TWA uniform, headed to Madrid or Cairo or Rome, felt like I was dreaming, every single time.

FLYING INTERNATIONAL at JFK, TWA's biggest international base, meant going back to reserve. Even with more than six years' seniority, I was junior on international. Really junior. I worked with flight attendants who had worked on Connies (the nickname for the Lockheed Constellations, which were propeller driven), before there were even jets. Some of those most senior flight attendants remembered when Howard Hughes owned TWA and told stories about him walking onto a plane flanked by movie stars, asking the passengers to get off, and taking the plane wherever he wanted to go, with the air hostesses along for the ride.

Just as I used to commute to work from Boston on New York Air, a lot of these senior flight attendants, their husbands now retired, commuted from Phoenix or Sarasota or Las Vegas, flying five or six hours to work an overnight transatlantic flight. Once I worked with a senior flight attendant who commuted from Sweden. She'd drive an hour to Stockholm to catch an SAS flight to Copenhagen, then take a TWA flight from there to London, and then another from London to New York, only to turn right around and work a flight from JFK to London. On the flight to London, she worked the other end of the bar cart with me. When I asked her if she had any more beer on her side, she didn't answer. I looked up and saw that she had fallen asleep—standing up. "The commute's not bad," she insisted later. "You get used to it."

Early on, I opted to bid for the flights senior people didn't want, which meant mostly London trips. Flights to London were relatively short, so you had to fly a lot of them to reach your minimum monthly flight hours. We would leave JFK at six at night, arrive in London at five in the morning, have that whole day and overnight there, then get picked up to go back to Heathrow at seven the next morning. Two days off and I'd do it all again. Despite the jet lag from so much back and forth,

I bid that route a lot so that I'd have a regular schedule, albeit a crazy one. After a few months, I had a regular hairdresser in SoHo and had seen most of the West End plays: Joan Plowright in *Mrs. Warren's Profession*; Ben Kingsley as Iago in *Othello*; Judi Dench in *Waste*; and a production of *The Seagull* with Jonathan Pryce, Vanessa Redgrave, and her daughter, Natasha Richardson, in her theatrical debut. I loved musicals, too, and got to see *Les Misérables* and *Me and My Girl* before they came to Broadway.

Covent Garden, the former open-air market in the West End, had recently reopened with new shops and restaurants and bars, and at one of those bars I met Oliver, a British guy with an impressively droopy mustache and deep laugh. I'd dreamed of dating a British guy ever since I was seven and fell in love with Paul McCartney, and meeting Oliver for dinner or sightseeing on my layovers fulfilled that fantasy—until I stopped flying London trips. He called a few times, but my flights were to Rome and Athens now. I couldn't help but think of Kathryn Cason's question in *How to Become an Airline Stewardess*: Would you like a boyfriend in every city in the world?

FLYING INTERNATIONAL meant working longer hours, for which my per diem was almost double what it had been on domestic. But the service was more complicated, and it was performed when I'd normally be asleep. Preflight, we'd walk down the aisles offering playing cards, magazines, and newspapers to the passengers. I remember passengers complaining if our issues of *Time* were a week old or if they'd already seen the movie we were showing, not realizing that in just a decade playing cards and magazines would be a thing of the past. We also had stationery—thick white paper with matching envelopes—with the TWA logo on them in a leather-bound portfolio in case a passenger wanted to write a letter during the flight.

Part of the job on long-haul flights was selling headsets in coach for the movie, which was free in first class. Movies were shown on big screens that dropped down from the ceiling in strategically located places throughout the cabin. Just one movie played, no options. If the flight was over six hours, we showed two movies.

"Not *48 Hours* again," a passenger groaned. "This is the third time I've seen it this month!" If he'd flown TWA three times that month, he was right—movies changed monthly.

"There will be a new one on the first," I said.

He grumbled and paid to rent the headset I was offering anyway. I was glad we showed the same movie all month. It gave me the opportunity to see a movie, albeit in a disjointed fashion, a pleasure that with my crazy schedule I rarely had time for. I couldn't sit in a movie theater with a pager that could go off at any minute, and I usually got back from flights too late for a show. But during slow times on the flight, I could tune in to the movie, often seeing the middle first, or even the ending, depending at which point I could pop on a headset for a few minutes.

After the movie, up went the cabin lights and in coach we did a lemonade service. Once on a flight back from Frankfurt the lemonade had not been brought on board and none of us noticed until the movie was ending and it was time to get out those trays and cups. When a flight attendant announced: "Ladies and gentlemen, we apologize but due to a commissary error we are not able to do a lemonade service today," passengers started to complain. Loudly. "Hell," the captain told us, "give them free drinks to settle them down." Out came the beverage cart and in no time we had a plane full of happy passengers.

On overnight international flights there was also a breakfast service before landing. From London it was scones with clotted cream; from Paris, croissants. In first class, of course, it was a full breakfast. But I didn't mind doing all of the little things that made first class on TWA international flights special—once I learned how to do them.

The nicer senior flight attendants walked me through duty-free shops and taught me what liquor to buy, what perfume to wear, which champagne was the best. In Rome and Paris, they brought me to the guys who sold Gucci and Chanel at cost; in London they showed me around Harrods. Here's what to order in Athens (moussaka) and Cairo (mezze). Get spaghetti carbonara in Rome and finish with sambuca con mosca, three coffee beans floating on top. I learned when famous stores in different cities had annual sales, how to ride the Underground and the Métro and the Metropolitana, the best places for high tea and street crêpes and tapas. The senior flight attendants shared what they knew—sometimes—but even more important I learned from exploring on my own. Even when I was a starry-eyed kid dreaming of walking around Paris or Madrid, I never imagined I would be brave enough, comfortable enough, happy enough to go out alone in a foreign city. But that was how I learned to buy discount theater tickets in the West End or where to catch a boat ride along the Seine—from watching and exploring, and taking chances, alone.

Usually the most junior flight attendant, most often me, worked E Zone, which was the very back of the plane in the tail. The 747 narrowed there, so the seating was different from the rest of coach, with fewer people. The person working E Zone worked it alone, zipping around the section with the bar cart and serving meals. I liked being back there, especially if the crew were all cranky senior flight attendants, nicknamed "dinosaurs" because they'd been around so long. The downside of E Zone was that it was an all-smoking section. As I walked down the aisle toward it, I could see it enveloped in smoke. I used to have to pack an extra uniform jacket in case I worked E Zone because the smell of smoke was too awful to wear the same jacket.

After several months flying London trips, I tried to hold other cities. But I was too junior so I ended up back on reserve. On international, that had its benefits. If I flew only three or four Cairo, Athens, Tel Aviv, or Bombay trips, I had enough flight hours to be finished for the month. Also, sometimes I could escape the smoke of E Zone and work in the hushed first-class cabin. Although the service up there was elaborate, with a full caviar course at the start and a cheese and port service at the end, the time went by much faster being so busy. When we finished, we could eat the leftover caviar or the extra lamb chops in peace.

The first time I worked first class on an international flight, I had to set up the serving carts. I stared a long time at an oddly shaped chunk of ice before finally deciding that it was worthless and tossed it. A couple hours later, the purser was screaming about not being able to find the ice mold for the caviar. Ice mold? Caviar?

"Have you seen it?" he demanded.

"No," I lied.

Just when I thought I was that glamorous woman I'd imagined, something else came along I didn't know. Not only did we dress our lamb chops in little gold foil stockings, but our caviar sat in a molded ice ring and was served with silver bowls of diced red onion and crumbled hard boiled eggs, with chilled vodka or champagne.

The next time I worked first class on an international flight, I perfectly set up the caviar service, that ice mold sparkling happily back at me with caviar nestled atop it.

I loved those flights. The busyness, the linens and silver, the hush of the 747 when we dimmed the lights, and even the caviar service. The long-haul flights on jumbo jets captured the part of me that had wanted to be a flight attendant in the first place.

ON A FLIGHT TO PARIS, I was working first class on a 747 and went into the cockpit right after takeoff to take their beverage orders. The captain asked me for two Jack Daniel's with ice. I thought he was joking. I took the first officer's order, then asked the captain again what he'd like.

He steadied his eyes right on me and said in a firm voice, "Two Jack Daniel's with ice."

One of the rules of flying is that the captain is in charge. If there's a problem in the back that needs authority, you get the captain. The captain decides if you can serve free drinks on a very delayed flight, if we need to divert because of a passenger's health, and how to handle the serious problems that can and do arise, like a passenger dying midflight. In other words, we were not supposed to question them, kind of like the relationship between doctors and nurses.

I took a deep breath and said just as firmly, "I'm not allowed to do that, sir."

The first officer kept his eyes averted the whole time. He was also not supposed to question the captain.

I left the cockpit, got the first officer's soda, and delivered it to him. The tension in the cockpit was thick. A few minutes later, the captain walked into first class, opened the liquor cart, and took two miniatures of Jack Daniel's and a glass of ice. I was terrified that the captain would drink more during the flight or crash the plane when we landed. I debated whether to tell another flight attendant, or if I should write the pilot up— a form handed in that reported crew infractions. In the end, we landed safely and I did nothing.

WHEN I FIRST STARTED FLYING, I was too self-conscious—mostly about the rest of the crew asking me what I was doing—to pull out my notebooks and write my stories. My dream of becoming a writer was still private, a secret I held close. But now I had an actual book contract, which gave me the confidence to work on my novel on board. I loved dimming the cabin lights after the meal service, grabbing a ginger ale, and sitting on the jump seat to write. On other jump seats around the plane, flight attendants picked out wallpaper from samples they'd gotten on the layover, did crossword puzzles, wrote letters, read books or magazines, studied French or for the LSATs or their real estate licenses.

We couldn't sleep, of course, though we wanted to. On flights over ten hours—from JFK to Athens or Cairo or Bombay— 747s had hidden beds for us to take an hour or more of "crew rest," decided, like everything else, by seniority. As the most junior on international flights, I often had to take my crew rest an hour or two into the flight, meaning I had to stay awake for the next seven or more hours, well into the night. Although that was tough, I used that time to write rather than rest.

Most international flights weren't long enough for crew rest, so we sat on our hard, upright jump seats as if they were our sofas at home and entertained ourselves. If a passenger pulled back the curtain and came into the galley, we had to drop our book or crossword puzzle and get up, ready to get them another beer or Coke or bag of peanuts. Sometimes, a passenger came into the galley because, like us, they were bored. After they got their drink, they'd start to talk, to tell us where they were going or where they had been. Sometimes I'd find myself talking for thirty or forty minutes to someone I would never see again, whose story I would quickly forget. Then it was time to raise the cabin lights, and do the next service or prepare for landing, my notebook of stories tucked into my crew purse once again.

. . .

ON MY FIRST LAYOVER in Cairo, the crew took great delight in the fact that I had never been there before, and they promised to show me around. They walked me through Khan El-Khalili, one of the oldest markets in Egypt, dating back to 1382. The onslaught of vendors trying to lure us into their shops, the smell of so many different spices, the crowds, and the architecture all dazzled me. A senior flight attendant named Karen showed me the hammered brass trays that came in all different sizes and patterns. "You buy a few of these and get legs for them back home to make cool coffee tables," she told me. "This is a great place to buy gold," a flight attendant named Simone said, pointing to one of the little shops. She showed me the gold bracelet and earrings she'd bought there and quoted the low price she paid. "Always bargain," she advised as we moved on. A flight attendant named Mark bought saffron and gave me half. "At home this costs like $2,000 a pound," he said. "Here it's so cheap." He explained that saffron came from the crocus flower and was costly because it took about two hundred thousand flowers just to get one pound of saffron. I wasn't sure what I'd do with the saffron, since I'd never used it before, but before I could ask, I had to catch up with the crew as they entered a tiny café for mint tea.

That night, we ate traditional Egyptian food and watched a belly dancer at a restaurant near the hotel. "This was such an incredible day," I said when we parted later. "Just wait until tomorrow," Mark said, and told me to meet them in the lobby at noon. When I arrived the next morning, a car was already waiting for us. Forty-five minutes later we were dropped off at a restaurant. I walked in and came to a halt. Behind me I heard Mark chuckle. But in front of me, out a wall of windows, stood the pyramids, rising out of the desert. Standing before something I had only seen in my elementary school geography textbook suddenly right there, I started to cry. Embarrassed, I apologized for getting so emotional, but Karen touched my arm and said, "I cry every time I see them." We had a long lunch of kebabs, kofta, and ta'ameya, similar to falafel but made with fava beans instead of chickpeas, everyone instructing me on what to dip into which sauce and detailing the ingredients in all the dishes I'd never tasted before—which was most of them. After mint tea and Om Ali and basbousa for dessert, we got back in the car and drove to a spot with a perfect view of the Great Sphinx. I gazed out at the sixty-six-foot-high statue, again feeling tears starting to fall. I had dreamed so long of seeing and doing things like this, of knowing how saffron was made or having a hammered brass table brought home from Egypt, of seeing all the world had to offer.

"It's forty-five hundred years old," Karen said.

"See how it's missing its nose?" Mark said. "Napoleon blew it off with a cannon because Egyptians believe the nose demonstrates power."

"I think that's been disproven," Simone said.

"Who cares?" Mark said, nudging me gently with his elbow. "It makes for a good story, doesn't it?"

THE NEXT MONTH, to my utter surprise, I held a line and was off reserve. I worked a flight that went from JFK to Rome and laid over; then from Rome to Athens and laid over; and then from Athens to Rome and laid over in Rome again; and then back to JFK. For me, this was a dream trip—lots of flight hours, long layovers in two of my favorite cities, and because the pairing was long—five days—I only had to work three of them to meet my required hours.

I worked my first trip, and as I usually did, I called my parents when I got back to JFK so they knew I was safe. That afternoon I gushed about how lucky I was to score such a great trip, how lovely Rome was in early June, how it was already hot in Athens but I could see the Acropolis from the Hilton rooftop pool.

I had a few days off, and then I did my trip again, leaving

JFK on June 11, scheduled to return on the fourteenth. Back at JFK, I went to a pay phone, eager to tell my mother about the leather bags I'd bought for us cheap in Rome. But when she answered and heard my voice, she burst into tears.

"Oh thank God, thank God, you're all right," she kept saying until my father took the phone from her and said, "There's been a hijacking on a TWA flight from Athens to Rome and we knew that's what you were flying."

"What? When?" I said, and then I noticed passengers looking at me the way people look at someone when something bad has happened.

My father was telling me all he knew from the news, but all I could say was: "I just did that flight yesterday."

There is nothing quite like the realization of how near you came to a catastrophe. Carol Quinn, the American Airlines flight attendant I spoke with, flew Flight 11 from Boston to Los Angeles in September of 2001. She missed being on the plane that flew into the World Trade Center on 9/11 by one day, and that close call led her to retire from flying.

As I stood in the phone booth at JFK that day, I thought I might faint or throw up, but people were watching me, so I took a deep breath and pulled myself together. I was a TWA flight attendant, in uniform, and I had to act like one. Not showing fear or worry was part of the job. I remembered my roommate Diane telling me about a flight she was working that experienced severe turbulence—so severe that it frightened the passengers. Everyone turned to look at her, the flight attendant, to see if she looked scared. Her face of calm made them feel calmer.

It wasn't until later, with the rest of the world, that I learned what had happened, and watched the seventeen-day ordeal unfold on the news. Flight 847, en route from Athens to Rome, was hijacked shortly after takeoff. With the captain held at gunpoint, the plane was diverted to Lebanon, where, after beating any military passengers, the hijackers shot and killed Robert Stethem, a U.S. Navy diver, and dumped his body onto the tarmac. Flight attendant Uli Derickson, as the only one who spoke German, helped negotiate with the hijackers, hid passports, and protected the 152 passengers on board throughout the ordeal. I had missed being on that hijacked flight by just two days.

No one wanted to fly TWA after that, fearful that we were a target for a new wave of hijackings. For the rest of the summer, I was back on reserve, working mostly empty 747s to Cairo, Paris, and Madrid. Some of those flights were so empty that we moved everyone into first class and gave them the full first-class service—caviar and champagne and chateaubriand. The passengers who did choose to still fly with us had decided it was safe, and so had the flight attendants. We knew from the first day of training, if not before, that catastrophic events like crashes or hijackings were possible. We were trained on what to do if they did happen, and like those passengers who still flew TWA that summer, believed in the statistics that proved we were safe.

MY FAVORITE LAYOVER was Rome, a city I loved from the moment I arrived. I loved, too, how the Italians on board always applauded and cheered when the 747 touched down at Leonardo da Vinci. They typically jumped up and started gathering their things while the plane was still taxiing, which drove some flight attendants mad. Maybe because I'm Italian, despite how dangerous that was and how hard I tried to get them to sit back down, with them I felt right at home in Italy.

On one of my first layovers, I tagged along with a few flight attendants who were going to buy fake designer bags. They let me join them but pretty much ignored me as we made our way through the crowded streets to an apartment building, through ornate gates, into a courtyard, and then back out the other side of the building where a guy had a table of rip-off Louis Vuitton, Gucci, and Chanel bags in all sizes and shapes. The other women started haggling with him, pointing out flaws in the bags and snapping them open and shut. I stared up at the building's ornate cornices, into the bright blue sky. What was I doing here? I had no interest in designer handbags, never mind rip-offs of designer handbags. I should be at Keats's grave in the non-Catholic cemetery, writing down the words engraved in his tombstone into my notebook. *Here lies one whose name was writ in water.* Or I should be sipping espresso in the Piazza Navona, gazing at the Fiumi Fountain, its name the plural of the very street where I grew up in Rhode Island, Fiume Street. At home, I always had to spell it and explain that it was Italian for "river."

"Aren't you buying one?" the loudest bargainer asked me. She had four bags lined up her arm. I looked at the interlocking *c*'s and double *g*'s and the *v* atop the *l* and decided it was better to be alone in a new city than waste my time like this.

However, knowing this didn't take the loneliness away if I flew subsequent trips with unfriendly crews. It meant a lot of time alone trying to figure out how to get places, where to eat, and battling the nervousness of getting lost. But that was the situation I was in one evening in Rome when I made my way to dinner alone after sleeping most of the afternoon away. I asked the front-desk clerk to recommend a restaurant. He did so, gladly and with great enthusiasm, happily putting me in a taxi and telling the driver where to take me. The city lights as we sped through Rome were beautiful, and I even caught a glimpse of the Coliseum, illuminated and crumbling. Beautiful.

But when I got to the restaurant, dreaming of a red-sauce spaghetti dinner to soothe my homesickness, I was confronted with a menu of unfamiliar things. There was spaghetti, but it was *carbonara*. I read the strange words—carciofi alla guida, verdure, suppli, coda alla vaccinara. Even the way the menu was divided— *primi* and *secondi*—confused me. Would you really eat pasta and then also meat and vegetables and potatoes? My gaze landed on one familiar item—bresaola—but from a layover in Rome when I worked for Capitol, I knew better than to order that.

Unlike this lonely night, on that layover the entire crew, more than a dozen of us, went to an outdoor restaurant, where we sat under twinkling lights and drank carafes of house red wine. The purser, who spoke Italian, ordered all the food, and the night was a blur of wine and delicious things that I couldn't name, ending with too many sambucas con masca and a giant hangover the next day.

One of the other flight attendants, my good pal Matt, was also Italian American, his family from southern Italy like mine. In our families, braciola was a flank steak stuffed with spinach, pignolis, garlic, and parmesan cheese, simmered in red sauce. Matt and I used to frequently buddy bid, which means bidding on the same routes with the more senior flight attendant dropping seniority to the same as the more junior's. I sometimes buddy bid with Diane too. It took some of the sting of homesickness away when you flew with a friend and were assured that you'd have company on layovers.

Forty years later, Matt and I can say one word or phrase to each other and still burst into fits of laughter at the memory. Once, on a layover in Frankfurt, plagued by jet lag, Matt suggested we check out the hotel's Olympic-size swimming pool on the roof. Up we went, giggling as we made our way through the hushed, dimmed hallways and up the elevator to the roof. I don't remember if we actually planned to swim or if we just needed an adventure, but as soon as we flicked on the lights and the beautiful pool illuminated a brilliant blue, a voice in a heavy German accent boomed at us. "The pool is not ready for inspection!" That line still makes us laugh and remember running out of there as fast as we could, back to the safety of our rooms and our insomnia.

In Rome, we had spent the day together touring the city, hopping on crowded buses and basking in the dolce vita.

At the restaurant with the rest of the crew, Matt looked at the menu and asked me if I'd have some braciola if he ordered it. I said of course. The tender stuffed flank steak was a favorite of mine from my family's Sunday suppers. Instead, a plate with a tangle of very red meat was placed before us. The musty smell drifted up to my nose in the warm summer air. "Is it raw?" I whispered. The purser laughed. "Air dried," she said. Matt and I looked at each other, took a bite, and pushed it away. This tasted nothing like what we were used to.

Many years later, on a book tour in Milan, I realized that

the two dishes are not only different, they're spelled differently. Bresaola is the air-dried, salted beef; braciola is the southern Italian rolled flank steak simmered in red sauce.

But this night, sitting alone with that menu in Rome, I didn't know that, or any of the subtleties of Italian cuisine. I grew up eating everything smothered in red sauce—parmigiana, pastas, even eggs. I didn't realize that southern Italy, home of luscious red tomatoes, used them in so many things because they grew there so plentifully. On that book tour in Milan, I learned that northern Italy ate more rice and polenta than pasta because those grains grew best there. They cooked with butter, not olive oil, because olive trees grew in the south. Each region's cuisine highlighted what grew there, but to me back then, Italian food meant something, anything, everything in red sauce.

When the waiter came to take my order, I landed on the one familiar word—spaghetti—and hoped carbonara, whatever it may be, was not as awful as bresaola had been. "Secondi?" he asked me. I glanced down at what was surely a list of meats, but I didn't want so much food. I shook my head no, sending him off in a fit of angry Italian. Why had I ventured out alone? I chastised myself. I knew the answer, of course. Loneliness. In my hotel rooms across the world, I read and I wrote my stories in my notebooks. I watched television on the only English-language channel I could find. To sit in this bustling restaurant, with the music of Italian drifting through the air, the well-dressed diners swirling pasta on their forks and drinking wine, was what I wanted deep down. I just wished I could get over my awkwardness.

The waiter appeared, still upset with me for not ordering *secondi*, and placed a bowl of spaghetti in front of me. Creamy and cheesy and flecked with what appeared to be bacon, it looked nothing like the spaghetti of my childhood. But it was a thing of beauty. I twirled some around my fork and took a bite. Surely it was the most delicious thing I had ever eaten. Even the waiter smiled when he saw my cleaned plate. I had to resist the urge to order another bowl. Instead, I paid and went outside to hail a taxi, intoxicated with spaghetti carbonara and a half carafe of house red wine.

How important these small triumphs felt to my young self! Taking a taxi through the streets of Rome to a popular restaurant, ordering something new, and then falling in love with that food had all made me giddy. So giddy that I decided to speak to the taxi driver with the little Italian I knew, gleaned only from growing up listening to everyone around me talking in Italian.

I gave him the address, adding what I thought was an Italian accent to it, then put the flourish of an enthusiastic *"Grazie mille!"* at the end.

"What?" he said in English, his eyes meeting mine in the rearview mirror.

I repeated everything, even the *grazie mille*, and added a *capeto?* Understand? Except in my dialect we say "capeesh" *(capisce)* and as soon as the word was out of my mouth, the driver had pulled over, clasped his hands to his ears, and ordered, "Get out of my taxi, you peasant! With that dialect your words hurt my ears!"

At home, we sprinkled "capeesh" at the end of many sentences. I knew it meant understand. Confused, I sat there.

"Out!" he shouted.

But we were on a busy road and I was not going to step out of the taxi. I guess he realized that, because he hit the gas and we were off, flying through the streets, him muttering and glaring at me. My small moment of triumph faded and in its place was the homesick girl, far from her family and everything familiar.

The spaghetti carbonara I tried to duplicate back at home, adding Oscar Meyer bacon and a good dose of cream. Terrible. More bacon, less cream. Also bad. Garlic. Not right. I scoured Italian cookbooks, which back then were not plentiful, until finally I found a recipe for it. To my surprise, there was no cream or garlic, just eggs and cheese and bacon (or pancetta or guanciale). All these years later, spaghetti carbonara is my signature dish for dinner parties, the meal my kids ask for most, and my own comfort food, reminding me of that young, scared girl I was and how those lonely nights and brief attempts at bravery made me the woman I became.

I SAW MYSELF grow and change as I flew more and more miles. I was no longer the person who would tag along to buy fake designer bags or who would be intimidated by a rude taxi driver. Slowly I grew more comfortable with myself, and if I worked with an unfriendly crew, I was happy to wander into a foreign city alone. I traveled on my days off too. Although I still went to London frequently, I also visited Athens and Madrid and Paris and more with ease and confidence. I taught myself how to figure out my way around cities, how to convert different currencies, how to be alone and happy. In much the same way, I realized years later, I taught myself how to write. Unable to enroll in an MFA program due to my schedule, I became an autodidact, learning to write by reading books and deconstructing them, immersing myself in the *Paris Review* writer interviews in the library, and practicing writing.

One June afternoon I got a call from crew scheduling with an assignment to Lisbon, a city I had not yet visited. Excited to see a new place, even the terrible flight there filled with angry, overly demanding passengers didn't deter my eagerness for exploring. At least I won't have to see any of them again, I thought as I fake-smiled my goodbyes at the departure door. The whole crew felt beat up by this flight, and on the bus to the hotel I asked if anyone wanted to go out. No one did. So be it. I was going to change out of my uniform, ask for recommendations at the front desk for what to see, and step out into this exotic city.

The week before I had gone to London with a friend for a few days and bought clothes on sale at Harrods—flowered capri pants and a scoop-neck moss-green knit T-shirt. I felt hip and pretty in my new British outfit with a long strand of pearls wrapped around my wrist in the trendy way I'd seen women in London wearing. In the lobby, I heard a group of passengers from my flight complaining loudly to the concierge. And I thought I would never see them again! I laughed to myself. Then I saw most of the crew, changed into street clothes, heading out somewhere. One of them spotted me and looked away, embarrassed. They did have plans after all. I just wasn't part of those plans.

I took a deep breath and walked across the lobby to the front desk. The clerk gave me a map, circling the different things to do and see. I exchanged a hundred dollars for escudos and I was off. My ever-present jet lag hit me as soon as I stepped into the warm sun, an almost pleasant whoosh that washed over me, leaving me a little dizzy. Luckily, there was a café right in front of me, and I decided to have a double espresso and study the map.

In those days before the euro, I had a special change purse just for all the foreign money. Liras, pounds (British and

Egyptian), marks, francs (French, Belgian, and Swiss), pesetas, drachmas, guilders, and now escudos. I kept a little cheat sheet in there too, with the various exchange rates written on it. But I'd forgotten to write down how many escudos there were to a dollar, which was about 150 at the time. When I went to pay for my espresso, I couldn't understand how much I owed and so began pulling out not just escudos, but all kinds of money. Like in a movie, a handsome man with longish sandy hair and green eyes appeared beside me, flashing a big smile and looking like someone in a toothpaste ad.

He said something, I guessed in Portuguese, and I shook my head.

"Italiano, no?" he said, cocking his head.

"American," I told him.

"Ah! Put all of that away," he said in perfect English.

He threw down some escudos and asked if I'd like to join him, pointing to a little table on the sidewalk. Why not? I followed him outside and we fell into easy conversation about who I was and why I was in Lisbon.

His name was Francisco and he worked in advertising. "Right over there," he said, nodding in the direction of a building covered in beautiful cracked tiles. The city was like that, I already realized. Beautiful and run down.

I showed him my map with all the circled things, and he carefully folded it up and put it in his pocket. "No," he said. "I will show you my Lisbon."

Francisco stood and pulled me to my feet.

"First I will have my office vouch for me, then we will begin," he said.

I was not a reckless woman, though I had done a few reckless things in my life. Remember the jojoba shampoo executive? But I followed Francisco inside the tiled building, up an ornate, rickety, ancient elevator, down a long hallway, and into a bright, modern office buzzing with people talking and xeroxing and typing.

"Hello, everybody," Francisco said, and people paused to listen to him. "This is Ann and she is only here from America for one day so I would like to show her our *belissima cidade*. Please let her know I am a nice guy, unmarried, and trustworthy."

"He is very nice," someone said. All around us people chimed in, telling me of his many virtues and showing me framed posters of his bright, bold work.

"Satisfied?" Francisco asked me.

I was.


THE NEXT MORNING, as I waited in the lobby for the shuttle bus from the hotel to the airport, the rest of the crew began to arrive.

"How was your layover?" one of them asked me. She'd been the one who told me she had no plans, who I saw later heading out with the others.

"It was great," I said.

"Did you order room service?"

"No," I said. "I met a guy and he took me all over the city." They all exchanged looks.

"Well, good for you," one of them said.

"How was your layover?" I asked them.

"We just went shopping and to the place down the street we always go," she said.

"Next time you should get out and explore the city," I said. "It's beautiful."

Next time for them was in seventy-two hours; this was their schedule for the whole month. I wouldn't return to Lisbon for another thirty-five years, when my husband and I went for our anniversary. Nothing looked familiar, as if that one night had indeed been magical.

In the rest of my years as a flight attendant, I ventured out alone and with crew members many times. I flew thousands more miles, saw many more cities. But that day and night with Francisco in Lisbon stands out as one of the best layovers I ever had. We rode a funicular to the top of a mountain overlooking the glistening harbor below, ate tiny clams the size of my pinky fingernail, drank rich Portuguese wine, climbed steep streets through different neighborhoods, sat with glasses of port as the sun set by the water, kissed wildly on his balcony as the warm breeze blew the curtains behind us and the moon rose full and golden above us. When I was twelve and dreaming of being an airline stewardess, wasn't this what I had dreamed of? A handsome man in a foreign, romantic city sweeping me off my feet? And walking down any street in any city in the world and finding endless possibilities?

# STRIKE!

ONCE THE SLOW WINTER on reserve on international passed, I once again was holding regular London trips. On March 8, 1986, I returned home from working a London flight, paused long enough to feed my cats and kick off my shoes, and hit Play on my answering machine. I was still dressed in my sharp Ralph Lauren uniform—dark-blue skirt, slightly rumpled white shirt, striped scarf, and my blazer with my flight-attendant wings pinned right above the pocket—and the taupe L'eggs Sheer Energy Control Top pantyhose I wore. L'eggs pantyhose came packaged in a silver plastic egg and I bought them by the dozens, storing them in my freezer because we were taught that helped prevent runs in our stockings.

There were the usual messages from my friend who cat-sat for me when I was away on trips and my boyfriend asking me to call whenever I got home.

The third message was from a representative of the flight-attendant union.

"TWA flight attendants are officially on strike as of midnight tonight," she said.

She gave more information—how and where to sign up for picket duties, for example—but what I remember most was staring at my answering machine as if it were a Magic 8-Ball, holding the answers to my suddenly uncertain future.

I was living in Manhattan, in the one-bedroom co-op on the undesirable end of Bleecker Street that my parents had helped me buy. Though it would eventually be called NoHo, back then the neighborhood was nameless, was neither the East nor the West Village. Probably due to its lack of a neighborhood, the apartment had been a steal at $85,000. The building had a doorman, an atrium lobby, a bank of swift elevators, curving walls along the hallways, and in many apartments—like mine—original brick walls that entitled us to historical status and a big tax break.

I was one of the first tenants in the building, so everything was shiny and new when I moved in, a great relief after years of subletting quirky apartments typical of New York City in the '80s, by which I mean bathtubs in the kitchen; iron gates over the windows; beds made out of doors, pieces of foam, and saw-horses; the lingering smell of roach spray; and no closets. But at 77 Bleecker Street I had an entire wall of closets in the entry hall and another in the bedroom, big windows that slid open wide and let in lots of light, and a real bed that I'd rescued from my storage unit, which was on the West Side Highway and held remnants of apartments in Boston, St. Louis, and Marblehead, Massachusetts.

Being on strike meant not getting a paycheck, which meant the possibility of losing this apartment I loved. Standing in the gray afternoon light that day, I looked around at my blue flow-ered couch—also rescued from the storage unit—and the boxy coffee and end tables I'd bought from This End Up, a store in SoHo that sold furniture made out of packing crates. My blue electric typewriter sat on the oak kitchen table with the pages of my novel stacked beside it. This was home.

As much as I loved traveling, I loved nesting, too, coming home to my purring cats, Daphne and Lewis, and the apartment I had so lovingly arranged. Since my brother died four years earlier, my childhood home had taken on a sadness, like someone had taken a paintbrush dipped in gray paint and washed the whole house with it. I'd had to create a new idea of home, and with my books on the bookshelves and my stories being written at the kitchen table, I was moving toward it. But standing there that March afternoon, actually being on strike scared the hell out of me. Ever an idealist, I had truly believed that even as the date to strike loomed nearer, we would somehow sign a new contract. I was wrong.

TWA's new owner, Carl Icahn, was a corporate raider whose hostile takeover of the airline in 1985 set TWA's ultimate bankruptcy in motion. When contract negotiations began, Vicki Frankovitch, the head of our union, the Independent Federation of Flight Attendants, described Icahn as "unreasonable at best, discriminatory at worst." He told the union that, "I could get nineteen-year-old girls off the streets to do your jobs." We were told unofficially that during negotiations Icahn said he would "de-cunt and re-cunt this airline."

Ultimately, in January, the male-dominated pilot and machinist unions agreed to a 15 percent pay cut. They also agreed that they would not support any flight attendant strikes and would cross picket lines. Although we agreed to the same pay cut as the other two unions, Icahn wanted flight attendants to take what amounted to a 44 percent cut in pay, work hours, and benefits, "because women are not breadwinners." This statement was troubling for many reasons, primarily its sexism. But it also showed how little Icahn knew about the industry he had entered.

As Icahn's opinion of flight attendants—and women— became known, the threat of a strike loomed large. Negotiations stalled and got rescheduled after cooling-off periods. After flights, and on my days off, I went to union meetings for updates and to listen to debates over concessions. Sometimes I worried that we were holding on to things we should give up to keep our jobs, like special advantages that pursers still had and flight attendants didn't. But our strategy was that once you gave something up, it was impossible to ever get it back. So we held on tight.

By the end of February, TWA was asking us for a 22 percent pay reduction, or about $8,000 less per year, and an additional eight hours of flight time per month. Those eight additional flight hours did not sound like very much, but they translated to an additional *eighty* hours away from home a month when time on layovers, time between flights, and pre- and post-flight duties were factored in. The union, rightfully I believed, held out for the same 15 percent wage cut that the pilots and machinists took. We learned that Icahn had secretly hired fifteen hundred people—those nineteen-year-olds off the street—who were put up in a hotel near JFK, where they were getting flight-attendant training even as negotiations continued.

Now we were officially on strike. I looked around my apartment, trying not to cry over the thought that I had just worked my last flight, possibly ever. That I might never again get off the crew bus at a hotel in Paris or London or Tel Aviv, or walk through Terminal 5 at JFK in my beautiful uniform, proud and confident. Twenty-four hours earlier I had shopped at Harrods and then met a British friend at a pub for dinner. With the city lights twinkling through the rain, it had seemed impossible that I might actually lose this job I loved. Carl Icahn seemed very far away. Surely, I had thought as I went to bed in that hotel in London, our union, which was considered among the strongest in the industry, would win this fight. If we lost the strike, we lost everything.

• • •

IN SOME WAYS, I was luckier than some flight attendants, like those husband-and-wife couples with mortgages and kids who had just both lost their jobs. I had sold my first novel, *Somewhere Off the Coast of Maine*, to Bantam Books for the princely sum of $20,000. I was still finishing it, but I'd received half of the advance, so I had a bit of a financial cushion—though not much. Once the enormity of what was happening sank in, I picked up the phone and set up my picket duties at JFK.

How I went from working a full 747 flight to JFK from London to marching in a picket line at JFK on a rainy March evening was because of the corporate greed of the 1980s and Icahn's relentless desire to run TWA into the ground and make a profit doing so. By the time he left TWA six years later, he had made a personal profit of around $470 million, leaving TWA with a debt of over $500 million.

But first, we had to fight for our jobs. Flight attendants had fought before and won—over pay increases; the lifting of weight, marriage, and age restrictions; the right for men to fly; the right to have children. Standing in my living room that

March evening, I was terrified, but I believed that we would win again.

Of our six thousand flight attendants, fourteen hundred did not go on strike. Icahn's goal was to cut half of us, believing that three thousand flight attendants working more hours could do our job. With those fourteen hundred, combined with the fifteen hundred strike breakers, or scabs, hidden in the hotel nearby, along with increased hours, TWA was still able to fly half of its flights. If we couldn't shut down the airline, we weren't going to win.

A few nights later, I put on my uniform and headed to JFK, taking my familiar route of walking west down Bleecker Street to the West Fourth Street subway stop, where I boarded the Train to the Plane, an express train to JFK. The turquoise circle with the airplane icon in it that decorated the train always made me smile. Usually on the hour ride to the airport, I wrote in one of my notebooks or buried my head in a novel. But this time I just stared at nothing and tried not to think about the long hours ahead of picketing in front of the TWA terminal that I loved so much.

I emerged from the Howard Beach–JFK stop into a rainy night. One of my favorite parts of my uniform was the dark navy-blue trench coat that we wore in cold or inclement weather, and I had it on that night. I pulled the belt tight around my waist and raised the collar, then waited for the shuttle bus to the terminal. No one on the bus seemed to notice me, a flight attendant without a flight, about to join a picket line in one of the most contentious strikes TWA or any airline had ever had. News of the strike was everywhere. The front page of the *New York Times* read: TWA CANCELS HALF ITS FLIGHTS AS ATTENDANTS

STRIKE OVER WAGES. In the article, Icahn said, "Within three or four days from now, we hope to be up to full capacity." Similar headlines and stories were in the *Los Angeles Times* the *Chicago Tribune*, the *San Francisco Chronicle*, and just about every other major newspaper, and Vicki Frankovitch appeared on television shows such as *Today* and *Donahue.*

The bus driver announced, "TWA," like everything was the same as always as he slowed in front of the terminal, adding to the surreal nature of what was going on. There it was, that beautiful Eero Saarinen–designed building, with passengers moving toward it as usual. Except marching in front of it was a picket line of flight attendants. I walked toward them, noticing how easily people crossed that line and went inside, barely looking at the picketers. A few minutes later, I was one of them.

The red crew bus pulled up and its doors opened, releasing a dozen or more flight attendants in TWA uniforms. Young and defiant, they linked arms and crossed right through our line. One tossed her hair and said loudly, "I am so excited to work my first flight." There they were, the nineteen-year-olds whom Icahn had hired to replace us. After another hour, a flight crew—pilot, copilot, flight engineer—arrived. The copilot and engineer looked downward, avoiding eye contact with us as they crossed the picket line.

But the pilot looked straight at us with a look of disgust. He pushed through the picket line, turned to face us, and spat. That spit felt more like a punch in the gut, taking my breath away. And with it, I understood that we were going to lose. I still picketed every week or so, putting on my uniform, riding the Train to the Plane to JFK, and taking my place in the line.

The last time I ever wore my TWA uniform was on a warm

May afternoon when I walked the picket line at JFK. A few days later, on May 20, seventy-five days after it began, our union declared the strike was over and ordered us to return to work. But TWA said the gesture came too late; they had hired three thousand new flight attendants at greatly reduced salaries. Stockbroker David Sylvester told the *Los Angeles Times*, "Unfortunately for the union people, it's all over but the shouting."

# THANK YOU FOR
# FLYING TWA . . .

GROUNDED ONCE AGAIN, this time I had a book to finish writing and a real book contract in hand. But I still missed flying. Post-strike, TWA agreed to hire us back by seniority when they needed more flight attendants. Despite my eight years of seniority, I had never moved into the realm of senior enough to get my first choice of flights or positions to work or even crew rest. It would be a very long time before I got rehired, if ever. Two years after the strike, flight attendants with nineteen years or more seniority were called back to TWA at the lower pay and increased work hours. TWA wasn't the only airline that had busted their union or reduced flight-attendant earnings. At Eastern, flight attendants were being paid $817 a month, almost half of my 1978 hiring pay.

With the first installment of my book advance I'd received almost gone, I had to get a job. But waitressing—especially in oversized ruffled panties—or working in a bookstore no longer appealed to me or fit my lifestyle. I was almost thirty years old. Then I read about Presidential Airways, a new airline, starting up at Dulles Airport. Their routes included Boston; Portland, Maine; New York LaGuardia; and several cities in Florida, including Miami and Sarasota. It wasn't the international airline I'd dreamed of as a starry-eyed girl, but they had a fleet of new 737s and a philosophy of all-first-class service at low fares. Their VIP lounge was called the Oval Office, and their uniforms were a snappy navy blue with red accents—the flight attendants could even wear snazzy red high heels.

Unlike those first interviews I went on as a twenty-one-year-old, this time I did not have the nervousness or the anxiety. Instead, I walked in with the confidence of a young woman who had flown for two very different airlines, traveled around the world, and who knew she was an excellent flight attendant. I was hired and trained in one of Presidential's first classes. At TWA and Capitol, I worked with flight attendants who had flown for Howard Hughes, taken troops in and out of Vietnam, started before there were jets. Now I was working with recent college graduates, so excited about having the job that their enthusiasm was infectious. At Capitol, underpaid and overworked, I had often felt exhausted. But at Presidential, I was having fun. After every meal service we baked chocolate-chip cookies and served them warm, a pleasure that never faded.

Work rules were easy too; when I landed in Atlanta or Savannah or Sarasota I wasn't too tired to explore. One of my best college friends lived in Portland, Maine, so I flew that route often and got to hang out with her twice a week. Eight years on airplanes pretty much full-time made me see how easy it was to visit old friends, see new places, go anywhere anytime. It's a perspective that has not faded a bit in all these years.

In just a couple of years, Presidential became a regional feeder for Continental, then for United, before claiming bankruptcy in 1989. But my novel was finally finished and scheduled as one of the two launch books for Bantam New Fiction in May of 1987, so I left Presidential to prepare for the next chapter of my life. As I began my new life as a full-time writer, TWA began its inevitable decline.

By 1989, Carl Icahn owned 90 percent of TWA. He sold its Chicago–London routes to American Airlines, then went on to sell eleven of its jumbo jets, and then the rest of the London routes—also to American—including JFK–London, once among our most profitable. I read about TWA's slow dismantling in newspapers, and my heart broke. Losing London flights and our 747s was like killing the TWA I knew and loved. How could I not think of all those times I walked into TWA's International Terminal at JFK, with its modernistic design evoking a bird taking flight? How could I not hear the rapid clicking of the Arrivals and Departures boards as planes landed and took off to and from all over the world?

In 1992, TWA declared bankruptcy.

WHILE CARL ICAHN was destroying TWA, my new life as a full-time writer was progressing. *Somewhere Off the Coast of Maine* was published with a lot of fanfare, and I suddenly went from asking a few hundred people "Chicken or beef?" every day to talking about my novel on *Good Morning America* and NPR. During interviews, the interviewer always got around to asking, with disbelief, "Were you really a stewardess?" (I always had to bite my tongue from correcting them that stewardesses had been called flight attendants for decades.) They asked it as if flight attendants couldn't possibly have the intelligence to write a best-selling book, especially the kind that got reviewed in the *New York Times*. Charles Trueheart wrote a feature on me for the *Washington Post*. In it, he described me as dazzled by the turn my life had taken—and boy, was he right! Trueheart continued, "Consider her concern for appearances. Dressed in flip-flops, black stretch pants and a polka-dot top falling from her shoulders, her hair a jungle . . . this certifiable warmth has survived Hood's interim career as a flight attendant, with its round-the-clock regimen of congeniality and zombified good cheer." I had corrected him during the interview when he asked me about being a stewardess. "Not stewardess. Flight attendant." In the article he wrote that "'stewardess' is a word that does not cross Hood's lips, or those of anyone in her company."

At first, almost every day as I slipped on a sparkly black dress for a party, or ate Chinese takeout cold sesame noodles in my jammies as I rushed to meet a deadline, I marveled at what my life had become. How I'd loved my other life with its duty-free stashes in my cupboard, hailing a taxi on Broadway at three thirty in the dark morning to get to JFK while drunk revelers spilled from it, walking across the TWA International Terminal in my uniform like a person going somewhere. This new life could not be more different, yet I loved it too. I loved staying in my pajamas all day with a cup of coffee, sitting at the oak table and writing my stories.

I had achieved that dream I held so dear, flown all over the world, had enough experiences to last me a lifetime. I got married and moved to a rambling third-floor apartment in a brownstone in Park Slope, Brooklyn. Then, out of the blue, three years after the strike had brought an abrupt end to my life as a TWA flight attendant, a letter with the TWA logo on it arrived. It looked very much like the one that had changed my life a decade earlier by telling me I'd been hired. I opened it, read it, then read it again. I was reinstated as a TWA flight attendant and scheduled to report for training in St. Louis (Breech Academy having been shut down a year earlier) in a month. And just like that, the fantasy returned. I could put on my Ralph Lauren uniform and once again glide down the aisles of a 747, heading to a far-flung city.

I immediately called flight attendant friends to confirm that it was true. Our case had ultimately gone to the Supreme Court, and we had won. With a series of moves in a short period of time, many of my updates from the union had been misdelivered or even returned. How TWA managed to get the right one, I don't know. But sitting on the sofa in my apartment, holding that letter, I was gripped by a desire to fly again that was so strong, I almost ran back to the phone, called TWA, and told them I would be there.

*Why not?* I asked myself. Before I got published, I had managed to write a novel while I worked as a flight attendant. I'd written in composition notebooks in the galley of 747s as the passengers slept. I'd written ravaged by jet lag in the middle of the night in hotel rooms in Zurich and Paris and Rome. I'd even written on the Train to the Plane. The job, I realized, still had its hold on me. I wanted to put on my uniform again and walk through that gorgeous TWA International Terminal. I wanted to stand smiling at the door of a jumbo jet, sleep in hotels, and eat in bistros around the world.

To my surprise, I started to cry, for even as all of these images and memories swept over me, so did the realization that this writer's life of deadlines and book tours and teaching at writers' conferences would not be tenable as a flight attendant. Sure, the writing part could get done. But not the rest of it.

There was a phone number to call to hold my place in the training class or tell them no thank you. I stared at it, and then I folded the letter and put it back in its envelope with the TWA logo. I would think on it, I decided, even though I knew in my heart I couldn't go back. Years later, my old roommate Diane told me she had actually called that number—frequently. She was undecided too. She knew the new life she'd built for herself wasn't compatible with being a flight attendant either, but still she wanted to go back. In the end, after vacillating and many phone discussions, she did not return. Neither did I. I put the letter in a drawer, as if someday I could still take it out and call that number.

Not long after—a year or slightly more—another letter with the red TWA logo arrived. This one informed me that although I had not returned to work, since I never actually said no and quit, I was now entitled to unlimited free travel on TWA for the rest of my life. With buddy passes. Again, I had to read the letter over and over. By not answering the last letter I'd somehow gotten my flight benefits back? I called my friends and learned that indeed that was exactly what had happened. Those who had resigned relinquished their benefits. The rest of us undecided people regained them. As proof, there were blank tickets included, like the ones that had arrived to fly me to all of my interviews long ago.

I used those tickets too. A lot. Flying to Barcelona, Madrid,

Lisbon, London, San Francisco, Vienna, Los Angeles. When I had my son, the two of us flew everywhere, anytime. I had one of the best perks of the job without having to work the job.

"Are you kidding me?" a friend said when I explained why I could fly anywhere I wanted, basically for free, anytime.

"I have free tickets for the rest of my life," I said.

"Your life, or the rest of TWA's," he said, only half joking. Little did I know he was exactly right.

•   •   •

AT ALMOST EVERY writer's conference where I teach, there is a flight attendant—former or present—studying to become a writer. I even met a TWA flight attendant, Alecia Nelson, in 1994 at the Bread Loaf Writers' Conference in Vermont. Bread Loaf, the oldest writing conference in the country, is known for its high standards for acceptance and for attracting new talent. As soon as I heard there was a student who was a TWA flight attendant, I sought her out. Alecia was writing a memoir about her sixteen years as a TWA flight attendant. She shared pictures and stories of her six-year-old daughter, Twyla, with me. Although she had stopped flying, like me Alecia still had non-revenue flight benefits, which meant you could fly if there were empty seats. Unpredictable as that could be, it was worth it to fly, often in first class, for next to nothing, and we had a lot of fun sharing stories of our free travels. Over the next few years we stayed in touch through a mutual friend, who updated me on Alecia's progress with her book and on her daughter Twyla.

I didn't realize it then, but so much of what I learned as a flight attendant affected my writing, so it really shouldn't be surprising that some of us became writers.

IN 1996, pregnant with my second child, I taught for the month of July at the Bennington Writers' Workshop at Bennington College in Vermont. Through old TWA friends and newspapers, I knew that TWA was, as usual, in financial trouble. It broke my heart when they sold their London routes, or when I learned that they had the oldest fleet of aircrafts of any major carrier—an average age of nineteen and a half years. Just a couple of years earlier, they'd laid off three thousand employees. But after claiming bankruptcy again in 1995, they had emerged—again—and Carl Icahn was gone. I believed they would pull out of this latest crisis, like they always had. As if to prove that, I read in the paper that TWA had announced profits five times greater than the previous quarter.

Shortly after I read about TWA's financial upturn, my parents were driving up from Rhode Island to visit us. Like me, they were always game for seeing new places, plus they missed seeing my son, Sam, who spent a lot of time with them when I worked or traveled. I planned to take them to Bennington Potters, where I knew my mother would fall in love with the blue or pink speckled pottery they were known for, and then to eat at the Blue Benn Diner. They arrived midafternoon on July 18, a sticky, hot summer day. I can still see them as they emerged from their enormous white Ford and made their slow way across the grass to me. I watched them and I knew something was wrong. Not only were they walking very slowly, but instead of the excited looks they usually had whenever they saw me, their faces were somber.

I ran to greet them, wrapping them both in hugs, and led them to a picnic table to sit and wait for Sam to show up with his father; they'd gone to a swimming hole to cool off.

"Have you heard the news?" my father said. When he saw my puzzled look, he said, "About TWA?"

My heart sunk. "You're kidding," I said. "They went under? For real this time?"

"Oh, no, sweetie. It's much worse," he said. "There's been a big plane crash, taking off from Kennedy. Everyone on board died."

They didn't yet have any details, though even that afternoon my father said there was speculation that it had been shot down. The chances of me knowing a crew member on that plane were good. As it turned out, the person I knew on Flight 800 was Alecia Nelson, whom I had met at Bread Loaf. She'd used her free passes for a flight to Rome with her eight-year-old daughter Twyla to attend a writers' conference. But she was bumped off the non-stop flight and rerouted through Paris on Flight 800 on July 17, 1996. Twelve minutes after takeoff, TWA Flight 800 exploded over Long Island, killing everyone on board.

Although TWA had survived years of mismanagement, fuel shortages, hostile takeovers, deregulation, labor disputes, and more, losing a 747, perhaps to terrorism, would be almost impossible to recover from. Just like the Pan Am crash over Lockerbie, Scotland, in 1988 had moved that airline closer to its inevitable bankruptcy, surely this would be the final straw for TWA. I remembered those empty 747s I worked back in 1985, after the hijacking. Who would want to fly TWA now?

UNBELIEVABLY, with another change in CEOs and the purchase of 125 new planes, TWA gasped along for five more years. On January 9, 2001, American Airlines announced it had bought TWA. On December 1 of that year, TWA flew its last flight, from St. Louis to Las Vegas. At eleven o'clock that night, all TWA signage was removed in airports and replaced with American's. At midnight, TWA disappeared. All of its flights were now and forever listed as American Airlines flights.

Breech Training Academy also became one more relic of TWA. In 1988 they had been forced to sell it for financial reasons. Still, on a book tour in Kansas City a few years ago, I asked my driver if he could take me there before we went to the bookstore.

He glanced at me in the rearview mirror, surprised. "Why would you want to go there? It's just a bunch of office buildings."

"I lived there when I was training—"

"You were a TWA stew?" he said, impressed.

"Yes, I was a TWA flight attendant."

Without any hesitation, he took me there. We drove along the winding roads of the campus, with its late 1960s-era stone, square buildings. I wondered if the companies inside now had kept the mod open floor plan with its TWA-red carpeting and wide staircases. What had become of the sunken living rooms with the TWA-red wraparound sofas where we'd sat and quizzed one another on emergency procedures and service rules? We passed a bold metal sign on a stone wall: WADDELL AND REED. *A financial management company.*

"Thanks," I told the driver. "I'm ready to leave."

As we made our way out of the campus, I turned around for one last look, as if I could glimpse that gaggle of twenty new hires, ready to take on the world.

ONE REMNANT OF TWA did remain, however, and came back to life in May of 2019: the iconic TWA International Terminal at JFK designed by Eero Saarinen that had opened in 1962 and was once called the Grand Central of the Jet Age. In a 1959 lecture, Saarinen said that rather than have the terminal "as a static, enclosed place," this was "a place of movement and transition." The glass walls leaned away from the building as if people were "looking out from a plane to the earth below," *ArchDaily* wrote. From it, jets took people all over the world. I was one of those people, stepping off a bus from Manhattan into the glass-and-concrete terminal, dressed in my TWA uniform and on my way to a faraway city.

From the moment I had my wings pinned onto my dark-blue jacket in 1979 to the day in 1986 when I hung up my uniform for good, being a flight attendant brought me everything I had dreamed. By the time I stopped flying, I had flown well over a million miles, much of it out of that terminal on 747s that took me to all those places I'd dreamed of visiting. But the job gave me things that I could never have imagined: the ability to talk in front of a couple hundred people and navigate the subways and streets of foreign cities with ease. It taught me to listen, to be kind and helpful and compassionate. For every honeymooning passenger I treated to a celebratory bottle of champagne, there was another whose hand I held as they flew home after someone they loved had died. For every love story I heard, there was a tale of cruelty, or a broken heart.

I learned that there are misogynists in the world, sure, but that most people are pretty wonderful. I learned to laugh at human foibles, and therefore to laugh at myself, and to stop taking small things too seriously. We forget bridesmaids' dresses and Christmas presents on airplanes, we lose our passports and our wallets, we spill coffee on our white pants and red wine on our suits. But we also offer to hold a stranger's crying baby or give up a seat so newlyweds can sit together. TWA made my childhood dreams come true and turned me into the person I am today, forty years later.

In 1994, the terminal was designated as a New York City Landmark. But like TWA, it closed in 2001. Once a marvel of modern architecture, it was now outdated, unable to be adapted for new aircraft. Two years later, the National Trust for Historic Preservation placed it on the list of America's Most Endangered Places, and two years after that the National Park Service placed it on the National Register of Historic Places, all in an effort to keep it preserved.

A little over a decade later, the TWA terminal was reborn as the TWA Hotel. There is a cocktail lounge inside a Lockheed Constellation—an airplane once thought to represent the future—and a museum with flight-attendant uniforms on display, as well as a replica of Howard Hughes's office. The Paris Café has reopened under the guidance of chef Jean-Georges Vongerichten. A shop sells everything from cocktail glasses to bathrobes with the TWA logo on them.

My husband and I stayed one night at the TWA Hotel. "I never thought I would sleep in the place where I used to work," I told him on the train to Terminal 5.

Check-in is at the old ticket counters. To get to the rooms, people walk along the red-carpeted passageways that used to lead to planes. From our room, we could see a runway, and watch planes taking off and landing as we sipped cocktails out of TWA crystal glasses.

We decided to go to the chalet bar, overlooking the infinity pool, for cocktails before dinner. Walking through the terminal, now teeming with screaming kids; loud, tipsy women at bachelorette parties; and families escaping a winter weekend at home in Queens or Long Island, the sophisticated, modern, bustling terminal I had called home felt more like Disney World. All the guests we spoke to were on "staycations," not there for fine food and respite in transit between exotic cities.

At the crowded chalet bar, we ordered Manhattans and chose Scrabble from the board games offered. There was a wintry mix falling outside the windows, and the empty pool glistened. Despite the kitsch and the cruise-ship atmosphere, I was suddenly struck by a strong feeling of nostalgia. Some small part of Jet Age history—of TWA—had been saved, and for that I was grateful. I stared out the window, where the view seemed to stretch on forever. All the way, perhaps, to a bright future.

# ME AND THE SKY

I LOVE FLYING. Whether that love grew on the job or it was born in me, I cannot say. I can only say how much I love it, all of it. I even like the waiting at the gate, the hum of strangers as they drink their coffees and turn the pages of their newspapers; the toddlers who run around laughing and the weary parents who chase them; the occasional announcements that give us warnings (*Boarding will begin in ten minutes!*) and orders (*Check your boarding pass to see what zone you are in! You must board with your zone!*) and threats (*If you are in zone 4, your bag will be checked at the gate*). I even like the annoying people shouting into their phones, using business-speak like it is a foreign language.

Then the plane arrives and the door opens and passengers start to spill from it, often into the arms of their waiting loved ones. Before 9/11, the people you loved met you right there at the gate, and remembering that I think of my father, dead too long—twenty-three impossible years—who always met me right there so that as soon as I stepped out of the jetway I was in an Old Spice–scented hug.

The passengers and crew deplaned and then the waiting crew got on. Everyone at the gate seemed to sigh a collective sigh when we filed on. A sigh that said, *Oh good, they're here, they're getting on the plane. Everything is OK.*

These days, as a passenger, I even like the time in the crowded jetway, a bottleneck at the boarding door. Airlines hang posters along the wall of the jetway, I guess to entertain us. Some of them are clever and some are of the beautiful places the airline flies—pictures of deserted beaches or cities with twinkling lights—and some are boastful, telling us how many times they've been voted customer favorite or most on-time airline. The jetway takes you out of the airport bubble with its moving walkways and smell of Auntie Anne's Pretzels. It's cold in the jetway in winter—sometimes rainy and snowy—and scorching in summer. But then you're at the boarding door and then, finally, you're on the plane.

The feeling of having the plane to myself that I got when I was a flight attendant was decadent, luxurious. All those seats stretching before me, everything neat and clean and quiet. I used to love that pre-boarding time, loved knowing where everything was, and that everything was in its place. As a passenger, I get bumped and jostled and held up on the way to my seat. I like aisle seats, but when I travel with my husband (aisle) and/or daughter (window), I am usually in the middle seat.

I travel heavy: laptop, giant bottle of Advil, hand wipes, AirPods, phone, chargers, three magazines, a book, the newspaper, a rain hat, and a small handbag all tucked into a bulging larger bag that fits perfectly under the seat in front of me. I can live out of that bag if I need to. "Always pack a bathing suit and a sweater, because you never know," they told us in training, and I still heed that advice.

But I love the actual flying most of all. I love to watch the flaps lift on the wing. I love the peanuts or cookies or breakfast bars. I like to have a cocktail and order the overpriced cheese plate with three cheeses that all taste identical and grapes that don't taste like grapes. I like to look out the window and see clouds, so close I could touch them. Or to look down and see the blue rectangles of swimming pools or the golden squares of crops growing or the jagged, snowy mountains. To my family's puzzlement, I like to sleep on planes, to pull the skimpy blanket over me and tuck the Chiclet-sized pillow under my head and sleep as people move up and down the aisles and the plane flies at an altitude of 35,000 feet.

On night flights, the cabin lights are dimmed and there is a feeling of such hominess, such coziness, that sleep is practically required. Sometimes voices cut through the darkness. A mother and child playing Uno. Old friends off on an adventure together. Teenagers giggling.

I REMEMBER WALKING onto a flight as a brand-new flight attendant, just a few weeks out of training and called at the last minute on reserve. The rest of the crew had already boarded and done the pre-check requirements for safety equipment and commissary supplies. They were just waiting for me to arrive. I stepped onto the plane, and there in first class, curled up in a seat wrapped in a red blanket with the TWA logo across it, was a flight attendant, napping. She looked like she was at home on her couch, comfortable and at ease. For me then, airplanes were still mysterious things that I was just beginning to unlock. All those compartments and drawers and overhead bins, the galley items and OAGs and passenger manifest lists. Everything was stored in its special place—coffee and soda and first-aid kits and life vests and safety demo props—the way everything has to be stored on a ship. Would I ever feel as at home on an airplane as this flight attendant did?

The answer, of course, is yes. Before long I, too, felt as at home on a plane as I did in my very own living room. That feeling has never left me. All these years later, I still fly as often as I can, happily comfortable on an airplane.

Never has the magic of flying been more obvious to me than on a long-ago December flight, right before Christmas of 1985. The captain of the 747 I was working from Rome invited me to sit in the cockpit for landing. He told me I had to be absolutely quiet the whole time. I strapped into the extra jump seat, already enjoying the view out of the large cockpit windows.

The pilots spoke to air traffic controllers. Things beeped. The 450 tons of metal and glass began to descend into the winter evening. As we descended, snow started to fall, small bright flakes, like fairy dust.

Then Manhattan came into sight, its snowy, illuminated skyline rising majestically before us.

The air grew tense, electric with voices and the crackles of the radio. The ground seemed to lift up to greet us, that glittery snow falling heavier, the lights of the runway and the jet brighter, until the wheels hit the ground, and the magic ended. We were back on Earth.

Overcome, my eyes teared up.

"It's something, isn't it?" the captain said softly.

I could only nod.

Few times in my life have I experienced something that felt

that majestic, that reminded me that I was alive. The lava from the Kilauea Volcano crashing red and fiery into the Pacific Ocean. Standing beneath the Great Pyramid at Giza. The feel of a baby sliding out of my body. Two babies, Sam and Grace. Then unbelievably holding Grace, dead, suddenly, at only five years old from a virulent form of strep. Three years later, in a sterile city hall in Changsha, China, holding my daughter Annabelle, an eleven-month-old baby girl we'd traveled halfway around the world for.

And that snowy landing, when I understood, or understood as much as we can, how sky and earth and snow and light and man coexist.

*   *   *

IN MARCH 2020, coronavirus arrived globally, and for the first time since I was sixteen years old, the world was no longer available to me, waiting to show me its endless treasures. As was typical with how I've lived my post–flight attendant life, I had trips planned throughout the year—a romantic anniversary trip to Paris with my husband, a family trip to Amsterdam, teaching in Ireland in July, another family trip to Ecuador later in the summer, and a research trip with my husband to London for a long weekend. All of them canceled, leaving me grounded for the first time in fifty years.

How I took for granted all those miles spent at 35,000 feet! How I ache to be on an airplane again, going somewhere, any-where, my husband beside me, my kids playing cards across the aisle, a big glass of mediocre wine and even those roasted pea-nuts all so sorely missed. This morning I asked my son, Sam, when he thought we'd be able to travel again by airplane. Like me, Sam, age twenty-seven, flies anywhere at a moment's notice. Last year alone he flew to Italy, Sicily, Budapest, and Brazil. He looked at me and shook his head. "This time next year? Maybe?" If that's so, it will be a year and half without me stepping on an airplane. Lately I've started saving articles about flight deals—cheap first-class tickets to South Africa, Bali, Australia. I read reviews of the airlines and their service, the food they serve, how to get vouchers for canceled flights. I close my eyes and imagine I am airborne again.

"Why do you think I do this job?" that 747 captain asked me on that long-ago December night. "We don't even fly these planes anymore. A computer does. But the thrill of takeoff and landing makes all the hours in between worth it."

I have thought of his words often in the thirty-five years since I first heard them. It seems to me that they are true for everything we do: cook a meal, write a book, raise a child. The thrill of takeoff and landing make everything in between worthwhile.

# ACKNOWLEDGMENTS

WRITING THIS BOOK has been a marvelous journey. With great delight, I searched my memories, watched old training films and airline ads, researched TWA and the ever-changing role of flight attendants, talked with my old flying buddies—all in an effort to recapture a magical time in my life and the life of aviation. Therefore there are many people to thank, and many resources to note.

With great pleasure, I reread *Coffee, Tea or Me?* by Trudy Baker and Rachel Jones (pseudonyms for Donald Bain) and *How to Become an Airline Stewardess* by Kathryn Cason. The books *TWA Cabin Attendants Wings of Pride: A Pictorial History 1935–1985*, compiled and edited by Gwen Nebelsick Mahler, Mary Lou Axcell Finch, and Marie B. O'Connor Trainer, and written by Donna Steele; *Flying Across America* by Daniel L. Rust; *Skygirls: A Photographic History of the Airline Stewardess* by Bruce McAllister and Stephan Wilkinson; *Skygirl: A Career Handbook for the Airline Stewardess* by Mary F. Murray; *Femininity in Flight: A History of Flight Attendants* by Kathleen M. Barry; and *The Ghost of Flight 401* by John G. Fuller gave me history and reminders of the job and the industry. I also happily rewatched the movie *Boeing Boeing*.

The Smithsonian National Air and Space Museum and the

TWA Museum are treasure chests of aviation and TWA history. The *New York Times*, the *Los Angeles Times*, the *New York Post*, the *Irish Times*, the *Boston Globe*, the *Chicago Tribune*, the *San Francisco Chronicle*, and the *Washington Post* all provided multiple articles and advertisements about the airlines, as did magazines, including *LIFE*, *Time*, *Vanity Fair*, *Forbes*, *BusinessWeek*, *Air & Space*, *ArchDaily*, and *St. Louis Magazine*.

Another great source of information were the Facebook groups Oh Stewardess!! and Stewardesses of the 1960's and 70's, where I connected with other former flight attendants Vicki Kirschner and Pat Kuehn. Fontaine Dubus introduced me to Carol Quinn, who generously shared her years as an American Airlines flight attendant with me. Sadly, Carol died before I got to hand her a copy of this book. My TWA pal David Sherry gave me invaluable information about male flight attendants in the 1970s. My friend Shannon Miles offered her memories of flying for Pan Am. Like all flight attendants, they were funny, smart, and happy to talk. Thanks to my old TWA roommates in Boston and St. Louis who shared the wild ride with me. I've lost track of some of you, and hope my memories make you smile and that I got it mostly right. Thank you, Howard Hughes, for creating the flawed but wonderful TWA and changing my life! And thank you, 47F. You changed my life too.

I have to give heaps of thanks to my old TWA roommate and dear friend, Diane Bloodgood, who opened her home and her heart and her mind to talk about the good old days at TWA with me. And more heaps of thanks to Tracey Minkin for reading this and offering wise comments and notes.

Sadly, I couldn't find some of my old pals to commiserate with, so I've changed their names here and hope I did them proud.

Undying love and gratitude to Matt Davies, who flew those wild Capitol Air trips with me, came on board at TWA, and stayed one of my best friends forevermore. And more thanks than I can say goes to Kate Heckman, who shared her own TWA air hostess stories with me, as well as delicious lunches and fun book clubs. This book is dedicated to them.

I am the luckiest writer around thanks to my agent and friend, Gail Hochman, who loved *Fly Girl* when it was just an idea; Drew Weitman, who has read many drafts of this book, always with encouragement, good humor, and insight; my dream editor, Jill Bialosky, whose friendship and trust and brilliance are invaluable; and my publicist, Erin Lovett, who gets as excited about old TWA menus, cocktails, and stir rods as I do.

How I wish I could get on a plane with my parents again and fly off to San Francisco or anywhere. I miss them every minute of every day, but their fingerprints are still on everything I do. While I'm counting my lucky stars, thank you to the best kids a mom could have, Sam and Annabelle. They have flown around the world with me and made more of my dreams come true. And they turned me on to the song "Me and the Sky" from the Broadway musical *Come from Away*, which gave me the title for my final chapter here. And finally, thank you to my husband, Michael: tireless reader of a multitude of drafts, fun-loving travel companion, sweetest man, best husband, love of my life.